THE MEANING OF
MARY MAGDALENE

The Meaning of MARY MAGDALENE

⊙ ⊙ ⊙ ⊙ ⊙ ⊙ ⊙

DISCOVERING the WOMAN at the HEART of CHRISTIANITY

Cynthia Bourgeault

SHAMBHALA
Boulder
2010

Shambhala Publications, Inc.
2129 13th Street
Boulder, Colorado 80302
www.shambhala.com

Excerpts from *Divine Feminine in Biblical Wisdom Literature:
Selections Annotated & Explained* are copyright © 2005
by Rami Shapiro (Woodstock, Vt.: SkyLight Paths Publishing,
www.skylightpaths.com).

Unless otherwise noted, all major gospel citations are from
The Christian Community Bible (Ligouri, Mo.: Ligouri Publications/Claretian
Publications). Short gospel citations and all epistle and Old Testament citations
are from the New Revised Standard Version (NRSV).

Excerpts from *The Gospel of Thomas: Wisdom of the Twin, Translation
with Introduction, Notes and Questions for Reflection and Inquiry* copyright
2004 by Lynn Bauman. Reprinted by permission of White Cloud Press. Excerpts
from *The Song of Songs: A Commentary on the Book of Canticles or the Song of Songs*
copyright 1990 by Roland E. Murphy. Reprinted by permission of Fortress Press.

20 19 18 17 16

Printed in the United States of America

Shambhala Publications makes every effort to print on acid-free, recycled paper.

Shambhala Publications is distributed worldwide by
Penguin Random House, Inc., and its subsidiaries.

Designed by James D. Skatges

Library of Congress Cataloging-in-Publication Data
Bourgeault, Cynthia.
The meaning of Mary Magdalene: discovering the woman
at the heart of Christianity/Cynthia Bourgeault.—1st ed.
p. cm.
Includes bibliographical references and index.
ISBN 978-1-59030-495-2 (pbk.: alk. paper)
1. Mary Magdalene, Saint. I. Title.
BS2485.B56 2010
226'.092—dc22
2010015530

To Gwen, Lucy, Ava, and Zoë
the earth, air, fire, and water of a Mother's heart
And
To Deborah Jones
whose graceful incarnation of Magdalenic energy
reassures me that everything I have written
in this book is possible.

CONTENTS

PART THREE

Mary Magdalene as Unitive Wisdom

PREFACE

When I told Abbot Joseph Boyle I was writing a book on Mary Magdalene, he looked at me long and hard, as only an old friend can, then said, "Go gently. Try not to leave me behind."

His words have come back to me many times during this project, and I am grateful for the moderating influence they have had. Joseph is the abbot of St. Benedict's Monastery in Snowmass, Colorado, and one of the most committed and transformed Christians I have ever met. "The heart of Jesus must be lived," he is fond of saying, and he has indeed lived it graciously for nearly five decades as a Trappist monk. But he is also a loyal son of the Catholic Church, bound not only by his vows of obedience, but because he deeply loves its teachings and traditions.

And Mary Magdalene is wild stuff, for sure, particularly now, when things are only just beginning to settle down after *The Da Vinci Code* mania swept the nation a few years back. In some of the more conservative corners of Christianity, even to mention Mary Magdalene's name is taboo. St. Benedict's Monastery is not one of those places. But like many Christian communities it comprises a wide range of opinions and theological sensibilities. And beyond the narrow confines of the role ascribed to her by Christian liturgy and scripture, the subject of Mary Magdalene can indeed drop quickly off the deep end. Out there in the wide world of contemporary pop spirituality she is hawked about as everything from an archetypal goddess of wisdom to a sexualized consort. The shadow side of Christianity's notoriously undealt-with issues around human sexuality and the feminine get projected directly onto her.

That is not where I am going in this book. I intend to stay within a historical time frame and within the bounds of the literature and scholarship generally acknowledged as germane to this conversation, although I will unsettle some by giving the gospels of Thomas, Mary Magdalene, and Philip equal footing with the traditional New Testament texts. The best of contemporary scholarship bears me out on this point, I believe, and my first goal in this project is one already widely recognized and shared within progressive Christian circles: to repair the damage caused by a heavy-handedly patriarchal (and at times flat-out misogynist) ecclesiastical tradition and reclaim Mary Magdalene's legitimate role as a teacher and apostle. My angle of approach is not as a feminist, however, but from the perspective of wisdom Christianity, with its emphasis on those perennial spiritual practices of transformation and inner awakening. The argument I will be making is that Mary Magdalene earns her place among the apostles because of all Jesus's students, she is the one who best catches the full unitive meaning of his teachings and is best able to "walk the talk."

The second part of my book will bring us to the eye of the needle, and it is here that I have found myself frequently repeating Abba Joe's mantra: "Go gently, go gently . . ." But can even the lightest of footsteps onto this forbidden turf be gentle enough to keep a door open? For I do indeed intend to open the emotionally charged question of a possible love relationship between Jesus and Mary Magdalene, and my conclusion is that such a relationship most likely did exist and is in fact at the heart of the Christian transformational path—one might even say, its long-missing key. But the kind of relationship I have in mind is not the sentimentalized melodrama our culture commonly holds up as love, but a spiritual love so refined and luminous as to be virtually unknown in the West today. And I am entering these shark-infested waters precisely for the sake of this love: because its healing and generative energy is desperately needed right now to heal the deep psychic wounds of Christianity.

In the third part of my book I will be looking at how this healing has unfolded, and continues to unfold, in the Christian

West through the largely unacknowledged infusions of Mary Magdalene's presence. The language I will be using—of Mary Magdalene as an archetype of divine wisdom, or of the divine feminine—may sound trendy, but again, I am not coming from the usual reference points. I derive my observations not from contemporary Jungian categories but from traditional wisdom teachings on the human soul as a bridge between the visible and invisible realms. These teachings are amply laid out in the gospels of Thomas, Mary Magdalene, and Philip and thus comprise the immediate frame of reference in which Jesus and Mary Magdalene would have been working, not a contemporary psychological retrojection. The "inter-cosmic" fluidity attested to in these texts is, I will argue, the real legacy of the love between Jesus and Mary Magdalene and the basis on which we are able to meet her, and, through her, him. As with all lovers who have lived to the full the wager that love is stronger than death, the faithfulness of their two hearts resonating across time and space forms a particular kind of energy channel through which divine compassion pours itself forth as wisdom and creativity. This is the real post that Mary Magdalene has always held—unacknowledged but irrepressible—and why her presence on the contemporary scene, at this critical juncture in the life of Christianity, is so important— and in fact, so predictable. When a new infusion of love is needed, Mary Magdalene shows up. Our only real choice is whether or not to cooperate.

I had to wear many hats to write this book: as a scholar and medievalist, as a contemplative, and as a student along the path of conscious love. Mary Magdalene is accessible I believe, only in this integral way. To neglect any strand of this wisdom way of knowing her is to lose the full picture, and this is ultimately the shortcoming of almost all the scholarship I have seen on her so far. Yes, she is an apostolic leader, but not only this. Yes, she is a beloved, but not only this. Yes, she is a feminine archetype, but not only this. Flesh-and-blood human being, beloved, teacher, spiritual master in her own right: all of these dimensions have to come together to reveal who she really is, and the enormity of the gift she has to bring us. To enter her world I have relied in equal measure on scholarly study, contemplative prayer, and the lived experience of my own heart. My hope is that my reader will be able to follow what may, from the point of view of strict linear logic, seem like wildly intuitive leaps, or like a tedious insistence on factual reality for those simply wanting to re-create the story as a romantic fantasy.

But if the gaps can be bridged, so that we can hold her being in its fullness, the payoff is huge. For when we see who she really is, we see what Christianity really is, what it could have been— and pray to God, can still become.

And yes, Joe, I have tried to go gently. The verdict on whether I have succeeded or not will be largely in the hands of sensitive and spacious Christians like yourself, and I suspect that even for a charitably disposed Christian audience I will be pushing the envelope in several places. But I have tried to state my case in as measured a way as is possible, given the subject matter, and my hope is that even at those inevitable sticky wickets my deep love for the Christian path and yearning for its reconciliation and wholeness will still shine through. When all is said and done, I want Mary Magdalene fully back within the church, not outside it. For here, I believe, is where her finest work is yet to be done.

PART ONE

⊙　⊙　⊙　⊙　⊙

MARY MAGDALENE
AS APOSTLE

I

MARY MAGDALENE IN THE CANONICAL GOSPELS

☉ ☉ ☉ ☉ ☉

HIGH ON AN ESCARPMENT crowning the medieval walled city of Vézelay, France, stands the magnificent basilica of St. Mary Magdalene. And virtually at the center of that basilica, in a chapel immediately to the right of the high altar, is a larger-than-life marble statue of the patroness herself. It is the quintessential portrait of Mary Magdalene as most of us in the Christian West have come to know her. She is buxom and voluptuous (as voluptuous as one can be in stone), somewhat falling out of her marble bodice, and her face is contorted with the dual burden of remorse and devotion. She carries in her arms an alabaster jar, filled with the precious ointment with which she will anoint her beloved before his crucifixion. Haunting and haunted, she peers forth in eternal witness to the poignant reality of human love.

"She was forgiven because she loved much," writes the author of the fourteenth-century spiritual classic *The Cloud of Unknowing*.[1] For Western piety, if you want to know the story of Mary Magdalene, you will find it ensconced in a drama of sin and forgiveness. She is a "sinful woman" (read: prostitute), healed of her wicked ways by Jesus and reborn as his most devoted disciple. Yet in her essential being she remains effusive and slightly unstable, given to large, symbolic actions and copious tears. Just beneath the surface of her redeemed and reordered life, the passions ran hard and strong, symbolized in the color red with which medieval artistry tends to paint her, and her devotion is tinged with an element of desperation.

Modern scholarship has tended to soften up the prostitute aspect; we will be looking later at the loophole through which that total fallacy slipped in. But the memory of a broken person whose conversion was synonymous with her healing remains front and center in the portrait of Mary Magdalene. She is the "type" of the recovering sinner. Even the contemporary liturgical prayers for the Feast of Mary Magdalene (July 22) maintain this emphasis on healing and restitution. As the opening invocation from the Episcopal *Book of Common Prayer* goes, "Almighty God, whose blessed Son restored Mary Magdalene to health of body and mind, and called her to be a witness of his resurrection: Mercifully grant that by your grace we may be healed of our infirmities and know you in the power of his unending life."[2]

It may be surprising, then, to discover that this theoretically "scriptural" portrait actually hangs on the very slimmest of scriptural threads. It is almost entirely a concoction of patristic and medieval Western piety (interlaced with some not-so-pious political agendas, a number of contemporary scholars would add). It's "real" to the degree that it actually came to life within the church and both did and continues to exert a huge influence on Christian spirituality. But it's not "true," if by true you mean faithful to what actually happened or to what the scriptural accounts themselves actually say or imply. What scripture actually says about Mary Magdalene is a lot more positive—and for exactly this reason, a lot more unsettling.

Many people think that the current Mary Magdalene craze has been fueled largely by the recovery of the so-called gnostic gospels (those of Thomas, Mary Magdalene, and Philip in particular). Now the word *gnostic* means many things to many people (we'll be clearing up these distinctions shortly), but the bottom line seems to be a risqué and definitely dangerous departure from the tried-and-true ground of Christian orthodoxy. And, yes, it's true that these recently recovered ancient texts do round out the portrait of Mary Magdalene in significant ways. But in no way do they actually *contradict* the picture already available in the familiar canonical gospels (Matthew, Mark, Luke, and John). Even if we had only these four texts to work with, there is still more than enough material here to warrant a complete revisioning of Mary Magdalene. The question is not about information; it's about how we hear and process it. And in the Christian West, sad to say, we have been mostly sleepwalking for nearly two thousand years.

What do I mean by this? Let me try to explain by sharing with you my experience of the moment when I actually woke up.

As part of the research for my book *Chanting the Psalms*, I was spending Holy Week 2005 on a "working retreat" with the Fraternités monastiques de Jérusalem, the innovative young monastic order in residence at the basilica in Vézelay. This mixed community of men and women monks is well known for the imagination and beauty of its liturgy, and toward the end of the Good Friday liturgy I witnessed an unusual ceremony that changed forever how I understood my Christianity.

The liturgy was long and intricate, performed with meticulous reverence by the brothers and sisters. The late afternoon shadows were already dimming the cathedral when we finished with communion, followed by the traditional stripping of the altar. And then came the ceremony I am speaking of. Two of the sisters brought forward a small *corpus*—the crucified Christ figure that traditionally hangs on Roman Catholic crosses. It was carved in wood, about two feet long. Tenderly they wrapped it in the altar cloth, laid it on the altar, and placed beside it an icon of the Shroud of Turin Jesus (the portrait of Jesus allegedly imprinted on his original burial shroud and revealed through radiocarbon dating). They set a small candle and incense burner at the foot of the altar. And then, as sunset fell, one of the monks began to read in French the burial narrative from the Gospel of Matthew.

Enchanted by the mystical beauty of all this—the smell of the incense, the final shafts of daylight playing against the great stone walls of the cathedral—I allowed the sonorous French to float by my ears while I drifted in and out, catching what I could. I heard the description of Joseph of Arimathea asking for the body of Christ, wrapping it (just as the sisters had just done) in a linen cloth, laying it in a tomb. And then out of the haze of words came "et Mary Magdalene et l'autre Marie restaient debout en face du tombeau . . ."

That's when I did my double take. *Mary Magdalene* was there? *That* was in the scripture? Why hadn't I ever noticed it before?

Thinking that maybe my French had failed me, I went back to my room that evening, took out my Bible, and looked it up. But yes, right there in Matthew 27:61 it read: "And Mary Magdalene and the other Mary remained standing there in front of the tomb."

Suddenly the whole picture changed for me. I'd thought I knew the tradition well. As an Episcopal priest I'd presided over many Good Friday liturgies, and as a choral musician, I'd sung my share of Bach Passions. I'd thought I knew the plot backward and forward. How could this key point have escaped my attention? No wonder Mary Magdalene came so unerringly to the tomb on Easter morning; she'd stood by in silent, unflinching vigil the whole time Jesus was being laid to rest there. Maybe she never left . . . Since that moment I have literally not heard the Passion story in the same way. It inspired me to go back to the gospels and actually *read* the story in a new way.

And that's where I'd like to begin with you as well. Like myself, a great many Christians have absorbed most of what they know about Mary Magdalene through the dual filters of tradition and the liturgy, which inevitably direct our attention toward certain aspects of the story at the expense of others. Even without the assistance of *The Da Vinci Code* or the gnostic gospels, there is more than enough deconstruction and reconstruction work awaiting us right in our own scriptural dooryard. Let's begin our exploration, then, by looking at what the four canonical gospels actually have to say about Mary Magdalene. We'll start with the incidents that are unanimous and fully attested and move on to the ones that are contested, partial, contradictory, or allusive. Then we'll try to make sense of what we see.

MARY MAGDALENE AS FIRST WITNESS
TO THE RESURRECTION

All four gospels identify Mary Magdalene as having been the first witness to Jesus's resurrection and they all single her out individually in this role. The specific passages are as follows:

Matthew 28:1–10
Mark 16:1–11
Luke 24:1–11
John 20:1–18

Of the four accounts, John's is by far the most extensive and dramatic. Mary arrives alone at the tomb in the early hours of the morning to discover that the stone blocking the tomb has been rolled away. She hurries off to find Peter and "the disciple whom Jesus loved,"[3] who race each other to the site, discover the tomb empty and the grave cloths rolled up, and return home in bewonderment. After the two of them have gone their way, Mary stays behind, weeping beside the tomb. Then, in a unique and immortally reverberating encounter:

She turned around and saw Jesus standing there, but she did not recognize him. Jesus said, "Woman, why are you weeping? Who are you looking for?" She thought it was the gardener and answered him, "Lord, if you have taken him away, tell me where you have put him and I will go and remove him." Jesus said to her, "Mary." She turned and said to him, "Rabboni"—which means *Master.* Jesus said to her, "Do not cling to me; you see I have not yet ascended to my Father. But go to my brothers and say to them: I am ascending to my Father and your Father, to my God and your God."

So Mary went and announced to the disciples, "I have seen the Lord, and this is what he said to me." (John 20:14–18)

It is on the basis of this announcement that Mary earned the traditional title of "Apostle to the Apostles." The first to witness to the resurrection, she is also the one who "commissions" the others to go and announce the good news of the resurrection. We will see this role confirmed and considerably developed when we come to the Gospel of Mary Magdalene in chapter 3, but the contours are already clearly visible in this Johannine account. Meanwhile, we experience in this unique vignette (it occurs in no other gospel) a touching and poignantly human drama, whose core modality is love.

For what it's worth, we see here exactly the same configuration that we will meet again in the Gospel of Mary Magdalene two chapters hence: Mary's authority as "apostle to the apostles" derives fundamentally from a "private" vision and instruction from Jesus.

The Gospel of Mark also specifically mentions that Jesus "appeared first to Mary of Magdala" (16:9). But a word of caution here: the final verses of this chapter (Mark 16:9–20) are seen by nearly all scholars as being added on later to soften the original disturbing ending in 16:8, which concludes simply with the discovery of the empty tomb and the women fleeing in disarray. If we stick with this earlier ending, we find the following account:

When the Sabbath was over, Mary of Magdala, Mary the mother of James, and Salome bought spices so that they might go and anoint the body. And very early in the morning, just after sunrise, they came to the tomb. (Mark 16:1–2)

Mary Magdalene is mentioned as one of the first visitors to the tomb, but she is not singled out for a private appearance (in this earlier ending, of course, there is no appearance!). Her role is within the collective.

In the later Markan account, we again see Mary functioning as "apostle to the apostles," but with mixed results: "She went and reported the news to his followers, who were now mourning and weeping. But when they heard that he lived and had been seen by her, they would not believe it" (Mark 16:10).

The configuration is basically the same in the other two gospels: Mary Magdalene accompanied by at least one or two other women, also named Mary. (Who are all these other Marys? We'll take up that question in chapter 2.) Matthew's account is highly dramatic: as Mary Magdalene "and the other Mary" are making their way to the tomb, there is a sudden violent earthquake, and an angel descends from heaven to roll away the stone and announce to them that the Lord is risen (Matthew 28:1–7). The two women are collectively charged with the task of telling the news to the disciples, which they do immediately "in holy fear yet great joy."

Matthew's account then adds its own unique twist:

> Suddenly Jesus met them on the way and said, "Peace." The women approached him, embraced his feet, and worshiped him. But Jesus said, "Do not be afraid. Go and tell my brothers to set out for Galilee; there they will see me." (Matthew 28:9–10)

This "peace" encounter, which in Luke and John is ascribed to Jesus and the twelve male disciples (Luke 24:36; John 20:19), is here assigned to Mary Magdalene, with a powerful and poignant effectiveness. Touch! Embrace! Worship! Even though Magdalene is "chaperoned" in this resurrection appearance, she and her companioning Mary are warmly invited to embody their joy, and the lofty implications of the "he is risen" message play themselves out in a wonderfully intimate moment of human reunion.

In Luke's gospel, Mary Magdalene is also specifically mentioned among the witnesses to the resurrection, but in an expressly collective way. The passage reads: "Among the women who brought the news were Mary Magdalene, Johanna, and Mary the mother of James" (Luke 24:10). These have earlier been introduced as "the women who had come with Jesus from Galilee (Luke 23:55).[4] Luke explains how "on the Sabbath day the women rested according to the commandment, but on the first day of the week, at dawn, they went to the tomb with the ointments they had prepared." There they encounter the angel, hear the proclamation that he is risen, and hurry to inform "the Eleven and their companions."[5] Unlike Matthew and John, there is no specific angelic charge to do so, but as in the "second ending" of Mark (which leans heavily on Luke), the effort turns out badly: "However much they [the women] insisted, those who heard did not believe the seemingly nonsensical tale" (Luke 24:11).

While the details vary, and the jury is split as whether this was a solo or group appearance, all four gospels mention Mary Magdalene *by name* as the first witness to the resurrection. Moreover, all four gospels portray her in the role of "apostle to the apostles," not only the first witness to the resurrection, but the first to announce it publicly. In two of the four gospels this is a charge to which she is specifically commissioned by Jesus himself.

MARY MAGDALENE AS WITNESS TO THE BURIAL OF JESUS

In addition to her prominent role in the resurrection narrative, three of the four gospels also specify that Mary Magdalene was a witness to the burial of Jesus. The specific citations are:

Matthew 27:61
Mark 15:47
Luke 23:55–56

In no case is this a solo witness. Mary Magdalene is always accompanied by at least one other of the group of holy women. Luke does not even mention her by name in this particular citation; she is simply one of "the women who had come with Jesus from Galilee." But since the names of these women have already been enumerated (in Luke 8:2) and will be repeated a few verses later (Luke 24:10), it is safe to infer that she is a member of the delegation. The text itself is brief but explicit, situating this act of witnessing within the context of "information gathering" in preparation for a return to the tomb the morning after the Sabbath to perform the ritual burial anointments:

> It was Preparation Day, and the star which marks the beginning of the Sabbath was shining. So the women who had come with Jesus from Galilee followed Joseph [of Arimathea] to see the tomb and how it was being placed. And returning home, they prepared perfumes and ointments. (Luke 23:54–56)

In Mark's account, there is no mention of a motivation for the action, only the action itself. The incident seems to be included primarily to explain why the Marys will be able to find their way back to the tomb on Easter morning:

> Joseph took [the body] down and wrapped it in the linen sheets he had bought. He laid the body in a tomb that had been cut out of the rock and rolled a stone across the entrance to the tomb. Now Mary of Magdala and Mary the mother of Joset took note of where the body had been laid. (Mark 15:46–47)

Matthew's account of this incident is only one sentence long, and as in Mark, the emphasis is on witnessing pure and simple: "Mary Magdalene and the other Mary remained standing there in front of the tomb" (Matthew 27:51). But this fleeting vignette is unusually vivid and allusive because of its strong visual imagery— and because of the absence of any mention of *leaving*. In a brief, almost haiku-like image, Matthew manages to evoke a powerful, mysterious energy of presence. It was this passage, you recall, that I heard enacted at Vézelay, and it has continued to reverberate within me as an icon of steadfast love.

The Gospel of John makes no mention of Mary Magdalene's presence at Jesus's burial—although, as we shall see shortly, it places her prominently at his feet during the crucifixion.

MARY MAGDALENE AS A WITNESS
TO THE CRUCIFIXION

All four gospels either directly mention or allude to the fact that Mary Magdalene was present at the crucifixion. The references are as follows:

Matthew 27:55–56
Mark 15:40
Luke 23:49
John 19:25

In Matthew and Mark the emphasis is on distance, both physically and functionally. Matthew specifies that "the women watched from a distance" and that "they had followed Jesus from Galilee and saw to his needs." Magdalene is singled out in this passage as belonging to this group, together with "Mary the mother of James and Joseph and the mother of Zebedee's sons."

In Mark the parallel passage reads: "There were also some women watching from a distance; among them were Mary Magdalene, Mary the mother of James the younger and Joset and Salome, who had followed Jesus when he was in Galilee and saw to his needs." In both Matthew and Mark, the mention of the women follows directly after Jesus's death and the dramatic pronouncement by the centurion, "Truly, this man was the son of God."

In Luke, Mary Magdalene is not specifically identified but is clearly included among those who bear witness "at a distance" during the final moments of Jesus's life. The account, which again takes place immediately after Jesus's final cry and the centurion's proclamation, reads as follows: "Only those who knew Jesus stood at a distance, especially the women who had followed from Galilee; they witnessed all this."

While distance is the motif in these first three gospels, the Gospel of John moves the action up close. It is specifically noted that Mary Magdalene stands at the foot of the cross, together with Mary, Jesus's mother, and Mary, the wife of Cleophas. Her presence is neither explained nor further developed, but her witness is specifically noted.

MARY MAGDALENE IDENTIFIED AS HEALED OF DEMONIC POSSESSION

Luke 8:2
Mark 16:9

Unlike Mary Magdalene's role in the Passion and resurrection narratives, which is attested to in all four gospels, the report of her former demonic possession comes to us only through Luke (echoed in Mark 16:9). The passage reads:

> Jesus walked through towns and countryside, preaching and giving the good news of the kingdom of God. The Twelve followed him, and also some women who had been healed of evil spirits and diseases: Mary called Magdalene who had been freed of seven demons; Joanna, wife of Chuza, Herod's steward; Suzanna and others who provided for him out of their own funds.

The reference in Mark 16:9 (which, recall, many believe to be added on later) simply recapitulates this information: "After Jesus rose early in the week, he appeared first to Mary of Magdala, from whom he had driven out seven demons." His information undoubtedly comes from Luke.

Now this Lukan passage is interesting both for what we hear in it and for what we don't hear. It is certainly curious that what would soon become the chief feature in the Christian West's portrait of Magdalene—that she was healed of some "illness of mind or body"—is in fact mentioned briefly in only this one gospel. No

mention of any infirmity is found in Matthew, John, or in any of
the gnostic gospels, which paint quite a different picture. Luke's
gospel tends to have a strong bent toward healing anyway, so the
emphasis on this dimension is perhaps understandable.[6] But it
still leaves one wondering why such a variant detail should assume such gigantic proportions.

Please note that Luke does *not* say anything about the seven
demons being "prostitution." Or about Mary Magdalene being a
sinner. We'll see shortly how the early church fathers came to this
erroneous conclusion. Within the context of the times, being
possessed by demons could imply either an emotional or a recurrent physical illness. In a modern commentary on Mary Magdalene,
Jean-Yves Leloup is able to turn this text back on itself, arguing
ingeniously that the fact that seven demons have been cast out of
her means that she's "done her psychological work" inwardly and
is hence prepared to be a disciple.[7] But within Luke's own frame
of reference, this detail seems more intended to subtly undercut
Mary Magdalene's credibility as the premiere witness and apostle
of the resurrection. It plants the first seeds of doubt—the vaguest
innuendo of something "off" in her character. As we shall see,
these seeds will soon spring up to take over the whole portrait.

This passage is interesting in another way, however. Notice
how the list is set up: "The Twelve followed him, and also some
women . . ." "The Twelve" are of course the male disciples familiar to all Christians. (And earlier did you catch Luke's reference
to "and their companions"? See endnote 5 for the by-no-means-
inconsequential implications of this seemingly casual detail.) But
unlike Matthew and Mark, who specify that the women follow
Jesus "to provide for his physical needs," Luke merely notes that
they *follow*—which is what disciples do. They are not second-class
followers; they are full-fledged followers.

It is important to note this because it flies in the face of our
conventional assumption that Jesus had an inner circle and an
outer circle, the inner circle open only to men. Certainly this was
a cultural assumption of Jesus's time, and going against it was
controversial—in fact, it frequently landed him in a lot of trouble!
But when you really look at the public ministry of Jesus, particu-

larly as portrayed in the gospels of Luke and John, it shapes up as a lot more egalitarian. There were simply followers: people Jesus healed, or revealed himself to, or dialogued with, and these were both men and women. "The Twelve" were men, but they did not constitute an inside track; in all four gospels they are counterbalanced by an opposite and equal female presence designated collectively as "the Marys." As with any genuine spiritual master, then or now, participation in the inner circle is determined not by gender but by the degree of understanding and commitment. And all four gospels infallibly place Mary Magdalene within that inner circle.

ECCLESIAL STARDUST

Why is it so hard to see this today? At the beginning of this chapter I spoke about a collective sleepwalking that has dulled our senses, particularly in the Christian West. If I were to elaborate, I would describe it more specifically as a kind of stardust thrown over the whole picture by our habitual way of hearing the gospels heavily filtered through nearly two millennia of ecclesial theology. The implicit assumptions here (reinforced each Sunday in the liturgy) are that Jesus came to earth to found the church, instituted its principal sacrament at the Last Supper, and appointed his male-only disciples to be its apostles and priests. When we hear the story through that heavily self-reinforcing logic, the role of Mary Magdalene naturally shrinks to a minor walk-on. But when we loosen our stranglehold on that picture, the role that actually emerges for her from the scriptures themselves is considerably more important.

First and paramount, we see that all four gospels witness to Mary Magdalene as the premiere witness to the resurrection—alone or in a group, but in all cases named by name. Given the shifting sands of oral history, the unanimity of this testimony is astounding. It suggests that among the earliest Christians the stature of Mary Magdalene is of the highest order of magnitude—more so than even the Virgin Mother (mentioned as present at the crucifixion in only one gospel and in none at the resurrection). Mary Magdalene's place of honor is so strong that even the heavy hand of a later, male-dominated ecclesiology cannot entirely dislodge it.

Second, all four gospels insist that when all the other disciples are fleeing, Mary Magdalene stands firm. She does not run; she does not betray or lie about her commitment; she witnesses. Hers is clearly a demonstration of either the deepest human love or the highest spiritual understanding of what Jesus was teaching, perhaps both. But why, one wonders, do the Holy Week liturgies tell and re-tell the story of Peter's threefold denial of Jesus, while the steady, unwavering witness of Magdalene is not even noticed? How would our understanding of the Paschal Mystery change if even that one sentence that I finally heard at Vézelay was routinely included in the Good Friday and Palm Sunday Passion narratives? What if, instead of emphasizing that Jesus died alone and rejected, we reinforced that one stood by him and did not leave?—for surely this other story is as deeply and truly there in the scripture as is the first. How would this change the emotional timbre of the day? How would it affect our feelings about ourselves? About the place of women in the church? About the nature of redemptive love?

And above all, why is the apostle to the apostles not herself an apostle? But for the antidote to that most flagrant piece of ecclesial stardust, we will need to search beyond the walls of traditional biblical Christianity.

2

THE WOMAN WITH THE ALABASTER JAR

☉ ☉ ☉ ☉ ☉

SO HOW DID WE get there? From apostle to penitent whore? If it's not in scripture, how did it become such a fixed datum of our tradition?

To dig into that question, we have to look at one incident that so far we have not considered. All four gospels make note of a disturbing and highly dramatic event that takes place while Jesus is at dinner with friends. A woman suddenly bursts into the dining room carrying a jar of precious perfume. She opens it and copiously anoints Jesus's head or feet, weeping all the while. The host attempts to protest—why waste such precious perfume?— but Jesus staunchly defends her actions.

Aha, you say . . . finally, the familiar Mary Magdalene of our Vézelay statue, complete with alabaster jar! Why didn't I include this set of scriptural citations in the earlier chapter?

The reason is simple. Not a single one of the scriptures themselves identifies this woman as Mary Magdalene.

Let's look more closely at the four citations in question:

Matthew 26:6–13
Mark 14:3–8
Luke 7:36–47
John 12:1–8

While the gospels are unanimous in their testimony that this
incident happened, the actual portrayal varies widely. And these
variations prove to be crucial to the subject of our concern.

THE ANOINTING IN MATTHEW AND MARK

Matthew and Mark's accounts are virtually identical and establish
our baseline narrative. Here is Matthew's version:

> While Jesus was in Bethany in the house of Simon the leper,
> a woman came up to him carrying a precious jar of expensive
> perfume. She poured it on Jesus' head as he was at table. See-
> ing this the disciples became indignant, protesting, "What a
> useless waste! The perfume could have been sold for a large
> sum and given to the poor."
>
> But Jesus was aware of this, so he said, "Why are you
> troubling this woman? What she has done for me is indeed a
> good work. You will always have the poor with you, but you
> will not have me forever. She was preparing for my funeral
> when she anointed my body with perfume. Truly I say to you:
> whenever the Gospel is proclaimed all over the world, what
> she has done will be told in praise of her."

In this account we see three telltale details: (1) the woman is
unnamed, (2) the anointing takes place at the house of Simon
the leper in Bethany, and (3) the event takes place shortly before
Jesus's crucifixion and is interpreted by Jesus himself as a burial
anointment.

THE ANOINTING IN JOHN

John's account follows basically the same plot line, but adds two
very significant twists: the incident is set at the house not of Simon

the leper but of Jesus's friend Lazarus, whom Jesus has raised from the dead in the chapter immediately preceding this one. And the woman who does the anointing is specifically identified as Mary of Bethany, Lazarus's sister. Again, the episode is set directly before the crucifixion and is seen in that context as a burial anointment proclaiming Jesus's own death. Here is John's version:

> Six days before the Passover, Jesus came to Bethany where he had raised Lazarus the dead man, to life. Now they gave a dinner for him, and while Martha waited on them, Lazarus sat at the table with Jesus. Then Mary took a pound of costly perfume from genuine nard and anointed the feet of Jesus, wiping them with her hair. And the whole house was filled with the fragrance of the perfume.
>
> Judas, son of Simon Iscariot—the disciple who was to betray Jesus—remarked, "This perfume could have been sold for three hundred silver coins and turned over to the poor." . . .
>
> But Jesus spoke up, "Leave her alone. Was she not keeping it for the day of my burial? (The poor you will always have with you, but you will not always have me.)"

John's unique and categorical identification of the woman performing the anointing as Mary of Bethany has stirred up its own rat's nest of trouble, as we shall see shortly. But for now, let's stay with the main thread of our argument and look at the far more portentous variations introduced into this account by Luke.

LUKE'S ACCOUNT

The seeds of a myth

As usual, Luke's account is the richest in detail and human interest. He deliberately sets up this anointing episode as a kind of teaching drama to illustrate the meaning of Jesus's parable: "The one who is forgiven more, loves more." Uniquely in Luke, the incident is separated from the Holy Week narrative, and set within the context of Jesus's public ministry, where it loses its expressly symbolic and ceremonial ambiance and becomes simply another in a series of teachings and healings.

The account runs as follows:

> One of the Pharisees asked Jesus to share his meal, so he went to the Pharisee's home and as usual reclined on the sofa to eat. And it happened that a woman of this town, who was known as a sinner, heard that he was in the Pharisee's house. She brought a precious jar of perfume and stood behind him at his feet, weeping. She wet his feet with tears, she dried them with her hair and kissed his feet and poured the perfume on them.
>
> The Pharisee who had invited Jesus was watching and thought, "If this man were a prophet, he would know what sort of person is touching him: isn't this woman a sinner?"
>
> Then Jesus spoke to the Pharisee and said, "Simon, I have something to ask you . . . Two people were in debt to the same creditor. One owed him five hundred silver coins, and the other fifty. As they were both unable to pay him back, he graciously cancelled the debts of both. Now which one will love him more?"
>
> Simon answered, "The one, I suppose, who was forgiven more." And Jesus said, "You are right. Do you see this woman? You gave me no water for my feet when I entered your house, but she has washed my feet with her tears and dried them with her hair. You didn't welcome me with a kiss, but she has not stopped kissing my feet since she came in. You provided no oil for my head, but she has poured perfume on my feet. This is why, I tell you, her sins, her many sins, are forgiven, because of her great love. But the one who is forgiven little, has little to love."

We can see how in almost every detail this episode has been changed—and of course, the lineaments of the future Mary Magdalene are already peering through this portrait. To begin with, Luke uniquely adds the fact that this unnamed woman is a sinner, and Simon the Pharisee's "if you knew what kind of a woman this was . . ." sets up that innuendo of what kind of sin we are talking about. While Matthew and Mark make no mention of the state of mind the woman was in when she performed her ablutions, Luke fills in this detail, painting the picture of an effusive emotionality: tears, weeping, kissing of feet—all the attributes of what we would today call a first-class drama queen.

Note that Luke does not name this woman; he does not identify her as Mary Magdalene (or Mary of Bethany, either, although that Mary, too, makes a brief appearance in this gospel).[1] But when you put the pieces all together, merging Luke's details with the composite portrait emerging from the other three gospels, you have an explosion waiting to happen. Like that old wives' cure for hiccups (where with arms outstretched you try to hold your two smallest fingers as close together as possible without touching), the collision is inevitable; there is too much energy arcing across the gaps. And so, as the mind races to fill in the gaps (particularly if you start with the assumption, as was nearly universal in biblical scholarship until less than a century ago, that the scriptures agree and tell one true story), one moves swiftly to the following conclusions:

1. The seven demons cast out of Mary Magdalene imply that she was a sinner.
2. Since the woman in this anointing incident was a sinner, and Mary Magdalene was also a sinner, they must be the same person.
3. Given the effusiveness of her personality and Simon the Pharisee's comment about "what kind of women this is," her sin must be lust.
4. Since this woman is also identified as Mary of Bethany, Mary Magdalene and Mary of Bethany must be the same person.

This, in short, is the pathway traveled during the first six centuries in the Christian West to arrive at the conflation that has become our image of Mary Magdalene. You can see the basic links in this train of assumptions already percolating in the writings of the Latin church fathers by the end of the fourth century. But it is Pope Gregory the Great who finally ties the pieces into one definitive package during a sermon preached in 594. The following sentences from Homily 33 would define the Roman Catholic Church's official position on Mary Magdalene for nearly fourteen hundred years (not until 1969 was the teaching that she was a prostitute finally repealed):

> She whom Luke calls the sinful woman, whom John calls Mary, we believe to be the Mary from whom seven demons were ejected according to Mark. And what did these seven demons signify if not all the vices? . . . It is clear, brothers, that this woman previously used the unguent to perfume her flesh in forbidden acts. What she therefore displayed more scandalously, she was now offering to God in a more praiseworthy manner.[2]

That, in a nutshell, is the "how" of it: the slippery slope along which we moved from Mary Magdalene, apostle to the apostles, to Mary Magdalene, penitent whore. The "why" of it is a bit more complicated. Karen King and other feminist scholars are inclined to see a deliberate plot here: In an emerging church hierarchy founded on the assumption of a male-only and celibate succession from the original apostles, Mary Magdalene's apostolate was clearly an anomaly and a threat. A means had to be devised to undercut her original authority and move from, as it were, apostolacy to apostasy. Luke handed them the raw materials on a silver platter.

I don't disagree, but my own take is that the process was not so much conscious sabotage as unconscious projection. Knowing something of how scriptural *lectio divina* works (lectio divina, or sacred reading, is the traditional monastic practice of "ruminating" the scripture in such a way that it enters deeply into one's unconscious imagination), I see the portrait of Mary Magdalene as penitent whore as primarily the work of the early church's collective unconsciousness, the inevitable shadow side of its increasing obsession with celibacy and sexual purity. Gregory's leap from "seven demons" to the seven deadly sins to lust is, in my mind,

characteristic of subconscious rather than conscious mental pro-
cessing, and his further imaginative flourish that the sacred un-
guent had formerly been used by Mary Magdalene "to perfume
her flesh in forbidden acts" reflects the highly visual and associa-
tive logic typical of the practice of lectio divina and the allegorical
interpretive mode it gave rise to. This is not in any way to try to
excuse the church fathers; if anything, it makes the picture even
bleaker, pointing the finger not at individual culprits but at a deepening sickness of the soul already clearly visible in the Western
church by the end of the patristic era. But it does soften the cloak-
and-dagger spin that the contemporary feminist-driven "hermeneutic of suspicion" will frequently put forward. In all eras, the
church remains the faithful mirror of its times—what cannot be
faced openly will find its way to the surface in the only way it can.

MARY MAGDALENE AND MARY OF BETHANY

Once the conflation of Mary Magdalene with the unnamed sinful
woman of Luke's gospel has been gently disentangled, the more
gnarly question still remains: how about Mary Magdalene and Mary
of Bethany? If the woman who performed the anointing ceremony
has been traditionally remembered as Mary Magdalene—except
in the Gospel of John, where she is specifically identified as Mary
of Bethany—could the solution to this puzzle lie in the fact that
the two Marys are actually the same person? In virtually all the
details of the Holy Week narrative John goes his own way, introducing significant variations to the meaning and sequencing of
key events;[3] and among the many mysteries of John, none offers
more fertile ground for speculation than the prominent role ascribed to this puzzling threesome (Mary, Martha, and Lazarus)
who are pointedly singled out as occupying a special category as
Jesus's "friends." What's the message here? Is this in fact some
sort of code language to describe Jesus's *in-laws*, a familial relationship created through marriage?

  In the recent explosion of *Da Vinci Code* speculation, the classic conflation of "Mary M" and "Mary B" has once again gained

favor; in fact, the assumption that they are the same person becomes the linchpin of the whole dynasty argument. The hypothesis basically runs that Mary of Bethany, a descendant of King
Saul and the tribe of Benjamin, and Jesus, a descendant of King
David and the tribe of Judah, were secretly married and formed
thus a dynastic union reuniting the separated houses of Israel. The
anointing at Bethany was both a ritual that a wife would perform
over her soon-to-be slain husband and at the same time a symbolic
coronation, announcing Jesus as the Messiah (that is, the
"Anointed One").[4] The scholar Margaret Starbird even suggests
ingeniously that the name "Magdalene" does not refer to a place
at all, a town in Galilee, but is rather a nickname—Magdal-eder,
"the tower"—suggesting Mary's towering role in the band of Jesus's disciples and the honor they secretly accorded her.[5]

So . . . what does one make of this argument?

I admit to having sat on both sides of the fence on this question. If Mary Magdalene and Mary of Bethany are in fact the
same person, this certainly creates a strong case for the "lost dynasty" argument, and explains the mystery and secretiveness that
hovers in the gospel around the special status of this so-called
Lazarus family. Arguing against this interpretation, however, are
two significant difficulties. First, the Gospel of John itself clearly
distinguishes between these two characters. There is no conflation in the author's mind. Mary of Bethany is the one who performs the anointing, named as such. And Mary Magdalene,
named as such, is the one who stands watch at the foot of the
cross and engages in the resurrection drama. If they were the
same character, it is hard to see how John would have failed to
make this point clear.

Second, as we meet these women in the gospels, it is difficult
to make the case that they are the same person because their energies seem so distinctly different. Mary Magdalene is bold and
brash, "out there," witnessing and proclaiming. Mary of Bethany's role is more "yin": inward, passive, gentle, and softer. Both
in John and in her cameo appearance in Luke 10:38–42, she simply sits at the feet of her master and *waits*. She is the icon of pure
contemplative attunement.

Over the course of the three-year process of writing this book, I have gradually come to my own conclusion about this matter, which I admit is a bit surprising even to myself. I now believe that Mary of Bethany is a red herring, given artificial historical plausibility by our failure to spot John's deeper symbolic purposes and the subtly veiled bridal mysticism at work throughout his gospel. When these factors are seen, she fades back into Mary Magdalene like a noonday shadow. I will develop this argument toward the end of this book, but for now it is getting way, way ahead of the game. There is considerable groundwork that must be laid before you will be able to see for yourself what has led me to this conclusion.

For now, it is important to keep our feet on solid ground, and that solid ground is determined by well-established scholarly methods and procedures. Whatever you personally feel about this admittedly ambiguous issue of "Mary M" and "Mary B," it does provide our first working demonstration of what I like to call "The First Law of Scholarly Hygiene"—namely, when evidence is conflicting and hotly contested, it is dangerous to build speculative castles on shifting sands. From unanimous testimonies (as, for example, Mary Magdalene's witness to the resurrection) strong cases can be built. But where the evidence disagrees, it is wise to err on the conservative side, advancing one's claims modestly and in such a way that the whole superstructure of the argument does not rest on one weak link. That Mary Magdalene and Mary of Bethany are the same person is not out of the question, but at this point it is definitely a weak link; and until research turns up some definitive new piece of evidence or insight, we would be well advised to proceed cautiously. We will invoke this same principle a few chapters later as we look at the question of Jesus's presumed celibacy.

WILL THE REAL MARY PLEASE STAND UP?

There are, of course, a lot of Marys running around the gospels: Mary Magdalene, Mary of Bethany, Mary the mother of Jesus,

Mary *her* sister and the wife of Cleophas, and Mary the mother of James. Even given the fact that Mary (Miriam) was a common Semitic name, how does one account for this multiplicity? Is it merely coincidence, or is there some symbolism at work here?

Unable to resolve this quandary in my own mind, I asked my longtime friend and teacher Father Bruno Barnhart for his opinion. As the former prior of New Camaldoli Hermitage in Big Sur, California, and a practitioner of monastic lectio divina for some forty years, he has perfected the art of this subtle contemplative listening. I figured that if anyone had a reliable intuition, he would. "Well . . ." he pondered, "it may be that all the Marys in the story are really one Mary: aspects of one eternal feminine."[6]

It is tempting to follow his lead here, and his comment may indeed be true at one level. But one has to be fair: I can't recall ever hearing it said that all the male disciples are aspects of one Jesus, the eternal masculine. We can't compare apples and oranges—male individuals and female archetypes. While the Marys are definitely collective in their actions, they are not merely archetypes but rather are historical realities. The Greek Orthodox Church meticulously sorts them out and keeps track of them in its liturgy and prayer. My own take, which I alluded to toward the end of the last chapter, is that they function as a counterbalance to "the Twelve"—a male chorus and a female chorus, so to speak, each taking its place within the greater whole that in totality comprises the body of Jesus's disciples. Like the Shakers of yesterday or the Fraternités monastiques de Jérusalem today, they bear witness to the fact that it is when men and women travel together on the spiritual path, each in his or her own order but in full equality, that the icon of the *anthropos* (or "completed human being") is most fully revealed upon the earth. In this regard Jesus was and remains light years ahead of his times.

Or perhaps, as some scholars suggest, the other Marys are added later, either to soften the intimacy of the resurrection encounter between Jesus and Mary Magdalene, or else to enhance its credibility by having multiple witnesses.[7] Again, the caveat about building castles on sand obtains. Since we do not know how they came to be part of the story, or for what purpose, it is safer to let them be than to try to explain them away.

Much later in this book I will return to Father Bruno's core insight that all these Marys may be aspects of just one Mary—which I believe is actually true, but in the mirror image of the way he intended it. Rather than a kaleidoscope of individuals adding up to one archetype, what if it were the other way around: a later distribution of the assets that originally belonged to one unique, individual woman? The contemplative attunement of a Mary of Bethany, the incorruptible spiritual purity of a Virgin Mary, the erotic devotion of a penitent whore—and of course, the bold and tenacious witness of the one so named as Mary Magdalene: could these all be facets of one flesh-and-blood woman whose very fullness breaks the mold of what our tradition has taught us is possible? This will indeed be the proposition set forth in this book, but it will take many chapters of careful bricklaying to build the case, so here I will merely plant the seeds.

THE MYTH OF THE PENITENT SINNER

A parting thought

"God sometimes writes straight with crooked lines," the old saying goes. While I would in no way want to be seen as approving of this process by which a powerful and faithful apostle is transformed into a repentant whore, its legacy in the West has by no means been a total disaster. When one explores the spiritual literature emerging from this transposition—from the early patristic legends of the "harlots of the desert"[8] to the medieval *The Cloud of Unknowing*—there is certainly more than a fair share of misogyny and slander. But in the most sublime representations of this genre, something else shines through as well. For the writers spiritually equal to the task, the archetype of the penitent whore seems to draw forth from them a clear understanding of the real energy and modality that Jesus's teaching works in: the unitive power of redemptive love. The third-century monastic legend of "Mary of the Desert," for example, offers what appears to be a classic allegory on the theme of gross sin, forgiveness, and a life of repentant wandering in the desert. But when after forty-seven years of solitary wandering, this particular Mary is finally discovered by an elderly monk, she emerges not only as forgiven but as a spiritual master. The monk quickly realizes he has met his match as she holds forth with an astonishing degree of mystical knowledge and insight. Her passion has transformed her into one of the initiated ones. And in *The Cloud of Unknowing*, the author recognizes this same quality of passion as the key element that not only frees Mary from her sins but catapults her into unitive consciousness and a state of continuous beatific communion:

> When our Lord spoke to Mary as a representative of all sinners who are called to the contemplative life and said, "Thy sins be forgiven thee," it was not only because of her great sorrow, nor because of her remembering her sins, nor even because of the meekness with which she regarded her sinfulness. Why then? It was surely because she loved much.
>
> . . . Even though she may not have felt a deep and strong sorrow for her sins . . . she languished more for lack of love than for any remembrance of her sins . . .
>
> . . . Instead [rather than sorrowing and weeping], she hung up her love and her longing desire in this cloud of unknowing and she learned to love a thing that she might never see clearly in this life, neither by the light of understanding of her reason nor by a true feeling of sweet love in her affection. Very often, in fact, she had hardly any special remembrance of whether she had been a sinner or not. Yes, and I hope that she was often so deeply immersed in the love of His Godhead that she hardly saw the details of the beauty of His precious and His blessed body in which He sat speaking and preaching before her with such great love.[9]

Again, this level of understanding is attained in only the most tough-minded of the mystics, those who have themselves attained to unitive consciousness. But where it is on the mark, it comes part and parcel with the realization that Jesus's core teaching is rooted in the ground of transformed eros and brings as its fruit not only forgiveness of sins but unswerving singleness of perception. Ultimately, it is not about "clean living" and purity, but the total immolation of one's heart. As early Christianity increasingly took its bearings from the monastic model of celibate renunciation, the repentant prostitute archetype keeps alive (albeit in distorted fashion) what is actually the true bull's-eye of the Master's teachings themselves. Here again, we will see why in later chapters. But if the choice had come down to a decision either to dress Mary Magdalene up in regal apostolic vestments and make her part of the celibate power structure, or to leave her as she was, bursting into the closed dining halls of ecclesial privilege with the raw immediacy of her love, surely tradition has chosen the better part. At least it gives us something actual of Jesus to work with.

3

THE "GNOSTIC" GOSPELS

⊙   ⊙   ⊙   ⊙   ⊙

To the victor belongs not only the spoils, but the right to tell the story. And by the fourth century of Christianity there was beginning to emerge a victor's circle, which could claim for itself the status of "orthodox." Not surprisingly, this circle began to form itself around the emperor Constantine, who in 313, by a single edict, converted Christianity from a forbidden cult to the state religion and thereafter made it his pet project. The energy toward clarification, unification—and yes, imperial pomposity—emerged primarily from that quarter of the Christian world. By 325 the church had its official creed, hammered out at the Council of Nicea in what is now southwestern Turkey and still in regular use by Christians today. And while it would still be another century and a half before an official "Bible" appeared, a consensus as to what belonged in it was already beginning to take shape. A list drawn up by the bishop Athanasius in 367 of the twenty-seven canonically authorized apostolic writings would eventually prove identical with the official New Testament canon. And as the church consolidated, it had a story to tell.

You know that story, if you've been raised Christian. It's not only in the Bible; it's in your blood, reinforced by the liturgy, the catechism, and the rich traditions of sacred art and iconography. The basic plot is laid out in the book of Acts. It begins with the hushed silence of Jesus being taken up to heaven, followed by the fiery descent of the Holy Spirit at Pentecost, which many Christians still celebrate as "the birthday of the church." The apostle Paul enters on the scene, at first a foe and then an indefatigable champion following his mystical encounter with Jesus on the road to Damascus. And then we watch as the disciples-now-apostles work out their differences and steadily spread the gospel—and the young church—to all the corners of the Holy Roman Empire.

Running through this story are several assumptions so powerful that they comprise what Karen King (drawing on the earlier work of German biblical scholar Walter Bauer) calls "the master story." Together these assumptions reinforce a singular point of view about how the faith and practice of the early Christian church took shape. In the powerful and eye-opening final chapter of her book *The Gospel of Mary Magdala* (a chapter that should really be required reading for all Christians), King summarizes the major tenets of this story:

1. Jesus reveals the pure doctrine to his apostles, partly before his death and partly in the forty days before his ascension.
2. After Jesus's final departure, the apostles apportion the world among themselves, and each takes the unadulterated gospel to the land allotted him.
3. Even after the death of the disciples the gospel branches out farther. But now obstacles spring up to it within Christianity itself. The devil cannot resist sowing weeds in the divine field—and he is successful at it. True Christians blinded by him abandon the pure doctrine.[1]

In other words, she writes, "This master story asserts that an unbroken chain stretching from Jesus to the apostles and on to their successors in the church—elders, ministers, priests and bishops—guaranteed the unity and uniformity of Christian belief and practice."[2] This "unbroken chain" is known in theological language as the "apostolic succession," and it is the cornerstone of ministry and authority in the church to this very day. (Please note that by the time this story emerges, the apostles had come to be seen as male only, the evidence of the scriptures themselves notwithstanding.) The developmental sequence, as King points out, thus moves in the following order: "unbelief, right belief, wrong belief." The apostolic mission began in the unity of fellowship and pure doctrine and only gradually fell into confusion and fragmentation. As these dissipating tendencies set in, what allowed the church to stand firm was the flaming sword of orthodoxy itself, vigilantly wielded by its apostolic fathers.

In the simplified version of this story that most Christians absorb through the skin, this amounts to the following tenets: Jesus came to earth to found a religion called Christianity, called his male-only disciples to be its apostles and priests, and gave them the sacrament of the Eucharist at the Last Supper. The obvious anomalies are overlooked—why Mary Magdalene, who was specifically given the first apostolic charge by Jesus himself to announce the news of his resurrection, was not included among the apostles, and why Paul, who was not at the Last Supper and never met Jesus in his earthly life, was. But such is the power of blinders. And if you doubt the hold that this story still has on the church, or its ability to inflict serious consequences on the lives of contemporary Christians, consider that in one Catholic parish of my acquaintance, during a recent Maundy Thursday service (where the central symbolic act reduplicates Jesus's washing of the disciples' feet), a priest refused to wash the feet of any women on the basis that only men were present at the Last Supper. The message being sent about the value of women and their full inclusion in the body of Christ is only too obvious. What's worse is that it's patently untrue.

THE NAG HAMMADI REVOLUTION

So seamlessly did this master story become the filter through which Christians saw the world that—understandably, after sixteen hundred years of consistent storytelling—it was all but impossible to see it any other way. But the time bomb was already ticking when, in 1945 in the deserts of Egypt near Nag Hammadi, a large urn was discovered in a cave containing scrolls dating from the early days of Christianity. They appeared to have been placed there in the late fourth century—probably in response to that edict by Bishop Athanasius designating the official New Testament canon. The scrolls were a collection of sacred writings that had once been in use in early Christian communities but failed to make the cut amid tightening standards of orthodoxy. Unwilling to destroy texts they still considered holy, the monks of some unknown monastic community hid them away for safekeeping. The recovery of these texts was destined to upset the apple cart, although it took a few decades for the implications to sink in.

The first response of the international team of Bible scholars assessing them was to dismiss them as "late" or "gnostic." They had been eliminated from the canon because they were "not orthodox." One distinguished New Testament professor went so far as to comment that if they had landed in the dustbin, it was because they deserved to be placed there! To Bible scholars who had grown up on the master story, the worldview emerging from these recovered texts looked like a theological version of *Alice in Wonderland*. They were staring at a Christianity that was simply unfathomable. Their circular logic was still invisible to them.

Little by little, that first charge was dismissed. The texts ranged in date, but they could not uniformly be dismissed as "late." Some—such as the Gospel of Thomas—proved to be among the earliest writings of the church: contemporary with or even earlier than Mark, the earliest of the canonical gospels. This, of course, increased the turmoil. Had the seeds of "unorthodoxy" been planted so early?

Elaine Pagels stepped forward as the pioneer in the revisioning effort. Her book *The Gnostic Gospels*, published in 1979, rightfully won the Pulitzer Prize for its groundbreaking efforts to make sense of these texts from a historical critical perspective. She realized that winners and losers in the canonical sweepstakes were determined not by divine edict—the triumph of "pure doctrine"—but in the far worldlier realm of politics. What we now call orthodoxy came into being through the tug of war of opposing viewpoints around developing issues of Christian order and doctrine. Prominent among these issues were the role of women, the question of apostolic authority, the relationship between the Old and New Testaments, and the meaning of the resurrection of the body. But as a scholar of her times, Pagels still saw the playing field as divided between "Jewish Christian" and "Gnostic" camps, each of which seemed to arrive with fixed positions and fully formed theologies. It would be another quarter of a century before the revisioning could mature to the point where Karen King could make the bold statement, "I never call the *Gospel of Mary Magdala* a Gnostic text for the simple reason that there was no such thing as Gnosticism."[3]

No such thing as Gnosticism? She has to be kidding, doesn't she? Not only is her statement here at variance with nearly two thousand years of apostolic teaching, it flies in the face of our own times as well. Gnosticism is highly fashionable these days, and in its current pop culture revival there is indeed an effort to portray it as a fully articulated alternative religion to Christianity, complete with its own theology and Mystery rituals.[4] Certainly the energy around *The Da Vinci Code* runs off this assumption. But while there may be short-range gratification (and even a kind of wicked glee) in recasting Gnosticism as the religion of the eternal feminine with Jesus and Mary Magdalene as its chief hierophants, in the long range this kind of fuzzy thinking does a lot more harm than good to the cause of Mary Magdalene. Karen King's point is intuitively brilliant, and once you see what she's driving at, it liberates the playing field far more sweepingly than even the most flamboyant of the neo-Gnostic speculations.

What King has come to recognize is that *Gnosticism is the inevitable shadow cast by the master story itself.* If one starts with the assumption of an original standard of orthodoxy against which all variants are weighed in the balance and found wanting, then these variants will inevitably tend to reify into an opposite and equal story whose collective name becomes "Gnosticism." But these are both, she claims, simply the view from the winner's circle: a mythological reconstruction of an earlier era of Christianity on the basis of theological and political agendas firmly in place by the time the myth was spun. Gnosticism came into being hand-in-hand with developing standards of orthodoxy, to be the scapegoat for "the devil sowing weeds in the field of pure doctrine," as stipulated by the master story. But the real culprit all along has been the master story itself.

When one moves this sacred cow gently off the tracks, the picture that emerges of the real origins of Christianity is far more fascinating and believable. Rather than an unadulterated "pure doctrine" handed on serenely from apostle to apostle, early Christianity was a riot of pluralism, as different in ethnicity and temperament as the Mediterranean lands themselves. There were Jewish Christians, Greek Christians, Roman Christians, a whole line of Syrian and Aramaic Christians that has largely dropped out of sight, initiates of Mystery schools, keepers of the Torah, millennialists and mystics, ascetics, misogynists, and matriarchs. Each community struggled within the terms of its own frame of understanding—its own *cosmovision* (to borrow a wonderful term from the contemporary scholar Raimon Panikkar)—to make sense of the Jesus event, and within each community that vision looked a little different. Far from bowing to some objective standard of orthodoxy, what gave these early Christian communities their seat-of-the-pants dynamism was that everything had to be worked out from scratch. What did Jesus actually teach? Who was an apostle and who was not? How did one tell? Needless to say, there were many local options, and the texts that circulated among these early outposts of Christians comprised an ongoing conversation rather than an unbroken monologue.

This revised picture is very good news for our study of Mary Magdalene, for it is against this backdrop of conversation and ferment that we can at last begin to hear her story. Certainly the new gospels that we will be meeting shortly confirm an environment of intense dialogue and debate—and they also give us a glimpse of the pressures already at work in the Christian community that will eventually diminish her role from first among the apostles to "best supporting actress." Most important, however, the new picture is more spiritually spacious, and it is far more comfortable with the idea of love as a spiritual path than was ever conceivable within the celibate and increasingly sexually phobic line of church fathers that eventually became the voice of orthodoxy. Within this more dynamic and culturally diverse backdrop there is room to reunite those three indivisible facets of Mary Magdalene's being which, through the lens of the master story, will always appear anomalous and fragmented: apostle, beloved, and soul mate. When the master story disappears, Mary Magdalene once again steps into view.

THE NEW MARY MAGDALENE GOSPELS

The treasure trove of writings emerging out of Nag Hammadi and other recent finds yields us up three very important new source materials for the study of Mary Magdalene: the Gospel of Thomas, the Gospel of Philip, and the Gospel of Mary Magdalene. The first two belong to the Nag Hammadi collection. The third, which is by far the most significant for our purposes, was recovered not at Nag Hammadi but in Cairo and made its way back into our awareness on a different but parallel track that I will say more about in the next chapter.

In the Gospel of Thomas, Mary Magdalene appears in only two places, but they are important ones. In logion 21[5] she asks the all-important question, "Tell us, Master, what your disciples are like," which leads Jesus to respond with the most succinct yet comprehensive description of the path he was teaching to be found among any of the gospel accounts, canonical or otherwise. And in the final logion (114), his response to Peter's assertion that "Mary should leave us because women are not worthy of this life" is not only an explicit validation of her spiritual authority, but a powerful summary of his vision of the fully realized human being as one who both integrates and transcends all gender identification.

The Gospel of Philip is the most ornate and intricate of the three—a parallel, in a different cultural stream, to the intricate brilliance of the Gospel of John.[6] The text is essentially tantric in its orientation (centered in the transformation of eros), but as in all tantric teaching, prudence and spiritual subtlety are required to catch the real meaning. This is the gospel in which Mary Magdalene appears most undisguisedly as Jesus's companion and beloved, and a disproportionate amount of titillation has been stirred by its comment that "the Teacher loved her more than all the disciples and often kissed her on the mouth."[7] But in this text even more than in most, it is dangerous to pull lines out of context in an effort to glean personal information. The whole gospel unfolds as a single tapestry around the theme of bridal mysticism as the core metaphor for the Christian spiritual path. Nothing in its contents can be separated from this overarching purpose. Because Philip's understanding of love as a transformative path is so brilliant and subtle, we will reserve our encounter with this gospel till the second part of this book.

The Gospel of Mary Magdalene is particularly important because it gives us a firsthand glimpse of that diversity and ferment at the heart of early Christianity (in fact, you might consider it "Exhibit A" for Karen King's argument). A good initial way of describing it would be to view it as a parallel version to the book of Acts but minus the master story. Like Acts, it unfolds after the physical departure of Jesus from the planet, and its focus is on the calling of the apostles and the preaching of the gospel. But whereas in Acts the heroes are Peter and Paul, here it is Mary Magdalene who clearly emerges as winner of the apostolic triple crown: deepest understanding of the Master's teaching, best ability to live out what she understands, and an ongoing relationship with the Master in the visionary realms that makes her privy to teachings the other disciples know nothing about. While the gospel itself is brief (and frustratingly, two major sections are missing, reducing the original seventeen manuscript pages by more than half), what does remain is of such importance to our understanding not only of Mary Magdalene but of the core path of Christianity itself that it will well warrant our careful attention in the next three chapters. On the basis of internal evidence (specifically, the absence of the master story as the ultimate court of appeal), King dates this manuscript early—to the first half of the second century.[8] As is also the case with the four canonical gospels, Mary Magdalene is probably the honorary rather than the actual author. But "honorary" is no small achievement; the designation clearly indicates that there were communities of early Christians who revered her memory and had absorbed their Christianity through her stream of apostolic teaching.

The Gnostic Conundrum

When we enter this other stream, however, we are definitely in a different cosmovision. And a cosmovision, remember, is not just a theology or metaphysic, but the whole worldview underlying it. Cosmovisions are cultural; they are filters through which different peoples and ethnic groups look out upon their world.[9]

The word traditionally applied to this other flavor of Christianity so different from our Western cosmovision is *gnostic*. Karen King has properly said that there is no such thing as "Gnosticism"— i.e., an organized counterbalancing religion (like Christianity only with the "wrong" doctrines). But while this point cannot be made strongly enough, there is still widespread confusion as to what *gnosticism* actually means, and when the term is used indiscriminately to describe an unfamiliar cosmovision, it winds up unfairly (for better or for worse) prejudicing our response to it. Since our quest for Mary Magdalene will by necessity carry us into these "gnostic" waters, I would ask you to bear with me for a few paragraphs as I attempt to clarify the terminology, at least as I will be using it. While this may look like a digression, I hope you will see that it is not.

The word *gnostic* comes from the Greek *gnosis*, which means "knowledge." It's a perfectly respectable scriptural word. Paul uses it repeatedly in his writings, including the celebrated lines from 1 Corinthians 13: "For now I see through a glass darkly, but later face to face; now I know in part, but later I will know even as also I am known." But the essential thing to keep in mind about this knowing is that it's participational—a "knowing even as also I am known." It is not just a knowing from the head; it's a knowing with the entire being. The Hebrew term which it translates is *da'ath*, which is also the word used for "lovemaking" (as in "David entered Bathsheba's tent and 'knew' her"). *Gnosis* speaks of a complete, integral knowing uniting body, mind, and heart—and by its very largeness connecting the seen and the unseen.

Please note that this "knowing" is not *initiatic* wisdom. It is not about Mystery rituals or secret initiation ceremonies where esoteric information is imparted. (And *da'ath* notwithstanding, it is not about sacred sex.) The difference between these two kinds of wisdoms can be summed up in a helpful distinction suggested by Ken Wilber—between "states" and "stages."[10] Initiatic rituals can briefly change people's states, transporting them into ecstatic visions and cosmic consciousness. But gnosis is about stages; it is integral knowledge brought about by the slow unification of one's being. In the wonderful words of the contemporary Jewish teacher Rami Shapiro, it is "not only an altered state of mind (moving from narrow to spacious), but an altered trait of behavior, moving from selfishness, fear, and narcissism to justice, compassion, and humility."[11] Jesus taught gnosis and was a master of gnosis, as we shall see shortly. But he did not change anyone's states, either by secret rituals or esoteric information. Rather, he set his disciples upon the only known path to integral transformation: the slow and persistent overcoming of the ego through a lifelong practice of surrender and nonattachment. His gnosis is gradual, conscious, and sober.

The problem arises when this generic meaning of the term *gnosis* gets confused with a later and much more specific strain in a very different cosmovision. *Gnosticism* as it was understood by the church fathers, and continues to be commonly understood today, is a specifically Greek heresy in that it depends upon a Platonic metaphysics of ideal forms and an inherent dualism between matter and spirit. In this complex metaphysical world of archons, emanations, and demiurges, salvation is a matter of freeing the immortal soul from its imprisonment in matter. As the fathers rightly noticed, this is at variance with what Jesus taught and practiced.[12]

So where does that leave us? You can see the difficulty we get into here. I may call the Gospel of Mary Magdalene "gnostic," meaning that its emphasis—as was Jesus's—is upon the gradual, integral transformation of being. But you may hear the word and think "dualistic," "esoteric," or "cultic"—which this gospel certainly is not.

My suggestion is that what we are really encountering in the gospels of Thomas, Philip, and Mary Magdalene is not gnosticism but a Near Eastern cosmovision. The Western mind has been formed in the Greek cosmovision, and within its parameters the terms *orthodox, heretic,* and *gnostic* all have specific reference points. But in these other gospels we are dealing with an entirely different frame of reference, a whole different way of making connections. My colleague Lynn Bauman, who taught in the Near East for nearly fifteen years and knows the culture well, has suggested that we call this other stream "Semitic." This is a helpful distinction as long as we bear in mind that he does not simply mean "Jewish" here, but is referring instead to the wider family of Near Eastern peoples and languages including Syrian, Aramaic, Arabic, and Persian.

Whatever one chooses to call them, the gospels of Mary Magdalene, Thomas, and Philip all clearly belong to the wider tradition of universal wisdom, or *sophia perennis,* with its core notion of conscious and integral transformation. Unlike the canonical gospels, which emphasize "right belief" as the basis for salvation, these wisdom gospels emphasize "right practice." They are transformation-minded. But they are not esoteric, dualistic, abstract, docetic (denying the reality of the body), initiatic, or elitist. So are they gnostic? Your choice. My own choice is not to use the word at all. After centuries of pejorative use as essentially a euphemism for "heretic," the term *gnostic* has become so convoluted and emotionally charged that it would be better to declare a moratorium on its use and simply allow these newly recovered texts to speak in their own right.

A DIFFERENT TAKE ON MARY MAGDALENE

We will soon be exploring in detail the portrait of Mary Magdalene that emerges from this other stream. But overall, three elements stand out in sharp contrast to the more familiar world of the canonical gospels.

1. Jesus's inner circle of disciples includes both men and women on an equal footing. There is no distinction made between a male group of disciples and a female group of camp followers, although there is certainly an acute (and sometimes painful) awareness of just how unusual this situation is. Inner and outer, as in all wisdom teaching, is essentially self-constituted, determined by the degree of understanding and commitment of the individual disciple. Mary Magdalene is clearly in the inner circle. Nor is there any conflation here: no Mary of Bethany or Greek chorus of witnessing and chaperoning Marys.

As I said earlier, this recognition is also implicit in the canonical gospels, particularly Luke and John. But here it becomes explicit.

2. Mary Magdalene is seen as "first among the apostles" not simply in a chronological sense (because she was the first on the scene at the resurrection) but in a more fundamental way: *because she gets the message.* Of all the disciples, she is the only one who fully understands what Jesus is teaching and can reproduce it in her own life. Her position of leadership is earned, and it is specifically validated by Jesus himself. (This again is confirmed in at least two of the canonical gospels, although it is consistently downplayed in tradition and in the liturgy.)

3. She is clearly in a relationship with Jesus that is in some way special: a "beloved disciple"—and this appears to entail an erotic component as well. "We know that he loved you more than all other women," says the apostle Peter in the Gospel of Mary Magdalene (6:1), and we have that passage from the Gospel of Philip that has caused the rumor mill to fly: "for Jesus used to walk with her and kissed her frequently upon the mouth." But

the fact of their relationship does not in any way undercut the second point just made. She is not his "consort" but his *companion* (specifically designated as such by Philip) and equal partner in the teaching and transmission. This tension is insisted upon. The intimacy Jesus and Mary Magdalene share exists, contextually, within the unitive love that grounds them—and all others open to it—within the kingdom of heaven.

How could this be possible? Beloveds and yet completely pure? Welcome to the world of Near Eastern kenotic spirituality— gnostic, if you insist. But to be able to hold this tension will not only make sense of Mary Magdalene, but shed a good deal of light on Christianity as a whole, as we shall soon see.

4

THE GOSPEL OF
MARY MAGDALENE

☉ ☉ ☉ ☉ ☉

IT IS AMAZING that something so tiny could pack such a punch. The Gospel of Mary Magdalene is tantalizingly brief—and frustratingly, two major sections are missing, reducing the original seventeen manuscript pages by more than half. Yet what remains is more than enough to radically overturn our traditional assumptions about the origins of Christianity. In four tightly written dialogues the gospel delivers powerful new revelations on the nature of Jesus's teachings, the qualifications for apostleship, Mary Magdalene's clear preeminence among the disciples, and the processes already at work in the early church that would eventually lead to her marginalization. Since it also contains a unique glimpse into the actual metaphysics on which Jesus based his teachings, this is a foundational text not only for devotees of Mary Magdalene but for all students of sacred wisdom.

The manuscript was not recovered among the Nag Hammadi trove. It first came to light in 1896, nearly half a century before the Nag Hammadi find, when it was discovered by a German collector in an antiquities market in Cairo. But due to a series of lengthy publication delays the first German scholarly edition did not appear until 1955. It would be twenty years longer before an English version appeared and still another twenty years before popular editions became available. For all practical purposes, therefore, the Gospel of Mary Magdalene entered public awareness at the same time as the Nag Hammadi material, and since they clearly belong to the same spiritual stream, it makes sense to consider them together. Particularly with the Gospel of Thomas, there are striking overlaps in both content and theology.

The manuscript itself is a fifth-century Coptic (i.e., Egyptian) version of what had almost certainly been an earlier Greek or even Syrian text.[1] In 1917 and then in 1938 two Greek fragments dating from the third century were indeed discovered, confirming the antiquity of the original text and the esteem in which it was held by the earliest Christian communities (only important manuscripts are recopied). As I mentioned in the last chapter, Karen King assigns the original text to the first half of the second century. If her argument is correct, this would place the Gospel of Mary Magdalene within the earliest strata of Christian writings, roughly contemporaneous with the Gospel of John.

Unfortunately, the Greek fragments did not yield any new material to fill the holes in the Coptic version; barring some unforeseen miracle, what was written on those ten missing manuscript pages (pages 1–6 and 11–14) is lost to us forever. But because of the thematic and structural tightness of the remaining material, the second of these two holes lends itself easily to imaginative reconstruction, and depending on how closely one assumes that this text echoes the Gospel of Thomas, the first six pages of Jesus's introductory metaphysical discourse can also be fairly well construed.

ENTERING THE TEXT

The Gospel of Mary Magdalene is in many ways much closer to drama than to narrative. It is constructed entirely in dialogue, and the exchanges are so lively that they lend themselves easily to a staged reading or even a full-fledged reenactment.[2] The five characters—Jesus, Mary Magdalene, Peter, Andrew, and Levi—all have clearly defined personalities and agendas, and even with more than half of its manuscript pages missing, the gospel still creates a unified impact largely through the strength of these dramatic interactions.

The manuscript's four dialogues (or "scenes," if you prefer to think of them that way) lay out as follows:

> (*pages 1–6 missing*)
> 1. Jesus's final teachings and instructions to his disciples. (manuscript pages 7–9)
> 2. Mary Magdalene's words of encouragement to the disciples. (page 9)
> (*pages 11–14 missing*)
> 3. Peter's invitation to Mary Magdalene to share with them some of the "secret" teachings of Jesus, and her visionary recital of "the soul's progress." (10, 15–17)[3]
> 4. The dispute among the disciples and its resolution; Levi's charge and words of dismissal. (17–19)

There are several translations now available to choose from, including Karen King's *The Gospel of Mary* and Jean-Yves Leloup's *The Gospel of Mary Magdalene*. In general, King's edition is the more reliable academically, while Leloup's, despite its sometime freehanded translations of the Coptic, is incomparable in its spiritual insight and knowledge of the Near Eastern wisdom traditions. I suggest that you buy both editions and lay them side by side in order to fine-tune your own interpretation. In this book I will be working from *The Luminous Gospels*, a new translation of the gospels of Thomas, Mary Magdalene, and Philip prepared by Lynn Bauman, Ward Bauman, and myself, published in 2008.[4] It more or less splits the difference in the interpretive spectrum: the translations are closer to King; the interpretive nuances closer to Leloup. After laying out each dialogue in its entirety, I will offer a brief commentary.

DIALOGUE ONE

. . . tell us about matter. Will it survive or not?

The Savior answered:

> All of nature with its forms and creatures exist together
> and are interwoven with each other. They will be resolved
> back, however, to their own proper origin, for the compo-
> sitions of matter return to the original roots of their na-
> ture. Those who have ears, let them hear this.

Then Peter said to him:

> Since you have explained everything to us, tell us one more
> thing. What is the sin of this world?

The Savior replied:

> Sin as such does not exist. You only bring it into manifesta-
> tion when you act in ways that are adulterous in nature. It
> is for this very reason that the Good has come among you
> pursuing its own essence within nature in order to reunite
> everything to its origin.

Then he continued:

> This is also the reason for sickness and death, because you
> embrace what deceives you. Consider these matters, then,
> with your spiritual intellect.
>   Attachment to matter gives birth to passion without
> an Image of itself because it is drawn from that which is
> contrary to its higher nature. The result is that confusion
> and disturbance resonates throughout one's whole being.
> It is for this reason that I told you to find contentment
> at the level of the heart, and if you are discouraged, take
> heart in the presence of the Image of your true nature.

Those with ears, let them hear this.

Having said these things, the Blessed One addressed them:

> Peace be with you. May my peace reside within you. Guard carefully that no one misleads you saying, "Look, he is here," or "He's over there," for the Son of Humanity already exists within you. Follow him, for those who seek him there will find him. Go forth, now, and proclaim the Good News concerning the Kingdom. Beyond what I have already given you, do not lay down any further rules nor issue laws as the Lawgiver, lest you too be dominated by them.

Having said this, he departed.

As we enter this dialogue, we are literally joining a conversation in midstream. From textual clues in this dialogue and the one following, it appears that the conversation takes place in temporal history sometime between Jesus's resurrection and ascension—the Gospel of Mary Magdalene's version of the "upper room" appearances in John and Luke.[5] In this energy-charged encounter Jesus gathers his students around him once again to reflect on the meaning of his passage through death and to leave them final instructions and encouragement before his departure from physical form.

The teaching style is clearly *sohbet*: "spiritual conversation" between a master and his students. This is a classic Near Eastern teaching style that even today is a mainstay in many schools of Sufism. In contrast to the "Socratic" method more familiar to those of us in the West, sohbet is not merely intellectual discourse, but rather it is a deep meeting of hearts and minds that also includes a direct energy transmission. For those familiar with the art form, the context of this first dialogue is unmistakable and speaks once again to this gospel's probable Semitic origins.

As manuscript page 7 opens, a student is clearly asking Jesus a question about the permanence of matter, and Jesus responds with a brief but remarkable metaphysical statement—something that

occurs nowhere in the canonical gospels and offers a fascinating
glimpse into the *theoria* (theoretical knowledge) on which his
practical wisdom rests. The student's question is probably not
theoretical; it follows directly from the resurrection appearance
itself with all its inherent paradoxes and consternation. Is Jesus
really here? Is this material body in which he stands before them
a solid reality or merely a veil that will soon dissolve? Jesus responds by affirming very strongly that the origin of nature (i.e.,
the material world) does not lie within this earthly plane. What we
take for solid reality is a *mixtus orbis*, a "mixed" (or "mixed up")
realm in which everything is "interwoven" (a statement that contemporary physicists and metaphysicians would heartily applaud).
At the end of their physical term, the forms of matter return to the
original "roots of their nature." But by this, we will learn shortly,
he does not mean they dissolve into their component atoms, quarks,
and/or humors. Instead, they return to an original template—or
"image"—whose place of arising is in another realm.[6]

Peter immediately jumps in with the next question. What is
sin? This is, of course, the classic Jewish philosophical preoccupa-
tion; you will find it vividly imprinted on nearly every page of Old
Testament prophetic and wisdom teaching and as the driveshaft
of the Pauline metaphysics upon which orthodox Christian theology rests. Whose fault is it that suffering and evil came into the
world? Who is to blame? How is it atoned for? Jesus rejects that
question out of hand: "Sin as such does not exist."

His answer would initially seem to place him solidly within
what we would nowadays identify as an "Eastern" rather than
a "Western" mindset: not sin, but ignorance of one's true nature,
is to blame for the sufferings of this world. But we must listen carefully to where he is headed in his comment. He does not go on to
state that sin is therefore an illusion, the typical Eastern thought
progression. To the contrary, he affirms that sin does indeed come
into existence—that is, it becomes objectively real—when one acts
in ways that are "adulterous in nature." And within his particular
frame of reference, acting in ways that are "adulterous in nature"
will prove to have a very specific meaning. It signifies a *failure to
stay in alignment with origin*: with that mysterious "root" (or

template) of one's nature he has already alluded to, which, while arising beyond this realm, seeks its full expression here.[7]

He quickly assures his students that this world is valuable and precious; indeed, this is the very reason the Good has come among them in the first place—"pursuing its own essence within nature [i.e., within this transitory realm] in order to reunite everything to its origin." There is important integrative work to be done here. But it all depends upon keeping a right alignment along what wisdom tradition typically refers to as the "vertical axis": the invisible spiritual continuum that joins the realms together. Nearly sixteen centuries later the German mystic Jacob Boehme would express this cosmological insight with poetic precision and beauty:

> For you must realize that earth unfolds its properties and powers in union with Heaven aloft above us, and there is one Heart, one Being, one Will, one God, all in all.[8]

When the realms are in spontaneous resonance—"one Heart, one Being, one Will, one God, all in all"—the music of the spheres bursts forth. When they are not, disease and disharmony inevitably ensue. As he quickly points out (again, with a contemporary feeling to the teaching), "Confusion and disturbance resonate throughout one's whole being," and sickness and death are the inevitable result.

IMAGE AND ANALOGUE

Like most of the world's great spiritual teachers, Jesus affirms that attachment to matter is the root of all suffering. But by building on his previous insight, he is able to offer a concrete explanation for this phenomenon:

> Attachment to matter gives birth to passion without an Image of itself because it is drawn from that which is contrary to its higher nature.

For the first time in this dialogue Jesus officially introduces the word *image*. The reference is brief here, but you will find ample elaboration in the Gospel of Thomas (particularly logia 83 and 84), which shares a virtually identical understanding. Within the particular metaphysical stream that Jesus seems to be working in, *image* corresponds to that primordial template mentioned earlier—"the origin" of each created form. Very cautiously, you might label it an *archetype*.[9]

At first glance you may be tempted to transpose this teaching into Platonic categories and assume that Jesus is talking about the "ideal form" of a thing. But be cautious in doing so, for there is a distinctly different dynamism at work here. For Jesus, the "image" is not merely a static blueprint, a preexistent prototype that its earthly analogue mechanically reflects. Between image and analogue there is a dynamic reciprocity as they simultaneously articulate the same reality in two different realms. Image and analogue are in a continuously creative tension receiving and fulfilling each other, and it is in the energy exchange that their indivisible wholeness is made manifest.[10]

Images do not arise in this realm, however (their origin is several cosmoses more subtle), and trouble begins when this fundamental cosmic law is forgotten. The problem with "attachment to matter," as Jesus explains, is that the passion it begets corresponds to nothing in the higher realm and is therefore a cul de sac, out of spiritual alignment and ultimately illusory. To be deceived by these mirages and spend one's time chasing after them is—in the blunt words of the Gospel of Thomas—"to make friends with a corpse."[11]

SEEING WITH THE HEART

The remedy Jesus sets forth for this cosmic malaise is to "find contentment at the level of the heart . . . in the presence of the Image of your true nature." The key to deciphering this all-important instruction lies in recognizing that the word "heart" is being used here in a highly specific way. In the wisdom traditions of the Near East, the heart is not the seat of one's personal emotional life, but *an organ of spiritual perception.* I have spoken about this extensively in my other books so I will be brief here, but the essential point is that the heart is primarily an instrument of sight—or *in*sight, as the case may be ("Blessed are the pure in heart, for they shall see God"). Its purpose is to navigate along the vertical axis and stay in alignment with "the Image of one's true nature." Itself a vibrant resonant field, it functions like a homing beacon between the realms; and when it is strong and clear, it creates a synchronous resonance between them.

"Those with ears, let them hear this," Jesus continues—his characteristic "heads-up." But as we remember our primary topic of interest in this book, Mary Magdalene, his warning is particularly well-timed: because how well you are able to grasp his teaching is exactly how well you will be able to grasp the basis of their relationship. To say that their hearts are intertwined is not at all to speak sentimentally. Rather, it is to affirm that Mary Magdalene has fully understood this principle of spiritual alignment through the heart and has been able to personally corroborate it within herself. This will directly explain her ability to stay present when he appears to her in visions and her ability to go about her earthly business with the serene confidence of one whose life is always flowing within that greater life.

THE UNITIVE GROUND

How would I characterize this teaching of Jesus? It definitely belongs to the wider stream of sophia perennis in its acknowledgment of many and more subtle realms of being whose energies impact our own—a concept traditionally known as "the great chain of being."[12] But it parts company from classic gnosticism (and even classic sophia perennis) by refusing to claim that this world is illusion, or fall, or error; or that its density places it at the tail end of the chain. We are not in Plato's cave. Rather, this world is good, worthy, and fully inhabited by the divine energies—"the Good comes among you"—so long as it stays united with its root.

The blending of incarnational and Platonic elements is a distinctive mix, which I believe is Jesus's original contribution to the metaphysics of the West. It presents itself as a profoundly incarnational, warm-hearted, and hopeful path, where the realms support and interpenetrate each other and divine fullness is accessed simply by keeping the heart in natural alignment with its invisible prototype. Unfortunately, his teaching went right over the heads of nearly all his followers, both then and now.

The subtlety of Jesus's metaphysics remains largely unknown to Christians—and sadly so, for it is the missing ingredient that makes his path comprehensible and doable. It is no secret that Jesus's teachings resonate with an extraordinary trust in the divine abundance and generosity, and Christians are asked to emulate that trust. But to try to do so without seeing what it is founded on is a bit like asking an elephant to fly, and Christians find themselves frequently caught in the gap between the incredibly high spiritual ideals of this path and their own ability to carry them out. In reality, the secret is simple. When the heart is aligned with its eternal image, abundance cascades forth from that place of origin, infinitely more powerful than the scarcity and constriction of this world. It is not a matter of believing in flying elephants so much as of purifying the heart.

"LAY DOWN NO FURTHER RULES . . ."

In the final lines of his discourse Jesus reinforces this teaching yet again. His parting instruction to his disciples opens with the plea that they remain present within themselves rather than chasing after mirages in the outer world, for "the Son of Humanity already exists within you . . . and those who seek him there will find him."[13] To remain in continuous union—the kind that Mary Magdalene will shortly demonstrate—is a matter of releasing the outer clamor and tuning in again and again through the homing beacon of the heart.

Then, as if knowing already that this is somehow beyond them, he adds a final practical caution: "Do not lay down any rules beyond what I have given you, lest you be dominated by them." From a textual criticism point of view, as Karen King rightly observes, this instruction situates the Gospel of Mary Magdalene at an early stage in the history of Christianity, when the contours of externally imposed hierarchy are just beginning to become visible in the dawning light of a brave new Christian world. From an artistic standpoint, it moves us directly into the second dialogue while at the same time setting the stage for the gospel's surprising and decisive conclusion.

DIALOGUE TWO

His students grieved and mourned greatly saying:

How are we to go into the rest of the world proclaiming the Good News about the Son of Humanity's Realm? If they did not spare him, how will they ever leave us alone?

Mary arose, then, embracing them all and began to address them as her brothers and sisters saying:

Do not weep and grieve nor let your hearts remain in doubt, for his grace will be with all of you, sustaining and protecting you. Rather, let us give praise to his greatness which has prepared us so that we might become fully human.

As Mary said these things their hearts opened toward the Good and they began to discuss the meaning of the Savior's words.

In this second and crucial dialogue, the predictable happens. The subtlety of Jesus's teaching is lost on his disciples, who return quickly to their conviction that Jesus is gone and that they are in extreme danger. They have completely missed the point of what he has just said.

As Mary Magdalene steps forward to encourage them, she demonstrates that she has fully understood what Jesus is saying and can apply it to her own life. "Do not let your hearts remain in doubt," she says, cutting immediately to the spiritual chase. For a heart in doubt—in two-ness and self-sabotage—becomes useless as that organ of alignment. To reconnect to the grace he has promised them is as simple a matter as opening to his presence right then and there in their inmost depths—"for those who seek him there will find him." And as she pointedly reminds them, "He has prepared us for this."

BECOMING FULLY HUMAN

In fact, her actual words are, "He has prepared us so that we might become fully human." "To become fully human" is a modern translation of the words "to become an *anthropos*," a completed human being. Both here and in the Gospel of Thomas this notion is at the very heart of Jesus's vision of transformation.

In modern psychological parlance building on a Jungian foundation, the concept of *anthropos* is generally interpreted in terms of an integration of the opposites within oneself—specifically, a bringing together of the male and female principles within the individual human psyche. While partially true, this understanding is far too limited to contain the cosmic sweep of Jesus's meaning. In logion 22 in the Gospel of Thomas, he lays out what he in fact has in mind for this integration of opposites:

> When you are able
> to make two become one,
> the inside like the outside,
> and the outside like the inside,
> the higher like the lower,
> so that a man is no longer male,
> and a woman, female,
> but male and female
> become a single whole;

when you are able to fashion
an eye to replace an eye,
and form a hand in place of a hand,
or a foot for a foot,
making one image supercede another
—then you will enter in.[14]

Obviously, there is far more at stake here than simply integrating masculine and feminine principles within one's finite humanity. The integration takes place on a cosmic scale and is accomplished through learning how to anchor one's being in that underlying unitive ground: that place of oneness before the opposites arise. Some traditions would call this the "causal level."[15] However one defines it, its origin is on the vertical axis, in a realm and mode of perception far more subtle than our own. It has less to do with what one sees than with *how* one sees; it amounts to a fundamental shift in perception.

When this level is attained, either by sudden spiritual insight or by a long, tough slog through the mine fields of ego, a person becomes "a single one" (in Aramaic, *ihidaya*: one of the earliest titles applied to Jesus): an enlightened or "fully human" being. The union of opposites Jesus is speaking of really pertains to the union of the finite and infinite within oneself, or the bringing together of the vertical axis with the horizontal so that there is "one Heart, one Being, one Will, one God, all in all." When this happens, the world does not pass away, but one is able to live in it as master, re-creating its external forms ("making one image supercede another") out of the infinite generativity of the One.

It is important to keep this wider definition of the anthropos firmly in mind because it is the key to everything in this gospel. Mary Magdalene moves among the other disciples as one who has "become fully human." She does not merely parrot the Master's teaching back to them, flaunting her specialness. Rather, she serves the situation. Flowing through the spiritual energy of her own alignment is a *baraka*—a grace that is able to actually shift the other disciples' emotional state. She is able to "turn their hearts to the good."

This short dialogue is the thematic epicenter of the Gospel of Mary Magdalene: the apostolic moment par excellence. "Apostle is as apostle does," one might say, and it is clear that in both her words and her deeds—her ability to comprehend, to calm, to convey blessing—Mary Magdalene has just proven herself an apostle: not just "first among the apostles," but in fact, the only one of them to authentically merit the title.

As we move into the challenging (and decimated) dialogue 3, it is important to keep firmly centered on this point. If Mary Magdalene does, in fact, enjoy a privileged access to the Master, she has certainly earned it: not because she is his special favorite (as Peter will shortly imply), but because she has been able so deeply to absorb and integrate his spiritual methodology. She has learned the secret of unbroken union with him across the realms, and she teaches from the same fount of living water that flowed in him—in fact, *still* flows in him, only now in a different energetic form. And thus, doing as real apostles do, she is able to lift her brethren out of their psychological paralysis and focus them once again on "the meaning of the Savior's words." Dialogue 2 ends on a note of strength and unanimity; for the moment, all is once again well. Unfortunately, that moment will prove all too brief.

5

DYING AND RISING

⊙ ⊙ ⊙ ⊙ ⊙

IN THE MELLOWNESS of the moment, Peter, ever the emotional weathercock, briefly rises above himself and invites Mary Magdalene to take the teacher's seat:

> Sister, we know that the Savior greatly loved you above all other women, so tell us what you remember of his words that we ourselves do not know or perhaps have never heard.

Brushing aside his flagrant "male logic" (that the only reason she would have received special teaching was because she was his girlfriend), Mary Magdalene seems happy to take him up on his offer. And what follows is one of the most extraordinary visionary recitals in the whole of Christian sacred scripture.

As fate would have it, this is exactly the place where that second major hole in the manuscript text occurs. Mary Magdalene has barely launched on her discourse about the mechanics of visionary seeing at the bottom of manuscript page 10 when there is a four-page gap; when we pick up again on page 15, she has seemingly moved on to a whole new topic. The loss of these four pages is particularly unfortunate, since this material promises to have offered important information on the inner workings of visionary revelation, one of the most critical and misunderstood topics in the early history of Christianity.

The more I work with this text, however, the more I suspect that there may not be as much missing as initially appears. By some creative application of the principles Mary Magdalene has already started to lay out, it is possible to intuit one's way a good deal of the distance across the manuscript gap. And the results are even more remarkable than one would at first dare to hope.

MEETING BETWEEN THE WORLDS

And she began to express these things to them:

> I saw the Master in a vision and I said to him, "Lord I see you now in a vision."
>
> And he answered me, "You are blessed, Mary, since the sight of me does not disturb you. For where the heart is, there is the treasure."

Buried within the intricate, quotation-within-a-quotation grammar lies the all-important issue of *when* this vision actually took place. It is clearly "earlier"—earlier, that is, than the resurrection appearance that they have all just experienced. But how much earlier? Conceivably, Mary Magdalene could be describing an episode that took place while she and the Master were both still in the flesh, but this seems a bit unlikely since the proximity of their actual physical presence would render the visionary mode of communication unnecessary.[1]

A second possibility is that she might be referring back to their powerful encounter in the garden on Easter morning when she became the first witness to the resurrection. The teachings she is about to share with the other disciples would thus be an account of what she herself received in that life-changing moment. But once again, this gospel seems to distinguish unmistakably between visions and resurrection appearances. What they have all just experienced in dialogue 1 is a resurrection appearance (when Jesus could and obviously did teach them himself), and what she clearly describes is a vision.[2]

If we keep in mind the primary characteristic of a vision, however—an exchange between two beings in different physical states (or "realms") of existence, then a third possibility presents itself: the vision might have occurred during those three days of Jesus's entombment, during which she kept vigil in the garden while he, according to tradition, "descended into hell."[3] For the moment I want to hold that possibility lightly. But note that this third possibility does fulfill all the requirements imposed by the text: an "earlier" encounter when communication in the visionary mode would make complete sense, since she and Jesus are temporarily on different planes of existence. And in this case, her teaching would assuredly be "words that we ourselves [the other disciples] do not know or perhaps have never heard," for she is reporting on a vision that came to her when Jesus was out of his body, in another realm, and she was tracking him graveside—an "insider's report," as it were, on his journey to the underworld.

THE EYE OF THE HEART

The remaining three lines of text before the manuscript gap contain fascinating, practical information on the methodology of visionary exchange. Jesus's first point—"Blessed are you, because the sight of me does not disturb you"—lays down a fundamental baseline (confirmed by virtually all spiritual masters): that the inner precondition for all visionary communication is a capacity to remain emotionally rock-steady, not allowing any waves of psychic excitation to ruffle the still waters on which the image will reflect. Any "Oh wow! Is this really happening?"; any curiosity ("How is it happening?"); any craving or excitement—and the vision is gone. The author of the fourteenth-century mystical classic *The Cloud of Unknowing* similarly warns against "any stressing or straining of the imagination,"[4] reminding his readers that it is love itself, not the personal ego, that makes the journey.

Long hours on the meditation cushion are the usual route to developing this absolute stillness of nonreflective presence that allows the deeper knowingness to flow.

The next line of text offers the important but puzzling completion of Jesus's train of thought: "For where your heart is, there is the treasure." The word translated here as "heart" is actually *nous*. It is a core concept in wisdom teaching and is often translated "mind" (as does Karen King). But that tends to imply a neo-Platonic "higher intellectual" contemplation, and such a degree of mentality does not accurately convey the real meaning of the term. The *nous* is a property of the heart, not the mind—the heart, as we have already seen, being classically regarded in the Near Eastern wisdom traditions as the organ of spiritual perception. Within it are understood to reside increasingly subtle levels and capacities of nonphysical perception, the nous being the most subtle of all. It is sometimes called "the eye of the heart"—a kind of mystical intertidal zone in which divine spirit and human spirit are completely interpenetrating. The contemporary Christian monk Thomas Merton describes this noetic territory well in the beautiful concluding lines of his essay "A Member of the Human Race":

> At the center of our being is a point or nothingness which is untouched by sin and illusion, a point of pure truth which belongs entirely to God, which is never at our disposal, from which God disposes of our lives, which is inaccessible to the fantasies of our own mind or the brutalities of our own will. This little point of nothingness and of absolute poverty is the pure glory of God in us. It is, so to speak, His name written in us, as our poverty, as our indigence, as our dependence, as our sonship. It is like a pure diamond, blazing with the invisible light of heaven.[5]

Merton's description brilliantly captures the functional essence of the nous. For this mysterious meeting ground does indeed belong to both realms, the finite and infinite. With regard to the finite, it is the highest and most pure point of divine beingness that can be enfleshed. With regard to the infinite, it is the "ombudsman," so to speak, of the divine life force as it expresses itself in each individual being, and it is the agency through which the heart is able to carry out its task of vertical alignment. When, through the nous, the vibrational field of a particular human heart comes into spontaneous resonance with the divine heart itself, then finite and infinite become a single, continuous wavelength, and authentic communion becomes possible. Bridging the created and uncreated realms within a human being, it is both a realm in itself and the means by which this realm makes itself known.

Imaginal and Imaginary

Before we delve further into the text itself, it is first necessary to underscore a very important point that Leloup raises in his commentary. Most of us, reared in the scientific objectivism of our times, tend to think of visions as "subjective." They belong to the realm of the personal and interior and, while perhaps illuminating the workings of an individual psyche, do not conform to anything in external reality. These, in fact, were precisely the criticisms that began to be raised during the third and fourth centuries, when visionary revelation was rejected as an authentic mode of knowing within the church. But in the original wisdom anthropologies, as Leloup points out, visionary knowledge is not an "experience," let alone a private or subjective one; it is "of an ontological reality entirely superior to mere possibility."[6] It emanates from an actual realm, a realm that is in fact more subtle and endowed with real Being than our own. In fact, in the reversal of our usual sense of things, it is the place of origin from which what we usually refer to as "reality" is merely the shadow projected into space and time.[7]

Many centuries later, when this implicit anthropology came to maturity in the work of some remarkable Near Eastern Islamic mystics, this realm would be given the title "the imaginal realm."[8] Imaginal does not mean "imaginary"—that is, fictitious or subjective. It means the realm in which the images—the eternal prototypes—reveal themselves in their full authenticity. Remember how, in dialogue 1, Jesus introduced the notion of "image" as a kind of primordial template? The imaginal is the realm from which these images emanate. Leloup describes it as "that in-between zone where spirits become embodied and bodies become spiritualized."[9]

The fine points of this cosmology may seem complicated. But the important thing to keep in mind, from the point of view of this teaching, is that when Mary meets Jesus in a vision, she meets him in an actual *place*—in "a reality that is neither the fruit of her projections nor some need to be filled with what remains of Yeshua in her memory."[10] It is both physically and spiritually "objective"—valid and truthful. Or so it would be perceived, at least, by "those with ears to hear."

THE GAP

> It is neither the soul nor spirit that sees, but the nous between the two that perceives, and it is this . . .

And there it ends . . . Just as Jesus is bearing down on his point comes that frustrating four-page hole in the manuscript. What would have been next? More on image and analogue? More on the realms? Further clarifications about the nous and mechanics of visionary seeing? We simply don't know.

When we pick up again, Mary Magdalene is midway through what appears to be a recital on the subject of the soul's progress through the realms en route to its ultimate liberation. This is a common literary genre in the world of late antiquity, and her rendition seems to be unfolding in the usual progression. Somewhere during the course of those missing pages she has already crossed the first realm (which we can infer from textual clues to be "darkness");[11] as the text resumes, we find her in confrontation with the powers of craving, then ignorance, then wrath. In each realm, an accuser appears and attempts to block her path; she successfully rebuffs him. Finally, breaking free altogether, she ends with a beautiful hymn to liberation, and falls back into silence.

The confrontation scene itself plays out as follows (for the concluding hymn, see ahead, page 67):

The force of Craving spoke:

> I did not witness your descent, but now I see that you are ascending. Stop, why lie to yourself, you are mine.

The Soul responded:

> It is I who saw you first, yet you never truly saw nor knew me. You took the garments that I wore to be me, but you never recognized my true Self.

Having said this, the Soul left rejoicing.

The Soul came under the influence of the third power, known as Ignorance, which again scrutinized it closely, saying:

> Where do you think you're going? You are the slave of wickedness, dominated by it, and lack discrimination.

But my Soul spoke:

> Why are you judging me since I have not passed judgment on myself? Indeed it is true, I have been dominated, but I myself have not sought to enslave anyone or anything. Though they never recognized me, I now perceive that heaven and earth will pass away and all things composed shall be decomposed.

When the Soul had overcome the third force, once again it ascended upwards encountering the fourth, where the seven powers replicated themselves. The first took the form of Darkness, the second the force of Craving, the third, Ignorance, the fourth, craving for Death, the fifth, enslavement to the physical Body, the sixth, the false peace of the Flesh,

the seventh, the compulsion of Rage. These are the seven
powers of wrath and demand of the soul, "Where do you
originate, man-slayer? Where do you think you're going,
space-conqueror?"[12]

On a first reading, this dialogue may feel very alien. In spite
of her vigorous protests against the use of this term elsewhere,
King unhesitatingly labels it "Gnostic." We find ourselves in a
strange, allegorical netherworld filled with shadowy accusers,
cryptic exchanges, and a kind of surrealistic, hall-of-mirrors quality as the seven powers of darkness ceaselessly reinvent themselves.
The response it will shortly elicit from the disciple Andrew—"this
stuff seems just too *weird*!"—may be our own as well, But if we
push harder, the dialogue gradually reveals its treasure.

What is the logical thread? So far, this gospel has proved itself
to be tightly organized; each dialogue builds clearly and coher-
ently on what went before. It is fair to assume, therefore, that this
visionary recital has not simply been dropped in from outer space
but is in some way logically connected to the dialogue that has
preceded it. If we can offer the text even this much benefit of the
doubt, the missing connective tissue is not hard to spot.

"Blessed are you, Mary, for the sight of me does not disturb
you." Dialogue 3 has opened hovering implicitly around a core
question: how does one get to have a vision? What are the inner
prerequisites for entering the visionary realm and sustaining an
encounter there? As we have seen already, a key factor in Mary's
inner readiness is that she has learned to remain "undisturbed,"
that is, completely still and inwardly composed, no matter what.
The obvious question, then, is what made her able to do this?

And in the light of this question, the material following the
gap in the manuscript begins to make a good deal more sense.

In her journey through the various nether realms Mary
Magdalene comes face to face with several of those entities that
very soon afterward in Christian experience would be labeled
"the seven deadly sins." Craving, ignorance, darkness, and wrath
are not only "places" in the hereafter—"climates," as Leloup per-

ceptively calls them[13]—but very real energies of the here and now. Collectively they comprise the gravitational field of what the contemporary spiritual teacher Thomas Keating has termed "the false self system."[14] They are the "stuck," needy energies that keep us trapped in our egoic selves, at the mercy of our inner demons. This section of the text quickly falls into line as soon as we stop seeing it as a stock "visionary ascent" of the soul after death and start seeing it as a dramatic allegory depicting the confrontation with the false self that must be engaged with here and now in order to attain to the state of inner singleness that makes visionary seeing possible. Mary Magdalene is now directly answering the question of how she got there.

THE GANG OF THIEVES

This section of the text lends itself handily to role-playing. Craving stakes the first claim: "Why lie to yourself? You belong to me!" The soul replies with a simple yet striking metaphor: "You never truly saw me or knew me. You took the garments I wore to be me, but you never recognized my true Self."

This is another of the many places where the Gospel of Mary Magdalene and the Gospel of Thomas are in close resonance. In logion 21 of the Gospel of Thomas, Mary Magdalene asks Jesus to describe what his students are like. He answers:

> They are like small children living in a field not their own.
> When the landlords return and demand, "Give us back our field!"
> The children return it by simply stripping themselves
> standing naked before them.[15]

In both texts, disrobing is a striking metaphor for Jesus's own kenotic path; it vividly conveys the absolute nonclinging at the center of everything he is about. Mary Magdalene has absorbed the lesson well. In her confrontation with the power of craving (i.e., compulsive clinging), she regains her freedom by applying the kenotic strategy and leaving her "clothes" (her egoic self) neatly behind.

The next confrontation is with the power of ignorance, which seems to be closely bound up with the act of judging. Again the opponent tries to gain the upper hand by issuing an accusation ("You are the slave of wickedness and lack discrimination"). And again the soul sticks to her kenotic path. Rather than contesting and defending (which implicitly exacerbates the state of divided-ness), she politely declines to participate: "You may engage in judgment, but I refuse to. I have not judged myself, nor have I attempted to judge others." Once again, she simply slips out of her garments and refuses to buy into the game.

The relationship between judging and ignorance may escape most readers, since judgment would seem to be an exercise of discernment and hence, wisdom. But the point usually not seen is that in this exercise of the power of "yes" and "no," acceptance and rejection, the world is inevitably divided up into opposing camps, and the deeper integrative wisdom that is capable of hold-ing the tension of the opposites is lost. Through the exercise of judging, dualism perpetuates itself.[16]

Again, Thomas Merton is helpful here. A week before his death, he wrote of a powerful mystical experience in the garden of the Three Stone Buddhas in Ceylon. After a lifetime of strug-gling with yes and no, he was suddenly "jerked clean out of [his] habitual half-tied vision of things" and able at last to taste the peace that comes from having "seen through every question with-out trying to discredit anyone or anything—*without refutation*—without establishing some other argument."[17] This is the peace that Mary Magdalene also experiences as she gently leaves her ac-cuser behind.

The final power, wrath, is something of a Medusa's head: it recapitulates the first three powers (darkness, craving, ignorance) and adds four more on top of these, "craving for death," "en-slavement to the body," "the false peace of the flesh," and "the compulsion of rage." All, of course, are forms of enslavement to the disturbed energy patterns of the false self. The desert fa-thers and mothers warned consistently against these deceivers:

"Beware the peace that comes from the flesh!" they wrote—in other words, steer clear of the slippery slope that ensues from trying to draw one's life energy on this treadmill of convoluted desire. For it is the chains of attraction and aversion, forged in the dominion of wrath, that bind us solidly to the gravitational field of this world.

In strange, almost science-fiction-sounding language, this final accuser confronts the soul—Magdalene—and tries to block her path: "Where do you think you're going, man-slayer, space-conqueror?"

The soul/Magdalene responds with one of the most beautiful poems in ancient literature, lifting high above the cloud deck on its wings of joy:

"What has bound me has been slain. What encompassed me has been vanquished. Desire has reached its end and I am freed from Ignorance. I left one world behind with the aid of another, and now as Image I have been freed from the analog.[18] I am liberated from the chains of forgetfulness which have existed in time. From this moment onward, I go forward into the season of the Great Age, the Aeon, and there, where time rests in stillness in the Eternity of time, I will repose in silence." And having said this Mary fell silent since it was to this point that the Savior had brought her.

In this last test, the key that springs the lock is remembrance. The sevenfold powers of wrath hold their dominion through "the chains of forgetfulness," deceiving us into forgetting our true origin in cosmic freedom and love.[19] But the soul has discovered the great secret: that she can tap directly into the image of her true nature (as laid out by Jesus in dialogue 1) and can manifest the freedom of oneness in the teeth of the gales of this world. She has discovered that root place beyond the multiplicity of the created realm: that place from which, as stated in logion 22, "You are able to make two become one."

With this final declaration of mastery, the soul sails forth to take its place "where time rests in stillness in the Eternity of time"—

or in other words, where the conditions of this world dissolve before the root unity of the next. She has found the place of origin.

DOING THE WORK

Viewed from this psychological perspective, dialogue 3 proves to be directly relevant to the core question around which this entire gospel encamps. Who is an apostle? How does one earn the title? The answer is simple and bold: *by doing the work*. Beneath its literary trappings, this visionary recital describes metaphorically the work of the "purification of the unconscious," and it does so with considerable psychological and spiritual acuity. If, as Leloup has pointed out, Mary Magdalene's traditional reputation as the one "from whom seven demons have been cast out" can be turned to the good, this is the moment when the turn occurs. We see her in the act of breakthrough. She has tamed the inner beasts, confronted the passions that hold human beings enchained to the powers of this world. The fruit of this work is not only psychological wholeness, but the capacity to see. Her clear heart is her intimate channel to the fullness beyond time.

Even with more than half of its pages missing, this third dialogue provides perhaps the most challenging answer in all of early Christian literature to the question of who has the right to be called an apostle. Apostleship does not lie in having been near Jesus, taught or studied with him, or attended the Last Supper. It lies in the inner integration ("singleness") which allows that person to live in continuous communion with the Master in the imaginal meeting ground through the power of a pure heart, so that "Thy kingdom come" is in fact a living reality.

THE HARROWING OF HELL

At this point I want to upset the apple cart. The foregoing explanation is certainly sufficient to account for the importance of dialogue 3 within the overall structure of the gospel, and most commentators are content to let the matter rest here. But is there another way of looking at this visionary recital that might lead us into even more fertile ground? While the following interpretation is admittedly speculative, I believe it is worth including here.

When the text breaks off at the bottom of manuscript page 10, Jesus is the one speaking. When it resumes on page 15, the speaker is identified only as "the soul." The assumption made by every commentator without exception is that the soul in question is Mary Magdalene; either allegorically or psychologically she is describing her liberation from the bondage of this realm.

But what if the speaker here, "the soul," is in fact Jesus?

As you start to wrap your mind around this new possibility, remember the suggestion I made earlier: that the most likely time for this visionary encounter to have occurred would have been in the suspended, intermediary state between Jesus's physical death on the cross on Good Friday and his return to the flesh on Easter Sunday—or in other words, on Holy Saturday. During this time, according to earliest Christian tradition, he is believed to have visited the underworld—the "harrowing of hell," as it's sometimes known—and there consummated his ultimate act of cosmic reconciliation. He is traditionally pictured as having done this alone. But as we have seen from our earlier investigations, this picture overlooks a significant other player. For as Mary Magdalene leaned and hearkened after him from her solitary tombside post, he was not traveling alone, nor was she. In the imaginal world, they again became traveling companions, and her heart was continuously "spotting" him as he made his underworld descent.

If this be the case, then what we have in the final pages of this dialogue is not Mary Magdalene's metaphoric description of her psychological work, but *Jesus's literal description of his own soul's passage through death and dismemberment and back to life again.* It is a unique and extraordinary record of his hero's journey through the bardo realms on behalf of all humankind. (If you're not familiar with the term "bardo realms," see endnote 13.)

In advancing this possibility, I am drawing heavily on the insights from the modern Jesuit mystic Ladislaus Boros, whose 1973 book *The Mystery of Death* is an extraordinary reflection on the cosmological atonement effected during Jesus's descent to "the heart of the earth." Here is a brief excerpt:

> In death the soul is planted firmly in that basis of unity which is at the root of the world. The soul's freeing from the body in death does not mean a withdrawal from matter. Rather does it signify the entering into a closer proximity with matter, into a relation with the world extended to cosmic proportions . . . When, in the way we have just explained, Christ's human reality was planted, in death, right at the heart of the world, within the deepest stratum of the universe, the stratum that unites at root bottom all that the world is, at that moment in his bodily humanity he became the real ontological ground of a new universal scheme of salvation embracing the whole human race.[20]

Remember Jesus's own earlier comment in the first dialogue: "It is for this reason that the Good has come among you, pursuing its own essence within nature in order to reunite everything to its origin"? If Boros's insight is correct, this would be the moment that Jesus's work of reunification would have been consummated and "the cosmos in its totality would have become the bodily instrument of the divine efficacy."[21] The cosmos would literally have been set on a new foundation.

Another Christian visionary whose insights seem to correspond uncannily closely to the Gospel of Mary Magdalene is the medieval mystic Jacob Boehme. To flesh out the details of Jesus's imaginal descent to the underworld, I could do no better than to refer you to Boehme's extraordinary "Sixth Treatise on the Supersensual Life" in *The Way to Christ*[22]—in fact, that is exactly the text I opened to as my primary resource for the reconstruction of those four missing manuscript pages that I am about to share with you. In particular, Boehme's comment that "God could not enter hell, but love could enter hell" may have a lot to do with why the evident separation of Jesus's divine Self and human soul (image and analog, in terms of the text) occurred in the first place, and why the ascent narrative makes perfect textual sense.

With Boros and Boehme as my primary guides, I would like to offer the following as a hypothetical reconstruction of what may likely have been contained in that second manuscript gap:

Page 11. After describing how the nous, once purified, is the gateway between the realms, Jesus speaks of the final moments of his earthly life, and he and Mary share their final admonitions as he prepares to embark on his cosmic ordeal.

Page 12. Jesus recounts the moment of his human death, the separation of his bodily members into their root elements (as described in dialogue 1), the temporary severing of image and analog, and the soul's descent to the underworld.

Page 13. Jesus describes "the turn": the planting of cosmic love in that place of utter darkness and the springing forth of this earthly realm on a new cosmological foundation.

Page 14. Jesus's soul begins its ascent, passing upward through the first climate, the one of darkness, in its return to the original oneness of image and analog.

The details themselves, of course, are open to fine-tuning. But if my hypothesis is basically correct, then the Gospel of Mary Magdalene becomes an even more sacred text than we first imagined it to be. For its pages originally contained an "eyewitness account" of that pivotal moment when universal salvation gushed forth from Jesus's cosmological act of atonement. This moment is preserved in visionary form through the pure, unflinching nous of Mary Magdalene.

The mechanics of this hypothesis work out well from a textual standpoint. If Jesus is the speaker (rather than Mary Magdalene), then his encounters with the three accusers from the under realms and his consistent kenotic response are a metaphoric description of the way in which he "reconciles all things to himself" (Colossians 1:20). And it explains wrath's curious salutation: "Where are you going, man-slayer, space-conqueror?" For these terms derive from the mythic traditions of the hero's journey to the underworld.[23] "Space-conqueror," in fact, coincides precisely with the more familiar epithet (thanks to George Lucas) by which

these conquerors were known in the Near Eastern shamanic traditions of the times: "sky walker." The powers recognize him as
a sky walker: one who has transcended the conditions of physical
space and time and healed the sickness of humanity by going to
its roots.

If this is true, then, the glorious final hymn describes the new
ontological ground. The analog—the human Jesus—has melded
back into his fully articulated image or Self (as it will for each of
us at the end of our human journey), and he "reposes" in the fullness of the imaginal realm, which surrounds this time-torn world
like a great womb of mercy. He will be ever present and intimately
available to all who can find their way there.

Having said this, he ends his speaking. And the text segues
perfectly, for as he stops speaking, Mary Magdalene also falls
silent—"for it was to this point the Savior had brought her." She
speaks no more than what is actively emerging out of the communion between them. When the conversation has ended, she
returns to silence.

This second interpretation works out far better from a dramatic standpoint as well. At our 2008 Wisdom School in Collegeville, Minnesota, we tested both options in staged readings. In
our version 1, Mary Magdalene was the speaker throughout. In
version 2, she began as the principal speaker, but during the
dialogue-within-a-dialogue on page 11 ("I saw the Master in a
vision, and I said to him, 'Lord, I see you now in a vision'"), Jesus
took over his own response ("You are blessed, Mary, since the
sight of me does not disturb you") and continued as the speaker
until the final hymn. At that point, we gradually reintroduced
Mary Magdalene's voice, at first speaking in unison with him.
Then Jesus's voice faded, so that the final "I will repose in silence" belonged to her alone. The results were both dramatically
and theologically compelling. It was unanimously clear to all
concerned that Jesus is the real speaker in dialogue 3.

Both interpretations are actually true, though on different
levels, and they are quite compatible. For Mary Magdalene to be
the bearer of such an extraordinary vision, she would have to have
done her spiritual work. But to think that this text may originally

have contained a visionary account of the epicenter of the Paschal Mystery is thrilling beyond belief. And even the possibility that this might be so lifts the question of Mary Magdalene's central importance within Christian tradition far beyond even the pressing contemporary issues around women's leadership and the feminine dimension in the church; it catapults her to the very center of the Christian Mystery. She becomes the keeper of a timeless gate through which the pure essence of Jesus's transfiguring mercy is always flowing.

At any rate, the possibility of this alternative reading suggests that we might want to take a close second look at those two holes in the text. Why is it that the two missing sections are precisely the cosmological teachings: Jesus's metaphysics on the root unity of all things and the discourse on the descent to the underworld? Why should these two teachings, which (based on surviving materials from other wisdom streams) most clearly link Jesus with ancient Near Eastern shamanic traditions of healing, be the ones to fall out? Was it pure chance? Or deliberate obfuscation?[24] Or was it pure synchronicity, suggesting that this riddle is something that had been intended all along to be worked out in our own times, when the message would finally make sense?

Whatever the answer may be, the longer I live with this gospel, the more Mary Magdalene becomes the finger pointing at the moon. What astounds me is not so much what this text says about Mary Magdalene as what it says about Jesus.

6

WINNERS AND LOSERS

☉   ☉   ☉   ☉   ☉

IN CHAPTER 3 we explored the notion of the "master story" at
the heart of the church's self-understanding. Deriving its energy
from the early scriptural accounts of Christian life, it depicts the
apostles as having all received a common faith and teaching directly from Jesus and working together in an astonishing unity to
spread the gospel throughout the world. Only later, so the story
goes, was this original Christian unity threatened by the seeds of
heresy sewn from outside the apostolic fold.

When I say "scriptural accounts," I am referring, of course, to
the *canonical* scriptural accounts, particularly the book of Acts—
which, Bible scholars overwhelmingly concur, is actually Luke/
Acts: a continuation of the gospel narrative of Luke, by the same
author. Particularly in Acts 2:42 this author paints an idyllic picture of the early Christian community united around a common
doctrine and practice: "They were faithful to the teaching of the
apostles, the common life of sharing, the breaking of the bread,
and the prayers." If there is dissent among the ranks, not a word of
it is breathed here.

The reason for all this harmony is not hard to spot: those
voices singing a different tune are simply silenced.[1]

Back in chapter 1 of this book, we noted how the author of the Gospel of Luke tends over and over to reduce Mary Magdalene to simply "one of the faithful women" who "followed Jesus from a distance." Her independent stature as an apostle is consistently undercut. And in the continuation of his story in Acts, she is not even mentioned (unless you consider her as being included in the brief reference in Acts 1:14 to "some women" accompanying the male apostles). The focus in this account is entirely on Peter and Paul, with the fledgling church portrayed as coming into being through their robust spirits and tireless labors of love.

But remember, that is the view from the "master story." The noncanonical traditions have a very different take on the subject. Both the Gospel of Thomas and the Gospel of Mary Magdalene bear witness to a powerful clash of perspectives (hardly a unanimity of faith and doctrine!) that was there from the very beginning, before a single apostle marched forth to preach the gospel. And they remember this tension as coming to a head in a clear power struggle between Peter, who represents a "stuck" or conditioned way of thinking, and Mary Magdalene, who has broken free.

Dialogue 4 presents the struggle in a succinct but highly effective format—bordering, in fact, upon déjà vu. In five brief exchanges, it anticipates and remarkably encapsulates two thousand years of lived Christianity, foreshadowing exactly those places where the stress cracks will eventually open up in the façade of the master story.

Dialogue Four

Andrew's response was to say to the rest of the brothers:

> Say what you will about all that she has said to us, I for one do not believe that the Savior said such things to her, for they are strange and appear to differ from the rest of his teachings.

After consideration, Peter's response was similar:

Would the Savior speak these things to a woman in private without openly sharing them so that we too might hear? Should we listen to her at all, and did he choose her over us because she is more worthy than we are?

Then Mary began to weep, saying to Peter:

My brother, what are you thinking? Do you imagine that I have made these things up myself within my heart, or that I am lying about the Savior?

Speaking to Peter, Levi also answered him:

You have always been quick to anger, Peter, and now you are questioning her in exactly that same manner, treating this woman as if she were an enemy. If the Savior considered her worthy, who are you to reject her? He knew her completely and loved her faithfully.

We should be ashamed of ourselves! As he taught us, we should be clothed instead with the cloak of True Humanity, and following his command announce Good News without burdening it further with rules or laws he himself did not give us.

After Levi had said this, they too departed and began to teach, proclaiming the Good News.

The "stillness of eternity" into which Mary Magdalene retires at the end of dialogue 3 barely has a chance to settle when a heated debate breaks out among the disciples. "Wait a minute!"—protests Andrew—"These things she's been telling us are just too strange!"

His response is in one sense completely understandable. For as we have just seen, the vision *is* strange. It doesn't work at the literal level; it requires "ears that can hear." In comparison to the "plain fare" of the beatitudes and parables that are the more familiar ground of Jesus's teachings—then and now—this new material doesn't fit. It is interesting how Andrew's basis for rejecting the vision—"it differs from the rest of his teachings"—implies an intuitive grasp of "canon"—that is, that there is already a standard of orthodoxy by which the authenticity of all other contenders can be judged.[2] But this is also, inherently, circular logic. Virtually the same response was called forth when the Nag Hammadi material made its appearance nineteen hundred years later: "This doesn't fit with what we know about Jesus's teachings; therefore it can't be valid."

Much of what makes this gospel seem so "different" is that it contains the metaphysics on which Jesus's more practical and earthy teachings are based. The same holds true for the Gospel of Thomas, and, as we have seen, the metaphysics of these two gospels are virtually identical. From a practical standpoint, the important point to bear in mind is that while these more abstract teachings may jar with our more familiar images of Jesus, they do not in any way contradict his practical teachings; rather they clarify and provide a context. All the same, however, they do cast a distinctly different light on his presence: less like a prophet and more like a sage.

"A Woman?"

Peter is quick to jump on Andrew's bandwagon, but his objections have to do with protocol more than with content. His issues are around why Jesus should confide his teachings to *a woman* and *in private*! Forgetting, evidently, that it was he himself who invited her to speak, he blusters on with his "just who does she think she is? Does she take herself to be more worthy than us?" Ever precarious in his self-esteem, he seeks refuge in the cultural conditioning of his times to reject her vision out of hand because the "wrong" person is bearing it.[3]

The Gospel of Thomas records an identical incident in logion 114 (the last one in this gospel) but expands its treatment of the subject to include Jesus's response:

Simon Peter said to them all,

> Mary should leave us,
> for women are not
> worthy of this Life.

Yeshua said,

> "Then, I myself will lead her,
> making her male
> if she must become
> worthy like you males!
> I will transform her
> Into a living spirit [*anthropos*]
> Because any woman changed
> In this way
> Will enter the divine realm."[4]

This particular logion has caused considerable distress to many feminist scholars, who hear Jesus saying that a woman must be transformed into a man (or led by a man) in order to enter the kingdom. But that is to fall prey to the same literalism that Jesus himself is trying to lift us above. He is not saying that Mary Magdalene must become a man; he is saying that she must become a "living spirit"—an *anthropos*, or a fully human being. You can almost hear the irony in the first part of his response: "If it is so all-fired important to you males that she be male—poof! Let her become male!, or a table, or a tree . . . whatever outer form you please!" The important point is the *inner* transformation. Any woman who succeeds in becoming anthropos will enter the kingdom (and presumably any male, too). As we have seen in logion 22, the real qualifying test is "when you are able to make two become one . . . so that a man is no longer male and a woman female, but male and female become a single whole . . . then you will enter in." So long as the disciples remain trapped in outer forms, they are far, far from the kingdom. In this sense, the final logion is both consistent with all Jesus has taught throughout the gospel and a fitting note on which to end—just as it is here. The church's failure to distinguish between outer forms and inner authority is, then as now, the story of its tragic inability to corporately walk forth along the path the Master has laid out for it.

"Magdalene Wept"

Mary Magdalene's response to this attack is a virtual replay of her confrontation with her second accuser in the visionary recital just before. In the face of this latest personification of the power of ignorance, she refuses to judge or counterattack. Instead, she weeps—just as Jesus is said in John 11 to have wept before raising Lazarus from the tomb, and for much the same reason. Her open, wise heart sees in this moment so clearly where things are headed. In Peter's inability to validate from within the authenticity of her visionary revelation, she recognizes that the tendrils connecting the disciples with their risen master are so very slender. The window of opportunity that has been opened for them at such precious cost is about to be wasted.

Rallying the Troops

The last words in this dialogue belong to Levi, who leaps into the fray to Mary Magdalene's assistance. If the name Levi puzzles you—you don't remember a Levi mentioned among the twelve apostles enumerated in Matthew 10:2–4—you are correct; his name is not included there. While a certain scholarly contingent claims that he is identical with Matthew, the tax collector named in that list (and by tradition the gospel's author), the point is actually better made if the uncertainty is allowed to stand. Remember how we saw that limiting Jesus's inner circle of followers to twelve male disciples is in fact a part of the master story? In reality the boundaries were much more fluid. Levi is simply another of the ones who belonged to Jesus's inner circle (like Mary Magdalene), and whom orthodoxy has now forgotten. Another silenced voice.

In either a synchronous or intentional way (commented on by King), this gospel pits the winners against the losers: the two accusers who will live on as part of the apostolic succession and the two losers whose voices will fade.

Within the context of this gospel, however, Levi's voice comes across loud and clear. It falls to him to deliver the final summation, packing into five short sentences the entire message and significance of what has gone before. His blunt opening words pinpoint the real cause of the tension: "You have always been quick to anger, Peter" (as the canonical gospels themselves would not deny; Peter's vision is easily clouded by his turbulent inner emotions). The effect of this hotheadedness is that he is now behaving like any other unenlightened mortal, covering his tracks with accusation and blame. Whatever became of the teaching they received from the Master? Having made his point, Levi moves quickly to the heart of the matter: "If the Savior considered her worthy, who are we to reject her?"

Twenty centuries later, that remains the heart of the matter.

His next sentence offers some further explanation of this point: "He knew her completely and loved her faithfully." His words here are more than just a touching description of human loyalty; as we will see in part 2, they are also a concise definition of what we will be calling "conscious love." Jesus knew her fully, inside and out, with complete transparency and wholeness. And the word "faithfully" (translated by King as "steadfastly") brings the strong connotation of a love that is not contained within the boundaries of this world, but extends its intimacy beyond space/time. In his own dazzling moment of lucid seeing, Levi recognizes that the person standing before them is not simply Mary Magdalene, but Mary Magdalene and Jesus flowing together as a single whole in the unbroken beauty of their inner communion.

That is what triggers his next comment: "We should be ashamed of ourselves!" Before this vision of the realized anthropos standing in their midst, the disciples' wrangling and posturing amount to a disgraceful forgetting of all they have received and been made accountable to. In the traditional way of epilogues, Levi redirects their hearts to the teaching itself. His final sentence is a succinct paraphrase of Jesus's core points in dialogue 1, ending with that challenging final instruction not to "burden" the Good News "with rules or laws that he himself did not give us." Once again, from a two-thousand-year retrospective, the irony is too pointed to overlook.

As at the end of dialogue 4, the temporary wobbling in the ranks seems to have been corrected. The disciples are back on track, the tension among them apparently resolved, and as the gospel concludes optimistically, "They all departed and began to teach, proclaiming the Good News."

If only it were so . . .

PART TWO

⊙ ⊙ ⊙ ⊙ ⊙

MARY MAGDALENE
AS BELOVED

7

RECLAIMING THE PATH
OF ROMANTIC LOVE

☉ ☉ ☉ ☉ ☉

NEARLY TWENTY YEARS ago, long before *The Da Vinci Code* uproar broke, I was serving as parish priest in a small Episcopal congregation in Colorado. When the gospel appointed for one particular Sunday in August was Luke's account of that anonymous "sinful" woman with her alabaster jar, I decided to take the risk of breaking open some of the insights that even back then were beginning to emerge from a growing spate of Mary Magdalene studies. My parishioners were a bright and intellectually curious bunch, so why not? During my sermon, I gently presented Margaret Starbird's assertion (in her book *The Woman with the Alabaster Jar*, named after this very gospel passage) that the anointing of Jesus's hands and feet described in the text was not simply a random act by a penitent woman, but an exquisitely symbolic ritual enacted between two lovers about to be separated.[1]

The firestorm was predictable.

I had tried to pave the way as carefully as I could. My point in raising those issues, as I made clear both in the sermon itself and in the discussion that boiled over afterward, was not to argue the case one way or another, but rather to get at some of the attitudes underlying the way we Christians do theology—and more important, the way we do love. "How do you feel about the possibility that Jesus had a human beloved?" I asked these parishioners. "Does it make you feel uncomfortable? Why?"

The responses were pretty much what I expected: "But if Jesus had sexual relations with a woman, he couldn't be sinless." "If he loved one in particular, he couldn't love us all impartially." "How could he be the son of God unless he gave himself completely to God?" The overwhelming consensus was that if Jesus had known erotic love, he could not possibly have also been the full embodiment of divine love. It would somehow disqualify him as the divine redeemer.

I could hardly blame the congregation for feeling that way. After nearly two millennia of reinforcement, these assumptions have become so much of the landscape of Christianity that they appear to be part of the seamless structure of revealed truth. But in fact, *assumptions* are what they really are—not core tenets of the faith, not anything that Jesus himself taught, but superimpositions of a male, celibate, priestly theology which for nearly two thousand years has been the only game in town.

The complicated history of how this situation came to be could fill a book in itself (and in fact has several times over).[2] The short version is basically this: during those first four centuries of Christian life, as leadership moved from a charismatic eldership model to the threefold sacramental ministry we know today (bishops, priests, and deacons), part and parcel of this evolution was an increasing tendency to view both Christ and his apostles through the prototype of celibate priesthood. This is of course a flagrant anachronism in light of the unambiguous scriptural references to Peter's mother-in-law (Matthew 8:14) and the only slightly more ambiguous allusions in Luke to the other disciples' "companions."[3] But counterbalancing the testimony of the gospels themselves was a growing discomfort with conjugal intimacy, a discomfort whose roots probably lie in the extreme Essene asceticism out of which Jesus himself most likely emerged (we will be exploring this topic in greater detail in the following chapter). Beginning as early as Paul, this unease was magnified in each succeeding generation by a chorus of Christianity's most influential thinkers including Marcion, Tatian, Jerome, and Augustine. The consensus grew stronger and stronger that sex and the sacraments simply didn't mix. By the fourth century edicts were in place forbidding married priests to have conjugal relations with their wives. Not long thereafter married priesthood itself dropped astern in Western Christendom, and celibacy became the entrance requirement for admission to the power structure of the church.[4]

It gives one a bit of a start to realize that for the better part of two millennia, Christian theology has been written, shaped, formulated, and handed down almost exclusively by celibates talking to other celibates. In that respect, it is extraordinarily monolithic. And from this exclusively celibate template emerges the only image of Christ our tradition has allowed us to entertain: of a celibate renunciate whose "sinless" purity would necessarily entail sexual abstinence.

THE MOTE IN OUR EYES

Like it or not, this template is the door through which we will enter as we move into the second part of this book. In the next several chapters we will be turning our attention to the highly emotionally charged premise that *in addition to* all those other roles to which Mary Magdalene can lay just claim—apostle, visionary, healer—that there is still one remaining to her, which may just be the most important of them all: soul mate.

Were Jesus and Mary Magdalene lovers? Were they secretly married? That, of course, is the claim laid out in *The Da Vinci Code* and a number of other books and documentaries and which the church angrily refutes.

In all honesty, we need to begin with the recognition that this question cannot possibly receive a fair hearing. Not in Christian

circles, anyway. It is one thing to argue the case for reclaiming
Mary Magdalene as apostle and wisdom-bearer, purveyor of
a sorely needed feminine presence to the church; it is quite another
to tie this claim to the theologically taboo subject of a romantic
involvement with Jesus. Two thousand years of dogma and tradition have left the field so thoroughly land-mined with negative
assumptions and stereotypes that it is virtually impossible to see
anything other than red, like my congregation that morning. The
question will inevitably be heard as an attack on Jesus and an act
of sabotage upon the Christian faith itself.

What's worse, there is a double jeopardy at work here that is
in its own way far more insidious. Because it has been so thoroughly programmed into us that celibacy is the highest Christian
way and that committed spousal love is a second-rate path or no
path at all ("better to marry than to burn," as Paul reluctantly allows), it is hardly surprising that our Western anthropology of
human sexuality is abysmal. In the secular version relentlessly
foisted upon us by contemporary culture, it's all about pleasure,
performance, gratification. In the bedrooms of the faithful, it's
still all too often about duty and shame: a begrudging debt to
future generations which even when carefully managed is still
tainted with carnal sin.[5] Mention "erotic love" and people will
immediately hear "sex," then immediately thereafter, "dirty."
The idea that there could be anything holy about this kind of love
is too alien to even consider. That's simply the way our ears have
been trained to hear it; we are all children of a cultural stream
whose vision of human love has been shaped by the shadow side
of celibate spirituality.

THE VIEW FROM THE GUTTER

It doesn't help matters, either, that most of the conversation going
on to date around the question of Mary Magdalene and Jesus has
been little better than scandalmongering. Amid the flurry of gos-
sip and speculation emerging from the current plethora of schol-

arly and pseudo-scholarly studies, we are really presented with only four options:

1. That Mary Magdalene was Jesus's mistress;
2. That theirs was a politically arranged marriage, strictly for dynastic purposes;
3. That they were sexual consorts in some gnostic Mystery religion, ritually reenacting the sacred *hieros gamos*, or union of the opposites;
4. That the whole story is purely archetypal, a great Sophianic myth depicting the integration of the masculine and feminine within the human soul.

Sex, power, cult, or myth: not a great set of choices. I have yet to see considered what in a sexually healthy culture would surely seem to be the obvious possibility: that they were faithful beloveds, whose lives were joined together in a fully enfleshed human love which was a source of strength and nurturance for both of them; which far from diminishing their spiritual integrity, deepened and fulfilled it. Why is it so hard to go there?

Well, obviously: because that is the one possibility our celibate template will not allow us to consider.

In the spirit, then, of some collective cleansing of the lens of perception, I would like to return to the welter of objections that came tumbling out of my congregation that morning. Rephrased slightly, these objections take shape as a set of four propositions—myths, I will argue, all firmly rooted in the soil of celibate spirituality—that together have subtly sabotaged our ability to see romantic love as an authentic path of spiritual transformation. While presenting themselves as "gospel truth," they in fact have little or no scriptural authorization in the teachings of Jesus himself but instead draw their credibility entirely from the circular logic of his presumed celibacy.

I will lay each of these out, together with a brief countering commentary. As I do so, I ask you to consider the extent to which you yourself may have consciously or unconsciously bought into these assumptions; to what degree they frame your own vision of romantic love. Once we've cleared the decks, I will then propose a simple methodology by which we might actually bring some new leverage to bear on this centuries-old rumor of a possible romantic involvement between Jesus and Mary Magdalene.

MYTH NUMBER ONE

Celibacy is the preferred means of giving oneself entirely to God

The notion that celibacy is the best means by which one can give oneself entirely to God has dominated the rhetoric of priesthood and monasticism almost from the start. Like so much else in the church's teachings on human sexuality, its scriptural origins lie in Paul's oft-cited admonition, "The unmarried man cares for the Lord's business; his aim is to please the Lord. But the married man cares for worldly things; his aim is to please his wife; and he has a divided mind" (1 Corinthians 7:33). Clearly this is a highly effective recruitment tactic for the religious life. Virtually every Christian monastic I know has entered upon the vocation espousing some variation of Thomas Merton's impassioned outpouring: "I want to give God *everything*."[6] Of course, from an operational standpoint Paul is quite correct: being in partnership makes the logistics of spiritual discipleship a good deal more complicated.

But the theology underlying this principle, if you really consider it, is monstrous. In fact, it seems to be saying that the wholehearted love of God and the wholehearted love of another human being cannot coincide; as our love for a particular human being increases, our love for God is proportionately diminished. Not only is this a theological nightmare; it is also a flat-out contradiction of Jesus's own dual commandment: "You shall love the Lord your God with all your heart, and with all your soul, and with all your mind . . . and you shall love your neighbor as yourself" (Matthew 22:37–39). Whatever the difficulty in juggling these sometimes contradictory demands, collapsing the tension between them is not an option.

The real solution to this paradox, I believe, comes in the gradual discovery that one cannot love God as an object. God is always and only the *subject* of love. God is that which makes love possible, the source from which it emerges and the light by which it is recognized. Thus, "love of God" is not one love among others, not love for a particular "one" to whom my saying "yes" requires that I say "no" to another. Rather, God is the all-encompassing One who unlocks and sustains my ability to give myself fully to life in all its infinite particularity, including the excruciating particularity of a human beloved.

It is not an easy notion to wrap one's mind around (it confounds the inherent structure of language itself),[7] but if the basic principle can be grasped, then the apparent contradiction between the divine and human beloved evaporates. God is the divine giving, who flows out and through our human expression to manifest love in all its fullness. And so the way to give oneself fully to God would be to give fully of oneself.

Myth Number Two

Love divides the heart

A few years back a friend of mine, a Roman Catholic monk, reported to me sadly that he had just terminated a long-standing relationship with a woman whom he loved dearly. His spiritual director had encouraged their friendship at first, telling him, "It will help your humanity[!]" But once friendship began to stray across the border into romantic love, he was ordered to cease all contact immediately: "Your heart is becoming divided."

It struck me as yet another case of spiritual striptease, and as a woman I wondered what it must have felt like from the receiving end. But there was little that any of them could do about it. The notion that erotic love divides the heart is so deeply engrained in monastic spiritual formation that renunciation becomes not only the imperative course of action but even a spiritual opportunity: the direct route to spiritual wholeness. The modern Jesuit John S. Dunne reflects this traditional view when he writes: "If I set my heart upon another person, then I cannot live without that person. My heart becomes divided. On the other hand, if I give my life to the journey with God, then my heart becomes whole and I can be whole in a relationship with another."[8]

The theology of self-unification through renunciation is such a cornerstone of monastic spiritual practice that one hardly dare breathe a word against it. And yet the question remains: *does love divide the heart?* If God is considered an object of one's love vying with other objects, then the crucial premise on which this theology hangs is true: yes, love would divide the heart. But if God is the *subject* of love, the place from which love emerges, then one could far more reliably claim—as poets, mystics, and lovers have claimed throughout the ages—that love does not divide the heart, but is in fact the sole force strong enough to *unite* it. What divides the heart is not the love relationship itself but the passions: the strong emotions and shadow side that are always present when love runs strong. But these are not grounds for renunciation; rather, they are grounds for purification.

What this purification might look like is captured with wrenching power in the memoir *Grace and Grit* by the contemporary philosopher Ken Wilber. In this remarkable autobiography he shares the story of his own love and transformation as he and his wife, Treya Killam Wilber, wage a five-year battle against her ultimately fatal breast cancer. As their ordeal intensifies, one watches them each being melted down and refashioned in the refiner's fire of their love for each other. Egotism, clinging, resentment—and other, darker shadows—rise to the surface and are released. Particularly in the last six months of Treya's life, Wilber writes, "We simply and directly served each other, exchanging self for other, and therefore glimpsing that eternal spirit which transcends self and other, both 'me' and 'mine.'"[9]

If this sounds like something you recall Jesus saying in the gospels, you're right.

MYTH NUMBER THREE

Human love is inherently different from divine love

It was Plato who first came up with the idea of classifying love by types, and his delineation of *agape* (impartial, disinterested love) from *eros* (desiring love) has basically laid the foundation for all such discussions for two and a half millennia since. But Plato never made the error of equating agape exclusively with divine love (given the notoriously riotous passions of the Greek divinities, that thought would probably never have occurred to him), or eros exclusively with human desiring. That particular reductionism, which has had such a pervasive influence on contemporary Christian spirituality, can be laid at the doorstep of Anders Nygren, a Swedish Protestant theologian of the 1930s whose monumental three-volume work *Agape and Eros* pronounced categorically that "eros is man's way to God; agape is God's way to man."[10] According to Nygren, eros is by its very nature filled with desire and neediness, hence impure; by contrast, God's way of loving is free, clear, and impartial, motivated only by the goodness of the giver.

With one deft stroke of the theological scalpel, Nygren essentially divided the core energy of love into two separate species and assigned to erotic love (the only love humans are by definition capable of) a permanent second-class status that essentially negates its value as a spiritual path. It is hard to escape the implication that if one is following a path of passionate commitment to a beloved, one is on an inferior spiritual track, or no track at all. This despite love's unassailable record as the most potent force at our disposal to unify the heart and transform the soul.

The best one can say about the damage inflicted by Nygren's pronouncement is that its influence is limited to the modern era. Whatever other shortcomings they may have had, earlier generations of Christian teachers did not make this mistake. For its first twelve hundred years, Christian spiritual theology stayed true to its wellsprings in eros, instinctively recognizing that this was the

transforming force, and one simply had to work with it. As John
Climacus wrote in the sixth century:

> I have seen impure souls who threw themselves headlong into
> physical eros to a frenzied degree. It was their very experience
> of that physical eros that led them to interior conversion.
> They concentrated their eros on the Lord. Rising above fear,
> they tried to love God with insatiable desire. That is why
> when Christ spoke to the woman who had been a sinner he
> did not say that she had been afraid but that she had loved
> much, and had easily been able to surmount love by love.[11]

The goal of "surmounting love by love" for a thousand years
formed the heart of the Christian mystical program of transformation, culminating in the twelfth century in the magnificent
"monastic love mysticism" of St. Bernard of Clairvaux and those
following in his wake (and notice that whenever eros is mentioned
in a text, the figure of Mary Magdalene hovers right in the background). To the extent that it still conceives of God as an object
that one can "concentrate one's eros" on, it ultimately falls victim
to that same dualistic fallacy we have already seen in the first
myth. But it is far, far better than what has been served up today
in the name of religious and psychological health: a gutless, pas-
sionless, numb "agape clone" that goes nowhere at all. Without
the quicksilver of eros nothing transforms: a secret which I believe Jesus himself knew and worked with in his teachings in a
profound way, only at a unitive rather than a dualistic level.

MYTH NUMBER FOUR

Celibacy is a state of greater purity

The mistake here—and it is one commonly made in spiritual teaching—is to confuse purity and clarity. Clarity has to do with attun-
ing the mind. Purity is about awakening the heart. The two can
overlap and reinforce each other, but they are not synonymous.

In Hinduism, where the practice of celibacy as an applied spiritual technology (known as *brahmacharya*) arose more than three thousand years ago, the objective has to do with conserving and concentrating *prana,* the vital energy or life force, so that it can be utilized for spiritual transformation. The modern Hindu master Swami Chidananda has restated the traditional wisdom by explaining it in this way: "*Prana* is the precious reserve of the seeker. Any sense activity or sense experience consumes a lot of *prana* [the sex act most of all, he claims] . . . The highest of all goals in life, spiritual attainment, requires the maximum pranic energy on all levels."[12]

With this goal in mind, he likens celibacy to a storing up or harnessing of other powerful natural forces: "A river may not have much power in itself. But if it is dammed up and its waters conserved, then it has the power, when properly channeled, to turn huge turbines. And the hot sun, even in summer, won't normally cause a fire, but if you concentrate its rays through a lens, those rays will immediately burn whatever they are focused on. That is what celibacy actually is."[13]

In the most ancient and powerful understanding of the practice, celibacy belongs among practices that can be classified as *enstatic*—those that have to do with conserving, collecting, concentrating. The positive side of this kind of practice is a significantly enhanced clarity—a relative freedom from the energy-consuming turmoil of the physical lusts and emotional passions and thus a greater capacity to stay present to the higher frequencies of spiritual energy.

For exactly this reason—that celibacy is a "storing up" process—its shadow side is avarice. One must be alert to a subtle tendency to withhold or "preserve" oneself, to hold oneself back from full engagement in the human sphere in order to have access to those higher realms of truth and light. Under all the aura of "selfless giving" with which the practice of celibacy generally cloaks itself, there can be a subtle spiritual acquisitiveness at work, betrayed in the very phrase "spiritual attainment." Which "I," one wonders, is this "I" who attains?

By contrast, the path that Jesus himself seems to teach and

model in his life, and particularly in his death, is not a storing up but a complete pouring out. His pranic energy is quickly depleted; on the cross, as all four gospel accounts affirm, he does not hold out even until sunset, but quickly "gives up the ghost." Shattered and totally spent, he simply disappears into his death. The core icon of the Christian faith, the watershed moment from which it all emerges, is not enstatic but *ecstatic*—love completely poured out, expended, squandered. In contrast to clarity, it is the archetypal image of *purity,* the complete self-giving of the heart.

The Path Jesus Walked

And right here, I believe, we come to the fundamental problem with these celibate models of transformation. It's not merely their monochromatic viewpoint or the implicit devaluing of a whole other stream of Christian spiritual wisdom whose roots are in passionate human love. Rather, it is the fact that at key points they seem to be slightly out of kilter with the path of transformation that Jesus himself walked and taught. One might say that this model points us toward John the Baptist rather than Jesus: toward those ancient and time-honored practices of renunciation, asceticism, and self-concentration through abstinence, whereas if we really look closely, we see that Jesus himself seemed to be constantly pushing the envelope in the opposite direction—toward radical self-abandonment, reckless self-outpouring, and the transmutation of passion in complete self-giving.

But it is right there, at the center of that cognitive dissonance, that a window of opportunity opens up. Rather than trying to smooth it over and pretend it does not exist, as the church has done for nearly two thousand years, we need to tune in and listen to it very carefully, for it gives us exactly the tool we need to proceed.

Were Jesus and Mary Magdalene lovers? To date, nearly everyone seems to be trying to solve that riddle from the outside, like good investigative journalists. It's all about finding new evidence: secret documents and societies, new gnostic gospels, purported lost tombs, hidden mathematical messages embedded in the lines of existent texts—some new piece of data that would settle the issue one way or another. Equally, those who are appalled by the very notion of a romantically involved Jesus build their case by recourse to doctrines and templates that did not exist until three or four centuries after he had left the planet. It's all external logic.

But there is another possibility, which has been sitting there right under our noses all along yet so far seems to have been consistently overlooked. That is to evaluate the evidence from the *inside*, on the basis of the path itself. For Jesus was, after all, a teacher, and the teaching itself is there to be consulted. Once one has compensated for the negative set and drift of the celibate current, it is merely a matter of asking a single question: In the light of what Jesus actually seems to have been teaching, is there anything in the teachings themselves that would have precluded such a love relationship?

If Jesus were indeed walking the path of classic monastic *brahmacharya,* then the answer is obviously yes; celibacy is an essential requirement of this path, and to diverge from this requirement would violate his integrity and sabotage his spiritual power.

But what if in fact he was walking a different path? A path difficult to identify because it was so close to its own headwaters that it was missed by nearly everyone both then and now? What if he was not an ascetic at all, but was in fact following a whole new trajectory, previously unknown in the West and with its own ways of understanding integrity and purity? Along this other trajectory, it might indeed be conceivable for him to be in a human love relationship, although that love would probably not look like that most of us are familiar with.

Let's see what the teachings themselves have to say.

8

THE GREAT
IDENTITY THEFT

⊙ ⊙ ⊙ ⊙ ⊙

To be sure, he *looked* like an ascetic when he set out upon his path. According to the gospels, he was born to intensely religious parents who dedicated him to God and supported his early gravitation to the consecrated life. One of the most indelible New Testament vignettes is of the boy Jesus sitting among the rabbis in the temple, listening and asking probing questions. Some Christians remember him as "Jesus the Nazarene." And while most people think this term refers to Nazareth, the town where he grew up, in fact the long flowing hair and white robe portrayed in the traditional Jesus portraits is in fact the mark of a *Nazirite*, a Jew who had taken an ascetic vow. Speculation has long linked him with the Essenes, a Jewish millennialist movement headquartered at Qumran, near the Dead Sea, noted for its visionary mysticism and rigorous asceticism.

With the recovery in 1947 of the Qumran scrolls, a major trove of sacred and juridical texts governing the life of this community, we now know a good deal about the spiritual climate in which Jesus most likely came of age. On a scale of one to ten (ten being the most difficult), the Essene version of asceticism would probably land somewhere around a nine. The combination of classic monastic renunciation with the well-known Jewish obsessions around purification and ritual cleanliness made for an edgy path, to say the least. While not all Essenes practiced celibacy (there were also married members of the community), those striving for the highest degree of holiness were strictly committed to the celibate path. Clearly evident in the Qumran writings is a predisposition to regard sexual activity as a spiritual defilement; laws prohibiting access to the temple to anyone who had recently had sexual intercourse are no doubt the immediate matrix from which Christianity's own deep ambivalence around genital sexuality would later emerge.

This Essene ascetic ideal is powerfully embodied in John the Baptist, Jesus's slightly older cousin. The portrait emerging from all four gospels of the "voice crying in the wilderness," clad in his animal skins, eating next to nothing, and thundering out his message of apocalypse and repentance, has in fact become our cultural stereotype of the quintessential renunciate. And it would appear that Jesus was destined for that track as well. The opening chapters of all four gospels quiver with anticipation of "the one who is to come," the one in whom the highest degree of attained holiness will be revealed. At the moment when Jesus himself steps into the Jordan River and receives his baptism at the hand of John, it indeed appears that he is destined to far surpass even his renowned cousin in purity, power, and luminosity—or in other words, in the fruits of ascetic rigor. He is to be the ultimate unfolding of the path of righteousness. John himself recognizes in Jesus a whole new order of spiritual magnitude and voluntarily capitulates to it: "He must increase; I must decrease" (John 3:30).

But it didn't work out that way—not in the orderly, hierarchical, and progressive ascetic unfolding envisioned by John. Something apparently went off course with this rising new star of holiness, and in the eyes of the Essenes he would become a bitter disappointment.

You have to read beneath the surface of scripture to see this, of course—but just barely beneath the surface. The gospels all

reveal a growing rivalry between the John and Jesus camps, evident in the very attempt to mask it as an orderly handing on of the
spiritual baton. In very short order, Jesus seems to have introduced serious confusion into the Baptist's ranks—"Are you the
one who is to come or should we wait for another?" (Matthew
3:11)—and was becoming an increasingly divisive presence until
the situation abruptly resolved itself in John's arrest and execu-
tion. That this falling out was mutual can be read between the
lines of the carefully hedged comment that Jesus offers as his final
eulogy for his fallen cousin: "Among the sons of women no one
greater than John the Baptist has appeared, and yet the least in
the kingdom of heaven is greater than he" (Matthew 11:11).

We know, moreover, exactly where the point of tension arose:
it was Jesus's notorious laxness, his failure to maintain the standards of purity (and not simply advanced, Essene purity, but the
fundamental requirements of the Jewish law). "The Son of man
came, he ate and drank, and people said: 'Look at this man! A
glutton and drunkard, a friend of tax collectors and sinners!'"
(Matthew 11:19). The complaints are all over the gospels. If the
chronology suggested by Qumran scholar Barbara Thierring is
correct (and to my mind, it seems quite persuasive), he is the one
being depicted in the scrolls as the "Wicked Priest," the one who
abandons the path and leads others astray—as over and against
the "Teacher of Righteousness," John the Baptist.[1]

Jesus himself does not deny this accusation, but he turns it
end for end. What is the point of all these ritual prohibitions, he
countercharges, if they do not lead to an increase in love? In the
words of one of his most powerful teachings:

> So then, you Pharisees, you clean the outside of the cup and the
> dish, but inside yourselves you are full of greed and evil. Fools!
> He who made the outside, also made the inside. (Luke 11:39)

It is not external observances or ascetic rigors that produce
purity, he teaches. There is only one purity: the purity produced
from within, by a refashioning of the heart:

Do you not see that whatever enters the mouth goes into the stomach and then out of the body? But what comes out of the mouth comes from the heart, and that is what makes a person unclean. Indeed, it is from the heart that evil desires come— murder, adultery, immorality, theft, lies, slander. These are what make a person unclean; but eating without washing the hands does not make a person unclean. (Matthew 15:17–19)

With this insight Jesus officially signals his departure from the classic ascetic path. If it had somehow been missed before, it is now perfectly clear that he is marching to his own drummer. Through all his teachings, disputes with the Pharisees, healings and miracles during the three years of his public ministry he will lay out a simple but revolutionary method for arriving at purity of heart from within.

The Way of the Heart

How did he come to know what he knew? It's surprising how rarely this key question is asked—probably because the overriding assumption "Well *of course* he knew everything: he was the Son of God!" precludes any developmental process. The gospels themselves point to the forty days of testing in the wilderness as the actual time when this knowing came to him, and their allegorical description of what he discovered is surprisingly good, although they do not say much about *how* he discovered it. In the following chapters I will be putting forth my own suggestions in this regard.

As we set out to consider the teachings of Jesus as an integrated spiritual method, we are entering territory that is both familiar and unfamiliar. Most people growing up in the Western cultural stream will have had some exposure to these teachings (if only as ethical precepts), but the apparent familiarity of the subject matter can blind us to its radical strangeness and difficulty. Perhaps more than any other spiritual teacher, Jesus requires a real beginner's mind, a willingness to unlearn what one already presumably knows and start with a clean slate. In this spirit, then, I would like to begin by describing what seem to me to be the three constitutive elements of the path Jesus discovered; then, on the basis of these characteristics, I will propose to identify what branch of the spiritual stream it most properly belongs to. I will of course be making use not only of familiar reference points in the canonical gospels but also the new resources opened up in the Nag Hammadi gospels that we began to explore in part 1 of this book.

These three constitutive elements are kenosis, abundance, and singleness.

Kenosis

Kenosis comes from the Greek verb *kenosein,* which means to empty oneself. It was Paul who first applied this term to Jesus. In a moment of intuitive brilliance he grasped the essential element in Jesus's methodology, and he described it in his immortal words of Philippians 2:6–11:[2]

> Though his state was that of God,
> yet he did not deem equality with God
> something that he should cling to.
>
> Rather, he emptied himself*
> and assuming the state of a slave
> he was born in human likeness.
>
> He being known as one of us
> humbled himself obedient unto death,
> even death on a cross.
>
> For this God raised him on high
> and gave him the name
> which is above every other name

---

* This is the place where the verb *kenosein* appears.

So that at the name of Jesus
every knee should bend,
in heaven, on earth, and under the earth.

And so every tongue should proclaim
"Jesus Christ is Lord!"
To God the Father's glory.

As Paul so profoundly realizes, self-emptying is the touch-stone, the core reality underlying every moment of Jesus's human journey. Self-emptying is what brings him into human form, and self-emptying is what leads him out, returning him to the mode of glory. The full realization of Jesus's divine selfhood comes not through the concentration of being, but through a voluntary divestment of it.

We have already seen this same self-emptying motion described in that brilliant "divestment" metaphor of logion 21 in the Gospel of Thomas. When asked to describe his students, Jesus responds:

They are like small children living in a field not their own.
When the landlords return and demand,
   "Give us back our field!"
the children return it by simply stripping themselves
and standing naked before them.[3]

Stripping oneself and standing naked: this is the essence of the kenotic path. And it is, in fact, precisely the strategy that Jesus employs during the famous temptation narratives of the canonical gospels. In each case Satan asks him to *take* (feed yourself by turning stones into bread; display yourself by drawing on your divine powers; advance yourself by letting me set you up as ruler of the entire world). Jesus responds by simply letting go of the bait being dangled, content to rest in his emptiness.

It is also the methodology he will reaffirm during his ordeal in the garden of Gethsemane ("Not my will but yours be done"), and which will carry him through the crucifixion, the "harrowing of hell" (if my reading of dialogue 3 in the Gospel of Mary

Magdalene is correct), and the final forty days of his time on earth following the resurrection.

Kenosis is not the same as renunciation. Renunciation implies a subtle pushing away; kenosis is simply the willingness to let things come and go without grabbing on. For all intents and purposes it is synonymous with nonclinging or nonattachment. But unlike a more Buddhist version of this spiritual motion, kenosis has a certain warm spaciousness to it; to the degree one does not assert one's own agenda, something else has the space to be. The "letting go" of kenosis is actually closer to "letting be" than it is to any of its "non-" equivalents (nonclinging, nonattachment, nonidentification, and so forth); its flow is positive and fundamentally creative. Between the "let it be" of kenosis and the "let it be" by which biblical tradition envisions Creation itself as having come into existence, there is a profound resonance.

ABUNDANCE

This second pillar of Jesus's teaching is often seen but rarely recognized. The kenosis Jesus has in mind is not a stoic stance against a pitiless reality; rather, it is a direct gateway into a divine reality that can be *immediately experienced* as both compassionate and infinitely generous. Abundance surrounds and sustains us like the air we breathe; it is only our habitual self-protectiveness that prevents us from perceiving it. Thus, the real problem with any constrictive motion (taking, defending, hoarding, clinging) is that it makes us spiritually blind, unable to see the dance of divine generosity that is always flowing toward us.

In this sense, then, kenosis is first and foremost a visionary tool rather than a moral one; its primary purpose is to cleanse the lens of perception. Letting go is not in order to get something better (the point Paul misses in the second half of his Philippians hymn); in and of itself it *is* the something better. For it immediately restores the broken link with the dynamic ground of reality, which by its very nature flows forth from a fullness beyond imagining.

Since this point is so fundamentally counterintuitive for our anxiety-prone minds, little wonder that Jesus takes every occasion to hammer it home. In virtually all his teachings the fundamental leitmotif is an "over-the-top" generosity that leaves its recipients not only satisfied but bedazzled. Think of all those well-loved gospel stories—the prodigal son, the good Samaritan, the loaves and fishes, the water turned into wine, the woman with the alabaster jar, the fishing nets cast in the Galilean Sea—and you'll see what I mean. It is not a question of "adequate," or "barely enough," but of a fullness "pressed down, shaken together, running over" (Luke 6:38).

In exactly the same measure, his implacable stance against any kind of greed or hoarding is because these motions lead to constriction, or in other words, to spiritual and physical death. Life is an exchange, and in this exchange the mercy of God is made real. (I am indebted to Helen Luke for pointing out in her marvelous book *Old Age* that the linguistic root of the word *mercy* is in fact the Old Etruscan *merc*, which means "exchange."[4]) The modern spiritual teacher Michael Brown succinctly summarizes the core principle at the heart of Jesus's practical teachings: "'Giving-is-receiving' is the energetic frequency upon which our universe is aligned. All other approaches to energy exchange immediately cause dissonance and disharmony in our life experience."[5]

To experience abundance is essentially to see from oneness. It is to know, intimately, the wholeness that underlies and belies our surface impression of separation and scarcity. In the Eastern traditions this realized oneness is known as nonduality, and while Jesus knew it by another name (we'll see what it is very shortly), he was clearly familiar with the state itself and yearned to impart it to his followers. "Do not be afraid, little flock," he urged (Luke 12:32)— "it is my father's good *pleasure* to give you the kingdom!" But this gift can be received only in a state of deep inner emptiness, for any grasping and self-assertion will shatter the unity of which abundance is the mirror. Between kenosis, abundance, and oneness there is in Jesus's methodology an unbreakable connection.

SINGLENESS

This unitive realization of this fullness ushers a person into a state that Jesus calls "singleness." In the canonical gospels the term does not stand out, but a whole series of teachings in the Gospel of Thomas (logia 5, 15, 18, 22, 23, 61, 75, 84, 106, 114) makes its meaning indisputably clear. It is Jesus's term for the attained state of nonduality. Logion 5 succinctly describes this state, in which one sees from the wholeness and lives from the abundance:

> Come to know the One
> In the presence before you
> And everything hidden from you will be revealed . . .[6]

It is fascinating how closely this idea resonates with what the Eastern traditions would call "enlightenment." Breaking through the egoic mind's compulsive need to divide the perceptual field into paired opposites (inside and outside, male and female, subject and object, and so forth), consciousness simply coincides with its source and looks at the world through a single lens of wholeness. To be able to "make two become one" in this fashion is to reunite with the creative principle of the universe itself:

> When you are able
> to make two become one,
> the inside like the outside,
> and the outside like the inside
> the higher like the lower,
> so that a man is no longer male,
> and a woman, female,
> but male and female become a single whole . . .
> —then you shall enter in.
> (logion 22)

> When you are able to transform two into one,
> then you too will become "Sons of Man,"

and it will be possible for you to say to a mountain,
"Move," and it will move.
(logion 106)

In the Aramaic language of Jesus's immediate followers, one
of the earliest titles given to him was Ihidaya, " the Single One,"
or the "Unified One."[7] In context, it speaks unmistakably of this
state of inner oneness; it designates the anthropos, the fully realized human being: the enlightened master of Eastern tradition,
or the monad or "undivided one" of hermeticism.

The "great identity theft" to which the title of this chapter
refers is that in remarkably short order this term, which was so
clearly intended to designate Jesus's attained state of inner oneness, should come to be interpreted as "singleness" in the sense of
being unmarried, "the celibate one."[8]

THE "GIFT" OF CELIBACY

But wait a minute! Didn't Jesus himself say that celibacy was the
higher way and that anyone capable of it should strive to accept
this gift? This indeed would seem to be the meaning of his words
in Matthew 19:3–20, the gospel passage generally cited as decisive
proof that Jesus approved of celibacy and recommended it as the
highest spiritual lifestyle.

But is that what he is actually saying? When we examine the
passage closely, the situation becomes a lot more ambiguous.

The dialogue begins, as so many of Jesus's teachings do, with
a challenge from the Pharisees:

Some Pharisees approached him. They wanted to test him
and asked, "Is a man allowed to divorce his wife for any reason?" Jesus replied, "Have you not read that in the beginning
the Creator 'made them male and female,' and he said, 'Man
has now to leave father and mother, and be joined to his wife
so that the two shall become one body?' So they are no lon-

ger two, but one body; let no one separate what God has joined." (Matthew 19:3–6)

In response to this first test, Jesus counters with the highest possible vision of marriage. The teaching itself is scriptural (Genesis 1:27, 2:24), but in the actual practice of his times marriage had become largely a matter of dynastic and economic alliances. Jesus brings the issue squarely back to the sacred meaning of marriage and actually ups the ante by adding his own injunction: "Let no one separate what God has joined."

This concept of "two becoming one" is at the core of all mystical love, and it is significant to note that in the context of this exchange with the Pharisees, Jesus leads with that concept forcefully. Clearly he does not disparage marriage; he regards it with the highest honor.

They asked him, "Then why did Moses command us to write a bill of dismissal in order to divorce?" Jesus responded, "Moses knew your stubborn heart, so he allowed you to divorce your wives, but it was not so in the beginning. Therefore, I say to you: whoever divorces his wife [unless it be for infidelity[9]] and marries another commits adultery." (Matthew 19:7–9)

The exchange here is telling. Jesus responds that Moses made this dispensation because men and women were unable to live up to the high demand that true marriage imposes; they were too "stubborn-hearted"—or as other modern translations put it, "too hardhearted."[10] And remember, in Jesus-metaphysics a hardened heart is one that is unable to hear; to align; it cannot follow a path back to its mystical origin. But *in the beginning* it was not this way, he avers. From the gospels of Thomas and Mary Magdalene, we have learned that the "beginning" he is referring to here is not in time but beyond it, at the origin. In the image, the original template, this discrepancy does not exist, and Moses's dispensation is in fact betrayal of the image itself. Again, the highest possible vision of marriage is presented.

The disciples said, "If that is the condition of a married man, it is better not to marry." (Matthew 19:10)

You can almost hear their collective "*Oy vey!*" If marriage is *that* hard, perhaps it's better not to get married in the first place.

Jesus said to them, "Not everybody can accept what I have just said, but only those who have received this gift. Some are born incapable of marriage. Others have been made that way by men." (Matthew 19:11–12a)

What gift? Christian tradition has universally read this passage as referring to the gift of celibacy. But celibacy has not even been introduced as a topic of conversation yet. Within the context clues, it is clear that the antecedent of the pronoun "this" (and hence the gift he is referring to) is *true marriage*, not celibacy. Furthermore, if you follow Jesus's train of thought closely, you'll see that he is also implying here that real marriage necessarily entails a sexual expression. Some are born incapable of marriage (either through hardness of heart or sexual incapacity). Others are disqualified in the second way by castration.

But there are others who have given up the possibility of marriage for the sake of the kingdom of heaven. He who can accept this should accept it. (Matthew 19:12b)

Only here does Jesus finally specifically mention celibacy, properly understood as a voluntary relinquishment of the path of marriage "for the sake of the kingdom." This is the path of John the Baptist and some of his Essene confreres, and it may have been Jesus's as well, at least at the outset. Yes, the path does exist. Then follows his cryptic final comment: "He who can accept this should accept it."

What does the ambiguous antecedent, this "this," refer to? Three possibilities are equally sustainable grammatically: (1) that it refers to the state of voluntary celibacy; (2) that it refers to true marriage, the central topic under discussion here and to which the earlier vague antecedent referred (not everyone can accept "this"—that is, true marriage); (3) that it refers to the entire teaching he has just given and functions here as the equivalent to his usual "those who have ears, let them hear." Any of these possibilities will work grammatically, and the meaning can be flipped with a mere change of intonation (try it yourself). In any case, even if one opts for the first interpretation, nowhere does it say that celibacy is the highest way: for Jesus that honor clearly belongs to marriage. For "those who can accept it," fine. But the passage contains absolutely no implication that this acceptance constitutes a higher or purer spiritual calling.

Thus, what the church has traditionally interpreted as a categorical, "straight from the mouth of Jesus" sanctioning of celibacy as the premier vocational path crumbles under closer grammatical scrutiny. What we see instead is that Jesus instantly recognizes the archetypal image of mystical marriage and responds to it with his whole heart.

Where would he have come to know this?

9

THE PATH OF
CONSCIOUS LOVE

⊙   ⊙   ⊙   ⊙   ⊙

IN THE LIGHT of those three interwoven threads—kenosis, abundance, singleness—it is clear that the path Jesus is laying out simply cannot be the classic upward-tending asceticism he was formed in. It is not brahmacharya. If anything, it is the polar opposite of brahmacharya in that the unitive point ("singleness") is reached not through the concentration of spiritual energy but through a "throwing off" or radiation of it. The direction of flow is centrifugal rather than centripetal.

Overall it bears some resemblance to a Buddhist path of nonattachment, but with a distinctly different flavor to it: a warm-heartedness and intrinsic relationality that lead one to suspect love rather than emptiness as its chief metaphysical operative. While in Buddhism nonattachment is the logical response to the perception that all form is emptiness, in Jesus's vision, "letting go" or "letting be" is the gateway to a fullness so extravagant that it fills the emptiness to bursting, like a rain barrel after a sudden deluge. The *pleroma*, as it's known in Christian mystical tradition—"the very fullness of God"—flows through every nook and cranny of this world, and while the world may ultimately prove to be an illusion, the fullness itself is real.

The name I myself would give to this teaching is "the path of conscious love." I have chosen the name deliberately. I could simply have called it "the kenotic path," identifying it by its dominant methodology. Or I could have taken a big risk and introduced the term that is actually the counterbalancing equivalent to brahmacharya and the generic category to which the path most closely belongs: tantra. But tantra is a huge scare word to most Christians, who have only heard of it in terms of sacralized sex, and there is no point in introducing any more fearfulness into the discussion than the topic of Jesus and Mary Magdalene in itself already produces.[1] "Conscious love" is a good middle ground. It emphasizes the life-affirming and implicitly relational nature of the path, and the word "conscious" makes clear that the touchstone here is transformation, not simply romance. Conscious love is "love in the service of inner transformation"—or if you prefer, "inner transformation in the service of love." Either way, this is exactly what Jesus was about.

So how did he come to this path? Clearly nothing quite like this had been seen in the Semitic lands before, and its divergence from the cultural and spiritual norms of the times was constantly calling people up short. How did he learn what he knew?

Certainly he could have come to this planet with the teaching already fully formed within him. For the high spiritual being that he clearly was (whether or not this extends to being the only son of God), such preexistent knowledge could be expected. Or perhaps the teaching came to him in a single overpowering revelation during his time in the wilderness. But my own hunch is that to a degree far more than is ever acknowledged, he learned it from Mary Magdalene. Or rather, they learned it from each other, through their combined efforts to stay true to this unexpected new invitation that God had dropped into their laps. The invisible current of their love is the measure of his deviation from the brahmacharya course. And the path itself is the measure of the integrity and beauty of what they discover together.

"AND THEIR EYES MET . . ."

Somewhere along the way, whether in Galilee, on an early teaching trip to Jerusalem, or somewhere in the wilderness between, Jesus and Mary Magdalene became acquainted. The gospels do not say how; she simply appears among the camp followers. Some scholars feel that Jesus's encounter with the Samaritan woman at the well in John 4:5–26 may in fact be a veiled description of his first meeting with Mary Magdalene, but the evidence supporting this inference is a bit technical and will need to await our fuller exploration of the Gospel of John toward the end of this book.

In the later traditions of gnostic Christianity, however, a story exists describing their first meeting. While most likely apocryphal, at both the psychological and spiritual levels it seems to ring true.[2] In this wisdom version of the classic "recovering prostitute" theme, the outstandingly beautiful and spiritually precocious Mary Magdalene had been promised in marriage by her worldly minded Jewish father to a wealthy Babylonian merchant. En route to Babylon, however, her caravan was attacked by robbers, and she was instead sold into slavery and prostitution. After a time she managed to regain her outer freedom, but inwardly she was still held hostage by hatred, rage, and darkness. At length a dream came to her telling her that she must return to the land of her birth and seek out the Anointed One, who would deliver her. She left immediately for the Holy Land, crossed the Jordan River, and found her way to the place where he was teaching.[3]

A crowd had gathered around him, and she hid herself in the back, hoping to remain unseen. But while the Anointed was speaking,

> . . . at one point he glanced at her, caught her gaze, and something passed between them. She was thunderstruck; an energy and vibration filled her whole body. Her sight opened and she saw his true form as light and fire and truth, and a love such as she had never known welled up in her.[4]

But can such a gaze ever pass in one direction only? The story makes clear that the impact of that "something" which passed between them is as compelling for him as it is for her. He sends for her immediately; there by the bank of the Jordan he performs his legendary exorcism of her seven demons, and their human journey together officially begins. Later, according to this legend, after a time of seclusion in the wilderness, in which he gives her teaching and initiates her, they are officially married and work together thereafter as mystically conjoined partners.

In real life, if something of this sort ever actually took place, it was probably a good deal messier, a good deal more ambivalent. For an emerging young spiritual master at the time self-identified as a Nazirite, one can only imagine that his first encounter with that "eternal gaze" through which true love announces itself must have been a replay of his mother's story some thirty years earlier, when that sudden visitation of an angel announces solemnly that one's life is not going to be a bit like what one thought it was. While he, too, ultimately made his way to that same "Let it be," I suspect he did not come to it without a good deal of interior struggle. Later in this book I will attempt to set out the pieces of evidence (mostly hidden in the deeper symbolic structure of the Gospel of John) by which I came to that intuition.

While the legend is almost certainly not literally true, its honesty lies in its fidelity to that initial moment of impact, as well as in its boldness in naming the actual nature of the impact. For despite all the later obfuscations on this point, one simply cannot read that deeply romantic, "love at first sight" energy out of the Mary Magdalene equation. There is *something* special about their relationship, something not simply reducible to teacher and devotee, and all attempts to hedge and prevaricate about its nature merely render its energy more palpable. The unspoken bond between them reverberates through even the highly muted accounts in the canonical gospels, while the Nag Hammadi gospels make no bones about naming this energy for what it is. "For we know that the Savior greatly loved you above all other women," Peter announces forthrightly in the Gospel of Mary Magdalene. The Gospel of Philip is explicit about the nature of their relationship:

she is his "companion," *koinonos*,[5] a term whose meanings can range from consort to spouse, but which at any rate implies a committed partnership.

As long as one is committed to shoehorning the Jesus path into a celibate monastic template, these facts remain anomalous and threatening. But the moment the path is correctly identified, the problem largely disappears. For while celibacy is certainly a requirement of the brahmacharya path, it is not necessarily so on a path of conscious love. The path comes in both celibate and noncelibate versions, as we shall see, and chastity is in either case a requirement. But chastity is not the same thing as celibacy. On a path of conscious love, chastity is guarded by purity of heart (as described in dialogue 1 of the Gospel of Mary Magdalene, as well as in the sixth beatitude: "Blessed are the pure in heart, for they shall see God"). It entails a primary commitment to the practice of keeping the eye of the heart clear and unencumbered in order to participate fully in that dance of divine abundance. Which version of the path Jesus would most likely have practiced in a committed relationship with Mary Magdalene will reveal itself gradually, of its own accord, as we move deeper into our exploration; there is no need to force its hand here. But it is important to realize that such a relationship would in and of itself pose no impediment to holiness on a path of conscious love.

THE FIFTH WAY

In fact, conscious love is probably the most inclusive of all spiritual paths. It can be walked by any and all, in any relational combination or none. It can be practiced by monks, by romantic partners both gay and straight, with children and aging parents, in a hermitage under the starry skies, with pets, and even with houseplants. The bottom line is not the "who" but the "how": the direction of the energy flow. On a path of conscious love the energy is always radiating outward; it is never self-defended or congealed. The contemporary teacher Raimon Panikkar succinctly captures the essence of this motion when he writes: "I am one with the source insofar as I too act as a source by making everything I have received flow again."[6]

Nevertheless, over the centuries there are those who have been intrigued by what conscious love might look like when specifically practiced as a relational path between romantic partners. Obviously, this exploration has been conducted mainly within the esoteric underground, since the institutional church has never been able to wrap its mind around the notion of relationship as an authentic spiritual path. But the fact that such a path has never been officially acknowledged does not mean that information about it is unavailable.

One thinker who clearly believed that such a path did exist— and has existed since the very beginning of Christianity—is a relatively obscure Russian esotericist by the name of Boris Mouravieff (d. 1966), whose three-volume *Gnosis* appeared posthumously in English translation in the early 1990s.[7] Mouravieff claimed to be making available for the first time in the West the hidden teachings of esoteric Christianity on the subject of conscious love as practiced in human partnership. He called this path the "Fifth Way."

Where Mouravieff actually came by his knowledge remains a bit mysterious. The term "Fifth Way" is itself a deliberate spin-off on G. I. Gurdjieff 's "Fourth Way" (or "Way of the Conscious Man"), the name by which the comprehensive spiritual method of this enigmatic genius (1866–1949) is familiarly known.[8] Mouravieff had obviously studied the Gurdjieff system closely, but he insisted that his own teachings had been handed down to him directly from the Greek Orthodox tradition of Mount Athos. Wherever he came by his knowledge, his dense and idiosyncratic work is the most complete exposition available in the West of courtly love as a spiritual path and of the way of transformation through mystical union with one's "polar being." While he stops short of saying that Jesus and Mary Magdalene practiced this path, he makes it clear that its headwaters lie deep within the marrow of Christianity itself, and he insists that it represents the purest and most sublime realization of the Christian spiritual path.

Difficult as his work may be, it at least puts some quantitative measurement around this particular pathway of spiritual realization, and its resonances with the heart of Christian mysticism are unmistakable. Without committing ourselves to the proposal that Jesus and Mary Magdalene were involved in a romantic relationship, we can say hypothetically that if they *had* been involved in such a relationship, it would have borne some resemblance to the Fifth Way as described by Mouravieff: a rigorous mystical path of conscious evolution practiced in committed partnership. And from that starting point, we can begin to imaginatively reconstruct what it might have looked like.

Perhaps even this starting assumption may by no means be obvious to all readers, so let me take a moment to explain how I arrived at it. Simply put, the state of singleness so clearly recognizable both in Jesus himself and in the Mary Magdalene who shines forth from the gospel bearing her name can only be sustained through a complete inner consistency. Whole is whole. There is no "time off for good behavior" (or bad behavior, as the case may be), no cheating on the path, and certainly no affairs or sexual dalliances. I have learned this, principally, through watching a number of contemporary spiritual masters at work. Any interior wobbling shows up immediately as a cavitation in the so-called master's energy field and can easily be picked up by those sensitive to it. I am personally convinced that in order for Jesus to have brought off what he brought off—a teaching which two thousand years later still reverberates with the energy of his presence—his singleness would have had to be impeccable. A relationship with Mary Magdalene, if such there was, could be embraced only with complete inner integrity and in accordance with the highest standards of the teaching itself.

For those reluctant to take on Mouravieff, fortunately the basic contours of the Fifth Way are confirmed by a number of later spiritual teachers, particularly in the superb work of John Welwood, whose *Journey of the Heart: The Path of Conscious Love* (1990) is in my estimate the finest practical guidebook available to partnership as a pathway of spiritual awakening. I will be drawing heavily on his insights, along with those of several other well-known contemporary spiritual guides, as we begin to orient ourselves along this path.

CONSCIOUS WORK

The first requirement of conscious love is, of course, that it has to be *conscious*—or in other words, anchored in a quality of our presence deeper than simply egoic selfhood. Nowadays we would identify this quality of consciousness as unitive, or nondual, awareness. Jesus's own term for this state, as we have seen, is *singleness*, and singleness in turn announces the emergence of the anthropos, or fully realized human being, the one in whom "image" and analogue have been brought together.

For Jesus as for all teachers of conscious transformation, then, the work with a partner is in service of this goal. It is not intended simply to fulfill physical or emotional needs, but to accelerate the process of awakening.

"A conscious relationship is one that calls forth who you *really* are," writes John Welwood. Instead of looking to a relationship for shelter,

> . . . we could welcome its power to wake us up in areas of life where we are asleep and where we avoid naked, direct contact with life. This approach puts us on a path. It commits us to movement and change, providing forward direction by showing us where we most need to grow. Embracing relationship as a path also gives us practice: learning to use each difficulty along the way as an opportunity to go further, to connect more deeply, not just with a partner, but with our own aliveness as well.[9]

As many of my readers will know, the great turning point in my own spiritual journey came when I was called into this type of relationship with a hermit monk just at the end of his life. Brother Raphael—"Rafe," as he was known—was an authentic spiritual warrior, and while the emotional healing experienced through our relationship was powerful for both of us, the fundamental contract between us was clear: all our interactions were to be food for seeing, for a growth of consciousness. At one point, I remember begging Rafe to let me tag along with him as he headed up to his hermitage for wood-splitting chores. "What if you *don't* come and see what happens next?" he asked me. All difficulties were opportunities for growth in self-knowledge, and it was precisely by cutting through all the relational game-playing that something qualitatively more real could begin to express itself.

Practically speaking, the ability to do this assumes the existence of a stable inner observer or witnessing presence, a place to regroup from. "You can't move a plank you're standing on" was an adage from my days in the Gurdjieff work; as long as the egoic self is the only self you know, you will cling to it like a life raft. In fact, without the development of a strong inner observer, surmises the contemporary pundit Eckhart Tolle, "all relationships are deeply flawed."[10] One automatically identifies with one's needs, agendas, and projections, that fatal stew which can instantly turn romance into armed warfare. The art of separation is essential to conscious love.

No doubt this advice from the masters will fall largely on deaf ears in a culture so geared to emotional gratification. But for those who have learned how to use the friction inherent in all intimate relationships as a stimulus for conscious growth, the rate of progress can be literally breathtaking. In fact, claims Mouravieff, this is one of the primary attractions of the Fifth Way: its incredible spiritual efficiency (he describes the path, in fact, as an "esoteric shortcut").[11] Functioning as foils and mirrors for each other, the partners can work their way together through inner logjams that might have taken years to navigate individually.

The trick, of course, is that one must *clear* these logjams rather than simply getting caught in them, and doing so requires keeping those skills of inner witnessing closely honed. Commitment to a daily practice of meditation or some parallel spiritual discipline is the usual means by which this is done and is hence the practical foundation for the path of conscious love.

KENOSIS IN THE FIFTH WAY

We have already seen that kenosis is the tie-rod of Jesus's entire teaching, connecting the inner and outer realms of our human experience in a single, unified gesture. "Greater love has no man than to lay down his life for his friend" (John 15:13) is one of his most celebrated dictums. But when that "friend" happens also to be one's uniquely beloved, one's romantic partner or spouse, kenotic practice takes on a particularly intense and even a sacramental character. This is because the root energy it works with is the transformative fire of eros, the energy of desiring. That messy, covetous, passion-ridden quicksilver of all creation is tamed and transformed into a substance of an entirely different order, and the force of the alchemy accounts for both the efficiency of this path and its terrifying intensity.

Vladimir Solovyov, that great nineteenth-century philosopher of love, was among the first to grasp the enormous implication of this point, which defines both the modality of the Fifth Way and its ultimate destination:

> The meaning and worth of love . . . is that it really forces us, with all our being, to acknowledge for another the same absolute central significance which, because of the power of our egoism, we are conscious of only in our own selves. Love is important not as one of our feelings, but . . . as the shifting of the very center of our personal lives. This is characteristic of every kind of love, but predominantly of sexual love [erotic love]; it is distinguished from other kinds of love by greater intensity, by a more engrossing character, and by the possibility of a more complete overall reciprocity. Only this love can lead to the real and indissoluble union of two lives into one; only of it do the words of Holy Writ say: "They shall be one flesh," that is, shall become one real being.[12]

In an earlier chapter I spoke of the dangers of trying to sever eros and agape into two different species, which is bad theology and even worse metaphysics. For the great secret of erotic love—which all true lovers instinctively know and which I believe Jesus also knew—is that *agape is in essence transfigured desire.* There are not two loves, one agape-based and the other eros-based. Rather, agape is what emerges from the refiner's fire when that surging desire to cling, possess, consume the object of one's adoring is subjected to the discipline of kenosis, self-giving love. One could almost express this as a simple mathematical formula:

$$A = E \times K$$

In which A is agape, E is eros, and K is kenosis. The greater the degree of eros present and the stronger the practice of kenosis, the greater is the magnitude of transfigured love thereby revealed.

The paradigmatic description of this process may well be that wonderful old O. Henry story "The Gift of the Magi," in which the two destitute lovers each willingly give up their most precious possessions to buy each other a Christmas present. She cuts and sells her beautiful long hair to buy him a chain for his gold watch; he sells his gold watch to buy her combs for her beautiful hair. A pointless sacrifice? To be sure. Unless love itself is the point. For those so attuned, the resonances with Jesus's own "pointless" sacrifice on the cross will not go unnoticed.

In practice then, erotic partners can and must ride the wild stallion of passion. The Fifth Way does not require one to renounce, suppress, or numb the energy that surges through romantic love, but merely to carve a deeper channel in which it can flow, through a meticulous commitment to the daily practice of laying down oneself for the other. Duty, sacrifice, making accounts, and, above all, keeping score are useless in this kind of love. As an old Baptist preacher I know back in Maine once quipped, "When I got married, they told me it was a fifty-fifty proposition. Wrong! It's one hundred–one hundred." Fifth Way kenosis is an exercise in the pure generosity of standing in the other's place, discovering what it means to love one's neighbor as oneself—not *as much as* one's self, as egoic consciousness always appends, but as the intimate expression of one's own being.

"In the end," Ken Wilber writes of his beloved wife, Treya, as they approach the finish line of her five-year ordeal with cancer, "we simply and directly served each other, exchanging self for other and therefore glimpsing that eternal Spirit which transcends both self and other, both 'me' and 'mine.'"[13] This is among the most beautiful descriptions I have ever come across of the Fifth Way followed all the way to conclusion, where those paradoxically intertwining threads of self-surrender and a complete fusion of being are finally revealed as one.

SHADOW WORK

Contrary to usual expectations, true beloveds do not live in peace and acquiescence. They fight and struggle, sometimes for dear life. But in their struggles with one another—rather like the Old Bible tale of Jacob wrestling with the angel—there is not the usual defendedness and posturing of egoic warfare, but an electrifying sense of something breaking free. Prison walls come tumbling down, and inner chains in which each of the pair had long been held captive begin to loosen.

I have always claimed that the real predictor of a couple's long-term success is not how well they can maintain tranquility but how honestly and vulnerably they can fight. For shadow work—dealing with those unseen but all-powerful chains—is the heart of the Fifth Way.

Welwood is again superb on this aspect of the transformative journey. "Love is a transformative force because it brings the two different sides of ourselves—the expansive and the contracted, the asleep and the awake—into direct contact," he writes.[14] In his own metaphor for this fundamental human predicament, he describes how each of us, in response to perceived threats to our psychological survival, constructs a "soul cage," an ego bastion of last resort in which our carefully constructed self-image resides. Like all cages, it creates an oasis of safety but is far too small to allow us to spread our wings.

When one meets one's authentic partner on a Fifth Way path,[15] perhaps the most striking telltale is an immediate trust, an intuitive recognition that this person is someone with whom it will be safe to open the door to the cage. And there is a yearning to do so, for the path of kenosis as walked between beloveds expresses itself in a deepening urge to hold nothing back. But as Welwood observes, "Though we may truly desire to connect with another soul-to-soul, our ego still prefers to promote and defend self-image."[16] Thus the approach-avoidance dance begins, as the clash between our deepest yearnings and our deepest fears sets the partners on an inevitable collision course. With honesty, trust, a huge amount of inner witnessing, and the mysterious alchemy of love itself, the two beloveds may finally set each other free.

While the tendency of contemporary spiritual teaching is to imagine the ego as a "false self" that needs to be dismantled, the actual process is a good deal more nuanced. Rainer Maria Rilke actually comes much closer to the truth when he writes in his *Letters to a Young Poet*: "Perhaps all the dragons in our lives are really princesses who are waiting to see us act, just once, with beauty and courage. Perhaps everything that frightens us is, in its deepest essence, something helpless that wants our love."[17] The soul cage forms around our original innocence—to protect what is most tender and vulnerable within us—and in the delicate surgery that takes down the walls, we must be careful not to destroy the bird as well.

True Fifth Way partners possess this delicacy. Because they see so deeply into the other's true nature and yearn so deeply for the other's becoming, they are able to touch that original innocence and reawaken its song. And this turns out to be the key to that expression of wholeness toward which this path is headed.

Did Jesus and Mary Magdalene do shadow work? The idea may seem outlandish to Christians used to thinking of Jesus as having arrived on this planet as a fully perfected being. But we have already noted an evolution in self-understanding (away from the Nazirite mold in which he was formed and toward a more dynamic and inclusive notion of spiritual purity), and we have already suggested that Mary Magdalene may well have been a significant factor in this evolution. His "soul cage" as an Essene ascetic melted before his eyes, and if we assume that this transition was not effortless but came at the cost of considerable inner struggle in the tension between his original self-image and the undeniable reality of his *koinonos* standing before him, then we are looking at shadow work in its classic form.

Here again the Gospel of John has been implicated. Beneath its surface may well lie a discreetly veiled anatomy of Fifth Way love (as I mentioned earlier, we will be exploring this proposal more thoroughly in part 3), and from this perspective not only the meeting with the woman at the well but also the wedding at Cana (John 2:1–12) describe distinct steps in the evolution of consciousness along this pathway. Symbolically at stake in the episode at Cana, as the British esotericist Maurice Nicoll points out in his book *The New Man*, is the issue of Jesus's psychological separation from his mother.[18] He arrives at the wedding feast in her company, and she calls the shots as she orchestrates his first public miracle, turning water into wine. While he meekly protests, "My hour has not yet come" (John 2:4), he also quickly capitulates. His mother has been his defender and champion, his closest friend, and as the text symbolically acknowledges, his consort; she embodies all that he has been conditioned to be and all that must be transformed—like water into wine—before he emerges into his full and authentic personhood. This brief vignette at Cana sets the baseline for Jesus's subsequent female relationships and foreshadows the road that must be traveled in order for him to come to the full personal realization of what it means "to leave father and mother and be joined to his wife so that the two shall become one body."

THE WEDDING GARMENT

With patience and committed practice, Fifth Way partners do gradually become "one body." As in all conscious practice, "singleness," that state of inner wholeness in which the warring factions of our being have been brought into alignment, becomes an abiding state of being. But on a Fifth Way path there is a unique aspect to this. At least in its Christian esoteric version, that "singleness" is not simply each partner's individual realization of the unitive state, but an actual union of their beings so that the two individual souls essentially yield themselves into one "abler soul,"[19] which jointly becomes the mirror of the image from which they have originated. The name traditionally given to this collectively attained singleness is "the wedding garment."

I realize that this teaching can be problematic. No doubt the Buddhists John Welwood and Ken Wilber would strongly disagree. Like most mystical teaching, it does not download easily into a space-time continuum. It can end up sounding like the old Platonic myth of the bipolar soul (see endnote 16, above)—or else simply codependency writ large! The usual way this ancient mystical insight is now handled is through Jungian means: as a symbolic description of the integration of male and female, animus and anima, within the individual soul. But in the original teachings, it is clear that the meaning is literal: two objective "others" (from the point of view of this realm) do actually choose to throw in their lot together to become jointly the true reflection of the "One" they sense themselves to be at origin. And this, in turn, creates a powerful open channel between the realms through which much spiritual blessing flows. This understanding of the true esoteric meaning of "one body" will be utterly essential as we move deeper into our consideration of Jesus and Mary Magdalene, and of the bridal mysticism to which Christianity so instinctively gravitates for the speaking of its deepest mystical truths.

10

THE BRIDAL CHAMBER

⊙　⊙　⊙　⊙　⊙

Only the single will enter the bridal chamber.
　　　　　　　　　—THE GOSPEL OF THOMAS, LOGION 75

Let not the Bridal Chamber be for animals, slaves, or harlots.
Rather, let it be for those both free and virginal.
　　　　　　　　　—THE GOSPEL OF PHILIP, ANALOGUE 47

FOR TRADITIONALLY RAISED Christians, the Gospel of Philip
is strong stuff—perhaps *too* strong. If it's true in general that
Christian mysticism seems to contain a "tantric gene"—a tendency to express itself in the language of transfigured eroticism—
in Philip the tantra is right in one's face. Both thematically and
structurally everything in this gospel flows in the direction of
nuptial union. And while the "marriage of opposites" consummated in the bridal chamber, the gospel's central image, clearly
transcends simply a sexual union, it also does not unequivocally
exclude it.

　　This is also, of course, the gospel in which the relationship
between Mary Magdalene and Jesus is portrayed in terms openly

erotic and spousal. Philip describes how "Jesus loved Mary Magdalene more than the others and many times would kiss her on the mouth." She is twice referred to as his *koinonos*, his companion or mate, and she is said to have "continuously walked with the Master." Whatever the nature of this nuptial union might be, they are obviously familiar with it and would appear to practice it together. The gospel thus lends itself easily to all sorts of extravagant projections, from those looking to find evidence here of a sexual Mystery cult at the heart of Christianity, to those wishing to reconstruct the entire Christian Mystery along Jungian lines as the archetypal reunion of animus and anima within the individual soul.

Neither of which, incidentally, has much to do with what this gospel is actually saying.

It doesn't help matters, either, that the text itself is obscure and in key places indecipherable. Words have a frustrating way of going missing or becoming illegible just at the moment when information is about to be delivered that would clarify how the complex symbolism of the bridal chamber is to be understood: literally, symbolically, sacramentally, or some combination of all three. That leaves us with little more than context clues and educated guesswork to work with, so it is not surprising that the two most important popular translations—*The Gospel of Philip* by Jean-Yves Leloup and *The Luminous Gospels* by Lynn C. Bauman[1]—in places read so differently that they seem like entirely different texts! Bauman and Leloup are both outstanding interpreters of the Christian inner tradition, however, and while their angle of vision may differ sharply on key points, their translations laid side by side provide a system of checks and balances that at least establishes the ballpark of the text's probable meaning.

If we are able to keep a level head while approaching the Gospel of Philip, it quickly falls in line with what is by now already familiar territory from our earlier explorations of the gospels of Thomas and Mary Magdalene. In fact, Lynn Bauman's thumbnail description of this text is that it is a "reflection upon and refinement of the tradition of Thomas,"[2] in much the same way that the Gospel of John is a reflection upon and further refinement of the tradition of the Synoptic gospels (that is, the gospels of Matthew, Mark, and Luke). I have already mentioned Bauman's intriguing proposal that each of these three primary wisdom gospels has its counterpart in the canonical tradition (Thomas parallels the Synoptic gospels, Mary Magdalene parallels the book of Acts, and Philip parallels John), so that in place of the unhelpful division of the field into orthodox and gnostic camps, we might do better to think in terms of a "Western canon" and an "Eastern canon": the same story told in parallel cosmovisions.[3] The Gospel of Philip belongs to this Eastern canon, and both its brilliant visionary imagery and the metaphysics underlying it reflect its Semitic frame of reference. If bridal mysticism this may be, it is definitely of a Near Eastern flavor.

Historically, most scholars see this text as emerging from the Valentinian community, possibly authored by Valentinus himself.[4] The Valentinians were a powerful stream of influence within the crosscurrents of second-century Christianity and among the first to incur the displeasure of the early church fathers and earn for themselves the approbation "Gnostic." But as Ward Bauman (Lynn's brother) points out in his introduction to this text in *The Luminous Gospels*, "Philip is gnostic but not Gnostic," since its teachings affirm a nondualistic view of the world and are "surprisingly positive about the physical body and its procreative and sexual aspects as part of Christian understanding."[5] Again, we have covered this point in chapter 3. Leloup in his introduction to this text prefers to keep his attention focused on Philip, whose name the gospel honorarily bears. Why should this be? Because, Leloup suggests, he is the apostle who, like Thomas, has been called to contemplate "the One who is before his eyes" (John 14:9),[6] and because his apostolic mission field is thought to have included Syria, Phrygia (around the Black Sea), and most likely Ethiopia: all those celebrated wellsprings of oriental light whose mysticism the gospel so richly reflects.

The Leloup edition identifies individual passages in the text by their original manuscript page, subgrouped into 127 numbered logia. Lynn Bauman departs from the traditional arrangement and groups the gospel into 72 sections that he calls "analogues" (or analogies), since they collectively comprise an interwoven set of metaphors, each one offering a slightly different access point to the mystery being unfolded. I will be using this Bauman numbering system to refer to passages in the text; the number in parentheses designates the analogue being cited.

THE COMPLETED HUMAN BEING

In the Gospel of Philip, as in the gospels of Thomas and Mary Magdalene, the backdrop against which everything else unfolds is the quest for the anthropos, the "completed human being." In Philip this quest is particularly strong. It is mentioned in the text at least a dozen times, and in terms that not only correspond exactly with the Gospel of Thomas but at one point quote him directly: "I have come to make the inner as the outer and the outer as the inner" (analogue 44, quoting Thomas, logion 22). The completed human being is the one who has reconciled the opposites, made two become one—

> the inside like the outside,
> and the outside like the inside,
> the higher like the lower,
> so that a man is no longer male,
> and a woman female,
> but male and female
> become a single whole . . .
> (logion 22)

Those who have attained to this Oneness of being, according to Philip, are "called the holiest of the Holy Ones" (analogue 48). They "come from that transcendent place beyond confusion" (analogue 44).

Philip makes expressly clear, however, that this two-becoming-one is not simply a union of opposites as we understand it nowadays: not simply the integration of masculine and feminine or any of other the great binaries. These are important, to be sure, but they are the *fruits* (rather than the cause) of a fundamental integration that occurs at a much deeper level.

The nature of this more profound integration is captured in a vivid but cryptic image at the end of analogue 14, concluding a discussion of Jesus's transfiguration on Mount Tabor:

> So when he revealed himself to his students in glory on the mountain . . . on that very day in an act of great thanksgiving, he cried, "O You who have united Perfected Light with Sacred Spirit, come bind our angels to our icons."

"Come bind our angels to our icons." This same striking image occurs again in analogue 41, here in specific reference to an inner reconciliation that must take place before "male and female sit side-by-side together in mutuality."

Once again we appear to be staring straight into the face of that curious teaching we first encountered toward the end of the first dialogue in the Gospel of Magdalene: the union of image and analogue. In Philip's terminology, *angel* corresponds to image and *icon* to analogue, but the template remains the same. Within the particular metaphysical stream all three of these gospels seem to be working in, the primordial union—the union underlying all other forms of "integration of the opposites"— is the union of one's temporal humanity with its eternal prototype or "angel" so that, in those uncannily relevant words of the seventeenth-century German mystic Jacob Boehme, which we have already cited earlier:

> earth unfolds its properties and powers in union with Heaven aloft above us, and there is one Heart, one Being, one Will, one God all in all.[7]

The foundational importance of this union may escape most Western readers, who have not grown up with this metaphysical tradition. The significance is perhaps best conveyed through a piece of Near Eastern wisdom that would eventually find its home as one of the *Hadith Qudsi,* or additional sayings attached to the Quran. God speaks: "I was a hidden treasure and I loved to be known, so I created the worlds visible and invisible." In a universe where everything exists "in, from, and toward" this unfolding tapestry of divine love, the intimate interwovenness of the visible and invisible realms is the medium in which this self-communication takes place; the warp and weft of theophany (divine self-disclosure). The strength and precision of the alignment is essential, not only for the attainment of one's personal "completed human being," but for the ultimate revelation of the "hidden treasure" that the divine heart yearns to make known.

Once this fundamental inner union is in place, all other unions flow rightly: the reconciliation of masculine and feminine, of male and female, and of flesh-and-blood men and women in a sacred embrace that encompasses all dimensions of their being, including their physical lovemaking. Once they have "awakened in this life to that in us which does not die" (in Leloup's words)[8] and become living conduits of Eternity flowing into time, then every one of their actions is imbued with transparency and grace. They become sacraments of wholeness—or in the language of this text, "virgins."

"THE HOLIEST OF HOLIES"

True to his Semitic heritage, Philip builds his elaborate symbolic edifice upon a central metaphor that comes directly out of Jewish mysticism: the vision of the heavenly temple. In analogue 48 he lays out the basic schematic:

> At the temple in Jerusalem there are three chambers to which one can bring an offering. One opens to the West called the Holy Place. The second opens to the South and is called the Holy of Holies, and the third opens to the East, which is the Holiest of all where only the High Priest may enter . . . The Holiest Place is the Bridal Chamber.[9]

Thus he situates his bridal chamber, anagogically, at the very center of the innermost and most holy and hidden place. Those familiar with the complex symbolic traditions of Semitic bridal mysticism will know that this "holiest of holy" places is also a traditional way of designating the human heart. Symbolically, then, Philip's bridal chamber is located in the heart.

To this already complex image Philip adds yet another layer of complexity, when he attempts to relate each of these three chambers to the five great sacramental mysteries of Christian life, which in analogue 44 he enumerates as baptism, anointing, eucharist, restoration to fullness of being,[10] and the bridal chamber. In analogue 48 (in those two lines previously omitted from the citation) he specifies: "Immersion or Baptism brings one into the Holy Place. Restoration to the Fullness of Being is the Holy of Holies, and the Holiest Place is the Bridal Chamber."

What makes Philip's overlay intriguing (and challenging) is that the matchup is not symmetrical. Baptism marks the entry into the first chamber and restoration to the fullness of being marks the entry into the second, with anointing and eucharist presumably guiding the journey between them. For the third chamber no sacrament is specifically mentioned.

It is important not to make the mistake of thinking of these sacramental mysteries as *initiation rites*. Philip makes clear that this is not so. While all sacraments are "outward and visible signs of an invisible grace" (in the classic definition from the Episcopal *Book of Common Prayer*), he insists that "it is truly imperative that one must not be reborn in symbol only" (analogue 44). Fullness of being is not a temporary ecstatic state produced through a Mystery ritual; it must be painfully ground-truthed in one's own life through a rigorous journey of purification. Otherwise, claims Philip, the "names" (temporary empowerment) that one has received through participation in the sacraments "will be removed" (analogue 44).

For a description of what this journey actually entails—and particularly, the mysterious transformation that is the work of the second chamber—one can do little better than to quote from Ward Bauman's excellent commentary:

Having received the Baptism to newness of life and the Anointing (which is Sacred Fire), and the Eucharist (which shifts one's perspective), one is ready to enter the second chamber, where everything is exposed so that all narrowness and limitation can be burnt away . . . The practice, then, is to bring the dark, hidden secrets of the soul to light, so that they can be immobilized (Analogue 68). Here the veil that keeps an individual from knowing his or her true Self is lifted. Stripped of the egoic self and exposed to the light, one is restored to "fullness of being," that is, to one's True Self, which makes the initiate ready to enter the Bridal Chamber. The perspective of self has now shifted from duality to participation in God, and the final transformation into nondual consciousness is now possible.[11]

Seen from this perspective, Philip's three-chambered mysticism falls right into line with the "purgative," "illuminative," and "unitive" stages of the classic formulation of the Christian spiritual path, and that profound melting and recasting of one's being in the refiner's fire of the second chamber corresponds to what is traditionally designated in the Christian West as "the dark night of the spirit." But at this point we must take note of one crucially important detail. You might think that the bridal chamber is the place where this union is achieved. But no, unity of being—the attained state of singleness—is forged in the holy of holies, and only then is one free to enter the chamber. The bridal chamber does not *confer* the state of oneness; rather, only those who have already achieved their singleness, those who are already "clothed" (a recurrent image in this text), can be admitted into its holiest inner sanctum, there to experience "the sacred embrace."

"A Further Union, a Deeper Communion"

But why should there be any need for a bridal chamber at all? What is this "further union, this deeper communion" (to borrow a phrase from T. S. Eliot[12]) that awaits one beyond singleness?

Isn't singleness itself by definition the fully attained state of non-duality?

Not according to this tradition. There is still one greater mystery to be revealed. It is the discovery that deeper than *at-one-ment* lies *comm-union*, love come full in the act of giving itself away. The nondualism of the Western metaphysical stream is a flowing unity—a "not one, not two, but both one and two," in which the continuous exchange of twoness and oneness in the dance of self-giving love captures the very dynamism of the divine life itself. To discover myself as a divine being is certainly a spiritual attainment, but to discover myself as the divine *beloved* is to discover something even more intimate and profound about the hidden treasure that God longs to make known.[13]

So it is inevitable, perhaps, that in all three of the great Western religions the bridal chamber becomes the core metaphor for evoking the actual feeling tone of our participation in nonduality. For it is intimate exchange in the "arms" of sacred embrace and not monism that most authentically captures the heart of Western nondualism. And for all our mistakes and false starts, our human lovemaking when it approaches these mystical heights is still, according to this gospel, our closest human analogue to the experience of the divine embrace itself.

COSMIC SERVICE

Before leaving the subject of the bridal chamber, it is important to mention one other perhaps minor detail that Philip nonetheless goes out of his way to stress. Admission to the bridal chamber, he makes clear, is not for our personal gratification or even our personal self-realization, but to equip us to "move forth *into the cosmos* as a Completed Being" (analogue 59). There is an expectation of servanthood, not unlike the bodhisattva vow of Buddhism, where an enlightened being voluntarily renounces his attained status and chooses to remain here on this earth plane in order to assist his fellow beings. Something of this sort seems to be being suggested in analogue 61, where Philip, again describing the completed human being, teaches: "Love is what uplifts and frees them, and yet in their freedom true knowledge also makes them slaves of love on behalf of those who are not yet ready to live in the freedom of truth." And in analogue 59 he warns, a bit cryptically, "It is crucial to become fully self-realized before moving beyond this world. Whoever receives this gift [and it is clear from the context that the gift he is referring to here is the bridal chamber] without achieving mastery in this domain will have no mastery in any other, moving forward through these transitions in an imperfect state. Only Yeshua knows what the destiny of such a person will be." While his meaning is somewhat ambiguous here, the gist of it seems to be that the state of mastery or "full self-realization" entails the capacity to give back—in terms that this world can receive—the gifts that one has so richly received.

VIRGINITY AND UNION

For Philip the bridal chamber is primarily interior, not exterior. The nuptial union takes place within the individual human heart, not as a literal coupling between two partners. And yet between these two spheres there is a direct and ideally an unbroken connection. This gospel sets forth what is in all probability the highest anthropology of marriage to be found anywhere in the sacred scriptures of the West. Analogue 40 states that "there is a magnificence to the mystery of marital union" and that "human society itself is grounded in marriage." Leloup's translation makes this point even stronger: "The mystery which unites two beings is great; without it the world would not exist."[14] Then, in the final sentence of this remarkable passage, Philip affirms that while the union of the "pure embrace" (that is, the union consummated in the bridal chamber of the heart) is infinitely more powerful, "its image, however, is found in physical sexual union."

What an extraordinary statement! After two thousand years of unmitigatedly phobic teaching from the church fathers that sexual intercourse is grounded in carnality and is itself a defilement, what a relief to hear it explicitly proclaimed that you *can*

"get from here to there"! Between our human lovemaking and
the most sublime experience of divine union awaiting us in the
bridal chamber the relationship is "icon to angel" (or analogue to
image)—or in other words, the human form both expresses and
becomes the authentic vehicle of its eternal archetype once the
two realms have been brought into alignment.

Herein, I believe lies the key to this entire teaching.

The translation of this passage is challenging. The phrase
that both Leloup and Bauman translate as "pure embrace" is in
fact "undefiled *koinonia*." (The Greek word *koinonia* essentially
means "communion" or "fellowship.") The Coptic phrase describing human sexual love is literally "defiled *koinonia*."

But wherein lies the defilement? As children of our own cultural stream, it is almost impossible to avoid leaping to the conclusion that the defilement lies in the sexual expression itself. But
in fact, Philip seems to be saying something quite different. In
analogue 49, his remarkable retelling of the fall of Adam and Eve,
he teaches:

> If the female had not been separated from the male, she would
> never have died with the male. Her separation, however, be-
> came the cause and origin of her death. It is for this reason
> that the Anointed One came that he might remedy this con-
> dition by uniting the masculine and the feminine [or male
> and female] together again. When the feminine and the mas-
> culine come together in spiritual union within the Bridal
> Chamber, therefore, they are no longer separated—a separa-
> tion that occurred when Adam and Eve united outside the
> Bridal Chamber.

In other words, if we follow Philip's train of thought here,
the problem is not that Adam and Eve united, but that *they united
outside the bridal chamber.* They had already separated from their
"angel"—the archetype of their collective wholeness—and hence
their actions were defiled not by their sexual expression itself, but
by their lack of alignment.

This directly accords with the teachings we have already met in the Gospel of Mary Magdalene during Jesus's metaphysical discourse in dialogue 1:

Sin as such does not exist. You only bring it into manifestation when you act in ways that are adulterous in nature . . .

And:

Attachment to matter gives birth to passion without an Image of itself because it is drawn from that which is contrary to its essence. The result is that confusion and disturbance resonate throughout one's whole being. It is for this reason that I told you to find contentment at the level of the heart, and if you are discouraged, take heart in the presence of the Image of your true nature.

In this particular metaphysical system, "adulterous" has the primary meaning of being out of alignment: severing what should by rights be the unbroken and mutually engendering connection between image and analogue. Eve fell into "defilement" when she "separated from Adam," not when she made love with him.

The name given to the state of restored alignment—of "singleness" or purity of being—is "virginity."

Once you recognize this, of course, it radically rearranges the playing field. We are used to thinking of virginity as something we begin with and then lose through sexual expression. In this teaching it is the other way around. Our early emergence into consciousness finds most of us scattered and confused, lost in a maze of self-images with not a clue as to who we really are. Many of us, tragically, remain in that state all our lives. The journey toward real self-knowledge (or *gnosis*), toward "restoration to fullness of being," is at the same time the painstaking reclaiming of our own virginity, which in this teaching bears the sense of "free, simple, and inwardly whole." Again, a wonderful phrase from T. S. Eliot comes to mind: "a condition of complete simplicity costing not less than everything."[15]

Virginity is essentially synonymous with "singleness" itself.
And it is the necessary prerequisite for entry into the bridal chamber, for only those who have reclaimed their own virginity can
truly become "one body."

Modern Fifth Way teachers would not disagree. In his famous counsel in *Letters to a Young Poet*, Rilke writes:

> Loving does not at first mean merging, surrendering, or unit-
> ing with another person (for what would a union be of
> two people who are unclarified, unfinished, and still incoher-
> ent?) . . . [Love] is a high inducement for the individual to
> ripen, to become something in himself, to become world, to
> become world in himself for the sake of another person.[16]

And Mouravieff, while affirming that the fusion of two beloveds into one "Real I" is indeed a true path to salvation, cau-
tions: "In practice, this can only happen when the two
personalities are very advanced, and both rich with the experience
each has acquired separately in exterior life."[17]

But in fact, it would seem that the distance between the
"image" of the pure embrace reflected in human lovemaking and
its full realization in the bridal chamber is exactly the Fifth Way
path itself. In Philip's categories, it traverses the territory between
the "holy" and the "holy of holies": from the confused and scattered false self to the "singleness" or virginity that heralds the
entry into bridal chamber. And while no one can create another
person's singleness *for* them[18]—and in its absence the true bridal
chamber cannot be entered—intimate Fifth Way partners can and
do accelerate their progress toward singleness through their
shadow work, self-giving love, and the mutual enlargement of that
"third term," the love between them, which will become their
jointly created wedding garment. As they travel the road together,
the distance between image and archetype gradually narrows, and
more and more their human lovemaking becomes not only the
dim reflection but the living sacrament of its eternal counterpart.

This is the good news according to Philip.

II

JESUS AND MARY MAGDALENE IN THE BRIDAL CHAMBER

⊙   ⊙   ⊙   ⊙   ⊙

Sacred beings are entirely holy, including their bodies.
                    —GOSPEL OF PHILIP, ANALOGUE 60

FOR THOSE INTENT upon discovering in the Gospel of Philip an implicit (or explicit) confirmation that Jesus and Mary Magdalene practiced this bridal mysticism as sexual partners, the results can only be seen as disappointing. Nowhere does the text depict them as entering the bridal chamber together, nor does it bring forth their names as an example of the masculine and feminine reunited (which we would certainly expect if it were so, since analogue 49 tells us that "it is for this reason that the Anointed One came"). In fact, nowhere at all in this text does the name Mary Magdalene ever occur in conjunction with the term *bridal chamber*.

Depending on how one interprets a very difficult analogue (50), it would appear to be saying that Jesus's own initiation into the bridal chamber occurred at his baptism[1] and would thus have been a "pure embrace" experienced directly between himself and his heavenly father, not with a human partner. When and under what circumstances Mary Magdalene experienced her own initiation into the bridal chamber is nowhere specifically stated (except, perhaps, in that Gnostic legend mentioned in chapter 9), but it seems reasonable to assume that Jesus himself initiated her at some point during their work together.[2]

But the text does make clear that they were intimate. She is described as his *koinonos*, his companion or mate, which of course derives from *koinonia*, the word used to describe the sacred embrace of the bridal chamber. A koinonos is one who on some level or another has experienced koinonia. Moreover the text expressly states that "the Master loved her more than the other students and many times would kiss her on the mouth."[3]

To our Western ears, this passage can hardly help suggesting an erotic attraction, but the meaning is actually a good deal more subtle. In the Near Eastern milieu from which this text emerges, kissing on the mouth was practiced (and is still practiced in some Sufi orders today) as a sacred exchange of being. "When a kiss is made on the mouth, one breath unites with another," Leloup explains, quoting from Jewish mystical sources[4]—and remember, in all the Semitic languages (as well as in Greek and Latin) the word for breath is identical with the word for "spirit." To kiss, to breathe together, is to share the same spirit. Leloup comments: "Thus Yeshua and Miriam shared the same breath and allowed themselves to be borne by the same spirit. How could it be otherwise?"[5] But it is more, even, than simply being borne by the same spirit, for it is not so much a matter of being born(e) as of *birthing*. As the Gospel of Philip itself states:

> The realized human is fertilized by a kiss
> and is born of a kiss
> This is why we kiss each other,
> giving birth to each other
> through the love that is in us.[6]

The Gospel of Thomas reflects this same understanding. In the distinctly eucharistic logion 108, Jesus states:

Whoever drinks what flows from my mouth
will come to be as I am
and I also will come to be as they are
so that what is hidden can become manifest.[7]

What flows from his mouth is of course his words and his sacred breath itself, and the kiss is a particularly intimate way of partaking of this communion—already, as Thomas indicates, a foretaste of "the two becoming one."

Philip's teaching on the kiss unfolds within a broader discussion of spiritual procreation, one of the gospel's recurrent themes. While the topic is too complex to delve into here, it is fair to say that within the particular symbol system of this gospel the fact that Jesus and Mary Magdalene are mentioned as kissing one another on the mouth is clearly to be understood as an indication that theirs is an engendering, begetting, fully incarnate, spiritually procreative friendship through which the sacred spirit flows. Their kiss represents a deep and intimate commingling of their beings on both a physical and spiritual plane.

". . . INCLUDING THEIR BODIES"

As spiritual partners who had both experienced (or were well on their way to experiencing) "restoration to the fullness of being," Jesus and Mary Magdalene would have approached that state of inner virginity in which, for each of them, "the image and the Archetype are united in mutuality" (analogue 41). Angel and icon would be firmly bound, so that the earthly image would become the "undefiled" vehicle of its heavenly archetype.[8] Thus, according to this text, their human koinonia would be continuous with their divine koinonia, and if as man and woman they gave sexual expression to this union, their lovemaking would take place within the bridal chamber. The "pure embrace" of their spiritual union would be reflected in the pure embrace of their human bodies. Equally possibly, they may have chosen *not* to give sexual expression to their koinonia. Having directly experienced the

heavenly bridal chamber itself, they may simply have consummated their union in the "Perfected Light" (analogue 14) of their
spiritual bodies without needing to download the experience into
its fleshly image. Either way, their spiritually conjoined singleness
would be a sacrament of wholeness.

Which of these alternatives is the more likely? Are there any clues
we can glean, either from the Gospel of Philip or within the wider
Fifth Way tradition itself, that might shed further light?

As if refusing to let us off the hook so easily, it is precisely at
this point that the tradition splits. Mouravieff is adamant that on
a Fifth Way path the ultimate realization of the bridal chamber
requires that "the two lovers . . . straightway renounce carnal
love"[9] and commit themselves irrevocably to a more spiritualized
expression of their eros, since it is through the power of their re-
directed sexual energy that their two beings will ultimately be
fused into one.

Leloup is not so sure. "It is easier to renounce sexuality than
to render it sublime through transfiguration," he writes in *The
Sacred Embrace of Jesus and Mary: The Sexual Mystery at the Heart
of the Christian Tradition* (2006). While adopting an officially
neutral stance on the nature of the relationship between Jesus
and Mary,[10] it is clear that his sympathies lie in the direction of a
probable sexual expression of their love. His court of final appeal
is consistently the adage of the early church fathers: "That which
is not lived is not redeemed," or in his own paraphrase of this
teaching, "That which is not accepted is not transformed."[11] In
other words, if Christ had not fully accepted and lived his human
sexuality (including his genital sexuality), he could not be the
universal redeemer of humankind. Railing against a pervasive
docetic tendency in Christian literature (the attempt to portray
Christ as less than fully human), Leloup quotes the Council of
Chalcedon (451 C.E.) as affirming: "Christ is at once perfect (*totus*)
in his divinity and perfect (*totus*) in his humanity." Thus, claims
Leloup, "to depict him as sexually defective should amount to
blasphemy."[12] While he perhaps moves too quickly here to equate
"celibate" with "sexually defective," most present-day teachers of

the Fifth Way would agree with his basic sentiment that sexual expression is a normal part of the path and potentially a sacramental one.

But if one is not renouncing sexuality, how does one "render it sublime through transfiguration"? Essentially, this is the work of the Fifth Way itself, through the application of those core practices laid out in chapter 9. Under the patient tutelage of kenosis, shadow work, and mutual commitment to conscious growth, the raw force of sexual desiring is gradually transformed into a sacred channel of conscious love. For partners well advanced on this path, their physical lovemaking becomes—in Leloup's words— "an act of the divine-as-human, or *anthropos*."[13]

It is rare to find descriptions of this type of sexual love. Obviously we are well beyond the familiar universe of sexuality understood as pleasure or performance. Nor can even the sublime allegories of monastic love mysticism help us much here, for the allegories gave way before the sheer physicality of the human encounter. But models do exist within the Fifth Way, and it is important to have some familiarity with them. Until we have a basic picture in our mind of what this "transfigured sexuality" might look like, it is really inconceivable even to raise the question of Mary Magdalene and Jesus as physical lovers.

"EUCHARISTIC SEX"

I was first introduced to this startling term by my friend Michael Bernard Kelly, an Australian priest and filmmaker. Once I got over my initial shock, I realized he had hit the nail on the head. "Eucharistic sex" basically equates to: "This is my body, given for you."

Along a Fifth Way path, sexual expression is characterized by two overarching qualities: total transparency and total self-outpouring.

Curiously, the most insightful description I have ever seen of this intrinsic relationship between the eucharist and human lovemaking comes from Carryll Houselander, an otherwise conventional Roman Catholic writer of the 1940s:

On the night before He died Christ took bread in his hand, blessed it and broke it, and gave it to his disciples saying: "Take it and eat it; this is my Body!" In giving himself to the world, he deliberately chose to emphasize the Body. Why? The body is, for us, the means by which we can give ourselves wholly. We say, "Go, my thoughts are with you," or "My soul is with you." And we know that though something of ourselves is with the traveler, essentially we remain separate from him. We can give someone devoted care, unfailing kindness, and all our worldly possessions, but we have still kept ourselves. But when we give our body willingly to another as a means of complete donation, then our union with the other is complete. We surrender our intimacy, the secret of ourselves, with the giving of our body, and we cannot give it without our will, our thought, our minds, and our souls. Christ surrenders the secret of himself to each one of us when he gives us his Body. In Holy Communion the surrender of the secret of Himself goes on.[14]

The Gospel of Philip would not disagree. In analogue 35 we read: "Yeshua is the Eucharistic feast, because in Aramaic he is called *faristha*: the one opened out and extended over all." The unbreakable link between self-outpouring, inner self-disclosure (the giving up of one's innermost secret), and the "this is my body" of the Eucharistic feast is at the heart of Christian sexuality sacramentally understood.

While this is true in a general way of all conscious love relationships, on a Fifth Way path the experience is predictably more intense—again because of the strength of the erotic bond and because of that uncanny sense of familiarity that so often attends these Fifth Way involvements. (As the poet Rumi says, "Lovers don't finally meet somewhere; they're in each other all along."[15]) One experiences oneself as already fully *seen,* and all the self-consciousness that typically surrounds the intimate self-exposure of lovemaking vanishes before the overpowering yearning to give all and the overpowering instinct that it is safe to do so. Next to the womb, perhaps, there is no space so completely safe and welcoming. Strengths, vulnerabilities, bodily fluids, soul cages—everything flows together in a single river of love. No shame or fear enters these precincts. In fact, while the egoic personalities themselves may still lag behind, lost in their well-worn defenses of self-image, there is a complete honesty to this earthly bridal chamber, which is itself a foretaste of the true Self. Partners who know how to recognize this foretaste and bring it back into their daily conscious work together may discover that their shadow work proceeds even more quickly since their bodies have already paved the way.

And of course, right there is the crux of the whole matter. For on a Fifth Way path, physical lovemaking can never be separated from the rest of the path itself. It is the daily experience of "this is my body given for you," lived out in the myriad opportunities for self-surrender and forgiveness, that gradually fashions a sacrament out of our human sexual passion. In this broader kenotic context sexual love offers a way of expressing, body to body, the deepening yielding of one into the other that is the essence of the path itself. Transfigured by the sincerity of the two beloveds themselves, it then participates materially in building up the "body" of that third term between them, their abler soul.

In fact, in many esoteric circles it is taught that this is actually the primary function of sexual love. "The sexual contact between a man and a woman is no casual affair," writes J. G. Bennett, one of the most accessible contemporary guides to this particular stream of esoteric teachings.[16] Embedded within the "outer" procreation that brings new humans into this world is a more subtle exchange of substances that becomes procreative with regard to the next. The realized "abler soul"—or "wedding garment," as the tradition variously names it—does in fact possess a subtle materiality that is nourished not only by the partners' faithful love but by the actual commingling of their substances during sexual intercourse, carried out primarily through the exchange of seminal fluids. Make of this teaching what you will, but if it contains even a vestigial remnant of truth, it might bring a newfound appreciation for the Roman Catholic Church's otherwise Neanderthal obstinacy in insisting that no artificial methods of birth control be used to inhibit this exchange. The bottom line may be correct; it's simply that the church has long since forgotten the real domain of its application.

At any rate, the Gospel of Philip falls right in line with this particular stream of inner teaching. One of its major themes, which we touched on already in our earlier discussion of the kiss, is the difference between "conception" at a physical level and "begetting" at a spiritual one.[17] The bridal chamber is portrayed not only as a wedding couch but as a womb, whose purpose is to bring forth "sons and daughters" (analogue 57) who "will be born into the light" (analogue 71). While the symbolism refuses to be precisely pinned down, it would appear that these children are the completed subtle bodies of the lovers themselves, whose birth announces the fruitfulness of the parents' spiritual labor and love. It is not the biological offspring of this life, but the "only begotten children of the bridal chamber" who are engendered in that mystical union of essences when human lovemaking becomes truly sacramental.

THE ROAD LESS TRAVELED

While this esoteric understanding of human sexuality may not be everyone's cup of tea, it is a relief, no doubt, to discover that the Fifth Way presents us with two alternative scenarios on the question of sexual expression, which are equally noble and equally difficult. It is not a question of "abstinence is holy and sexual expression is dirty"; both are holy. It is a question of one's fundamental aim and understanding.

There is a voluntary celibacy—a celibacy undertaken for the sake of higher union—which is a complete outpouring of sexual pattern at a level so sublime and intense that every fiber of one's being is flooded with beatitude. That is the "baptism of fire," which, according to Mouravieff and those who belong to his school, actually fuses the two beings into "one flesh."

And there is a sexuality which, clarified of its craving and attachment, is truly eucharistic—"This is my body, given for you"—

a drawing near to the other with all that one has and is, in conscious love, to give the innermost gift of oneself in the most intimate foretaste of divine union that can be known in human flesh.

Both paths exist legitimately within the Fifth Way. Either can be attained—or both can be attained—with pain, confusion, false starts, forgiveness, and grace—by partners who know that the only absolute law on this path is the law of absolute self-giving.

While it is tempting to speculate which version Jesus and Mary Magdalene might have practiced, in the end, this turns out to be the wrong question. Either way they would have been fine. But if you are curious about where my own inner pendulum has come to rest on this question, the tipping point for me lies in that perhaps minor detail I mentioned in the previous chapter. For Philip, the bridal chamber is never just about personal self-realization. One comes forth from the chamber as a cosmic servant, a bodhisattva, with a mission to help all sentient beings. The form and shape of this mission may change from age to age, but its basic set toward liberation remains constant.

Whichever way, then, that would lead to the highest possible outcome for the greatest number of people is the path they would be bound to follow.

12

SUBSTITUTED LOVE

⊙ ⊙ ⊙ ⊙ ⊙

There is no greater love than this, to give one's life for one's friends.

—JOHN 15:13

THERE IS ONE other aspect of the path of conscious love I have not yet mentioned, although really it is the most important of all. At that point where the line of *kenosis*, self-surrendering love, intersects with the line of *exchange*, the free flow of all things, there we find the practice of *substituted love*. And in substituted love the meaning of the entire path becomes exquisitely clear.

The idea of "substituted love" is one of the theological cornerstones of the work of Charles Williams, that remarkable British Christian mystic of a generation or two ago. What he means by the term is actually quite simple: the bearing of burdens. One person voluntarily chooses to carry the burden of the other person, so that the other is relieved of carrying it. If I carry my elderly neighbor's heavy bag of groceries from the market, then she does not have to carry it herself. Fundamentally, it is as simple as that.

The complexity enters, of course, when this simple, concrete notion is transported to the psychological and spiritual realms. If I bear another person's emotional pain in their place—if I voluntarily take on their fear or neurosis—does this mean they are relieved of carrying it? If I voluntarily agree to carry another person's guilt or crime, if I take the punishment in their place, does that mean they are relieved of it?

Most psychologists and spiritual teachers would say "no." One person's actions can ease the burden for another, can bring clarity and support, imbue the other with courage and strength, and sometimes even confer baraka, a direct transmission of spiritual energy that temporarily raises their state. But in the end, we each carry our own burdens, our own karma. "Every mutton hangs by its own leg," my Sufi teacher, the son of a butcher, insisted.

Charles Williams thought "yes." He believed that this total bearing of another's burden was not only completely possible within a Christian self-understanding, but in fact held the key to Jesus's luminous life and death. Again and again he returns to this theme in his novels, as he lays out the lineaments of what he somewhat curiously refers to as his "theology of romantic love."[1] In Williams's 1937 novel *Descent into Hell,* the poet Peter Stanhope willingly takes on the neurotic terror of his neighbor Pauline, so that she finds herself released from it. In the 1945 novel *All Hallows' Eve,* Lester rescues her friend Betty from a vicious attack of black magic when she willingly stands by the bedside of the sleeping Betty and allows the spell to fall on her instead. "Mystical substitution" (as he sometimes also names it) is at the heart of Williams's understanding of mature Christian love and of the "way of exchange" that Jesus has called us to.

But why "romantic love"? Because, I believe, like so many others we have heard from in these chapters, Williams could sniff that at the core of real Christian self-sacrificing love lies a quality of exchange that bears the unmistakable fragrance of eros. In this final chapter of part 2, I hope to be keeping an eye on how these three great threads—kenotic love, the Fifth Way, and the Christian Paschal Mystery—are ultimately woven together.

SUBSTITUTED LOVE IN ACTION

The Fifth Way has no exclusive claims on the practice of substituted love. It belongs to the entire path of conscious love and can in fact be seen as the normal maturation of this path. Mature Christian understanding can be said to have arrived as one gradually discovers there is no "as much as" in the command "Love your neighbor as yourself." It is simply "love your neighbor *as* yourself"—continuous, interchangeable. In substituted love you and your neighbor simply exchange places.

"And who is the neighbor?" That question, asked of Jesus in the gospels, elicits from him the parable of the good Samaritan, with its surprising response. The practice of substituted love does not require a previously established friendship or personal intimacy. The traveler on the road to Jericho in Jesus's parable is a total stranger. In Williams's *The Descent into Hell,* Stanhope takes on the burden of a woman who is little more than a casual acquaintance. In Fyodor Dostoyevsky's sublime exploration of this theme in *The Brothers Karamazov,* Dmitri Karamazov, falsely accused of murder, comes gradually to a conscious willingness to stand in the place of an unknown stranger. And lest I be giving the impression here that this path exists only in the literary mode, one need not search very far within the ranks of Christian saints and martyrs to find courageous unsung heroes such as the civil rights activist Jonathan Myrick Daniels, who in a standoff with police officers in Meridian, Mississippi, simply stepped before the assassin's gun and took the bullet aimed at his black companion.

In the Fifth Way version, however, substituted love does indeed unfold within a milieu of deep personal intimacy, and this brings to the practice its own distinctive taste. When Ken and Treya Wilber, nearing the end of their ordeal with her cancer, can report that they "simply and directly served each other, exchanging self for other," it is not a one-time act of generous self-donation, but the culmination of a long journey of self-giving love which has been ground-truthed in every aspect of their relationship: spiritual, emotional, physical. If you recall my earlier suggestion that agape is in fact fully ripened eros, this Fifth Way substituted love bears both its fragrance and its dynamic energy. These qualities are responsible for its mysterious beauty—and also, as we shall see shortly, for its unexpected cosmic efficacy. When two partners practice substituted love as the ultimate sacrament of their love, its reverberations are felt well beyond the human sphere.

LOVE AND DEATH

"Love and death have a common root," writes Ladislaus Boros, in *The Mystery of Death*. "The best love stories end in death, and this is no accident. Love is, of course, and remains the triumph over death, but that is not because it abolishes death but because it is itself death. Only in death is the total surrender that is love's possible, for only in death can we be exposed completely and without reserve. That is why lovers go so simply and unconcernedly to their death, for they are not entering a strange country; they are going into the inner chamber of love."[2]

The bridal chamber? At death's doorstep? These are strange and unsettling words, and yet they ring with a clear truth. While it is certainly possible that a couple on a Fifth Way path may live to a ripe old age together, the whole aspect of brevity seems to be built in. The stronger the eros, it seems, the stronger the internal drive to move swiftly toward this ultimate configuration, "the total surrender that is love's." Boros assumes that this is so simply because in the end, love and death are merely two variations on the same theme of total freedom through total self-surrender. But there is actually another operative at work here that turns out to be the most important factor:

The abler soul.

I have spoken about the abler soul several times already in this book. Basically it is the "third term" that comes into play when two people love each other: the reality of their love itself. Boros himself gives as good a working definition as can be found in his short essay on "Love" from his book *God Is with Us*:

When two people say "we" because love has made them we in reality, a new sphere of existence is created. The whole world takes on a new dimension, a new depth. This new sphere of existence is not simply "already there"; it comes into existence as a function of the free self-giving of one person to another.[3]

What he fails to recognize, however (though one can hardly blame a classically trained Catholic theologian for being unfamiliar with the Christian inner tradition, where these teachings are found), is that this "sphere of existence" is not simply an energy field, but in fact a body—or to put it more accurately, an energy field *is* a body. There is a subtle substantiality involved here, a kind of "flesh within the flesh" that has been variously described in the sacred wisdom traditions of the West as a "subtle body," "second body," "light body," "resurrection body," and "wedding garment." In the preceding chapter we looked at some of the esoteric teachings around spiritual procreation, particularly the idea that this body is built up not simply by the acts of loving self-surrender between the partners but by the actual commingling of their substances during their physical lovemaking. In other words, it has a real though subtle materiality to it which is equally at home in this realm and the next.

As long as both partners are alive in this physical world, the abler soul remains hidden within as that invisible "third term." But when both—or even more powerfully, when *one*—of the partners dies, it emerges forcefully from the form that has veiled it and takes palpable shape as a body. The hidden dynamism of their love now reveals itself as a substantiality—still an energy field, yes, but an energy field so charged with presence that its physical existence is unmistakable. And in this particular configuration, its sacramental power becomes very strong and universal.

"True love demands sacrifice because true love is a transforming force and is really the birth-pangs of union on a higher plane," writes an anonymous contemporary Christian mystic.[4] This "union on a higher plane" is for the lovers themselves the final fusion of their abler soul, which will henceforth exist as a permanent vibratory field within the cosmos, available not only to themselves but to the world itself, as a "cosmic seeding." Its purpose is to sow love; sow it deeper, sow it vaster. Wherever its vibration sounds, love is its issue.

THE ROAD TO CALVARY

Let us continue, then, exploring our working assumption that Mary Magdalene and Jesus are Fifth Way lovers; that in all the ways we have described so far, theirs is a particular subset of the path of conscious love, practiced with greater intensity and higher stakes because of the presence of eros as the sacramental leaven. Like all disciples on this path, they work within the basic principles of conscious love—consciousness, kenosis, exchange, abundance—but practice them within the turbocharged milieu of eros transformed in the fires of self-surrender. What, then, does that do to the final chapter of their human life together? What does the Passion look like when viewed from that perspective?

Ten years later, I still remember clear as day the sense of star- tlement that went through me in a small Catholic church in Sel- dovia, Alaska, when I suddenly found myself standing before a bas relief carving of the fourth station of the cross—Jesus bidding farewell to his mother—and suddenly realized with every fiber of my being that it was not his mother he was bidding farewell to, but his *beloved*. What told me this I can't tell, or whether the sculptor even intended it. But something in the body language between them, the quality of the yearning one could still feel arc- ing through the restrained gestures, made the picture absolutely clear. Since then, I have never experienced the Paschal Mystery in the same way. Suddenly, in addition to all those other crosscur- rents running through that great Holy Week drama—messianic pretensions, political intrigue, betrayal, abandonment, sacrifice, cosmic redemption—there is also a wrenchingly personal dimen- sion: "Lovers, going unconcernedly to their death . . . the inner sanctum of love."

And so it is *love* standing at the foot of the cross, *love* follow- ing the small entourage that takes his body from the cross and places it in the tomb; *love* holding vigil when everyone else has gone home. Not just a pious disciple or distraught camp-follower, but Jesus's koinonos, his uniquely beloved partner, with their hearts now stretched taut to accommodate the vast distance that has suddenly opened up between them.

And it is *love* that remains there for those entire three days (for where else is there to go?), holding his tether like falcon and falconer as he descends into the underworld. The sheer tenacity of her presence is not the result of ordinary human courage or even the detached equanimity of one who has attained to his level of mastery. It is an act of substituted love, as instant by instant she gives herself that he might be well. For those three days she holds in her own heart all that death has left unresolved in him—the swirling events of that final week, the anguish of betrayal and abandonment, the wrenching final "My God, my God, why have you abandoned me?" She takes his anguish into her own heart, so that he might travel freely to accomplish the cosmic task he has been given to do.

Now as explained earlier, one of the most striking aspects of the abler soul connection is that it is remarkably stable in that inter-realmic position. Already by predisposition a "sky walker," the heart instantly soars across the divide between life and death searching for its beloved, following the well-honed curve of their mutual yearning. It is the moment where mature erotic love comes magnificently into its own. The two beloveds, one in time and one in eternity, become truly "pancosmic," in Boros's beautiful term; they are a natural energetic bridge connecting heaven and earth.

John Donne, the great English metaphysical poet—who, you remember, is the one who coined the term "abler soul"—speaks of this configuration so beautifully in his "A Valediction: Forbidding Mourning":

> Dull sublunary lovers' love
> (whose soul is sense) cannot admit
> Absence, because it doth remove
> Those things which elemented it.

But we, by a love so refined
That ourselves know not what it is,
Inter-assured of the mind,
Care less eyes, lips, and hands to miss.

Our two souls, therefore, which are one,
Though I must go, endure not yet
A breach, but an expansion,
Like gold to airy thinness beat.[5]

What a remarkable way to picture the vastness of the energy field holding Jesus and Mary Magdalene together during those three days: "like gold to airy thinness beat." In that configuration she receives the remarkable vision recounted in the Gospel of Mary Magdalene, as "undisturbed" ("inter-assured of the mind," as Donne has it) she holds the still mirror in which is reflected the mystical epicenter of the Christian faith: the moment when, deep in the heart of the earth, Christ's act of cosmic redemption is consummated.

Donne speaks also of the return journey, using the image of a mariner's compass to describe the subtle give-and-take that links these "two souls which are one" during their time of physical distension:

If they be two, they are two so
As stiff twin compasses are two;
Thy soul, the fixed foot, makes no show
To move, but doth if the other do.

And though it in the center sit,
Yet when the other far doth roam,
It leans, and hearkens after it
And grows erect as that comes home.

So wilt thou be to me, who must
Like the other foot obliquely run:
Thy firmness draws my circle just,
And makes me end where I begun.[6]

And so it is on the morning of resurrection, her firmness drawing his circle just, that with an astonished cry of "Rabboni!" she recognizes that he has, indeed, ended where he begun. She is the last person he sees before he leaves the human realm and the first person he sees upon returning.[7] Together again, in that garden where life and resurrection life have become a single flowing river, they once again gaze into each other's eyes, exchanging their unspoken joy. Then, with a forceful "Go and tell the others," he sends her forth from the bridal chamber to take up her post as a cosmic servant.

ATONEMENT OR SUBSTITUTED LOVE?

Please do not misinterpret what I am up to here. I am not proposing that the whole sacred drama of Christ's Passion and resurrection, the epicenter of the Christian mystery, is *only* a love song, only a tryst between two lovers. It would be absurd and demeaning to make that claim. I am only saying that it is *also*, among other things, a love song, and that romantic love is an essential element in its unfolding.

It becomes an even more essential element as we try to fathom the true sacramental meaning of Jesus's self-offering.

What do I mean by this? Well, for many contemporary Christians, the hardest part of accepting and entering into the Paschal Mystery is the atonement theology it is usually based on. Atonement theology presents Christ as the spotless and unsinning "great high priest," whose death on a cross would take away the sin of the world. This theology is laid out chapter and verse in the New Testament book of Hebrews; it pictures Jesus's sacrifice as an expiation for human sinfulness, an idea deeply rooted in the Old Testament cultic traditions. And what I am describing here is only atonement theology in its most bland and affirmative version; in the darker version that dominates so much of fundamentalist theology, we hear it said that God was "angry" and demanded the sacrifice of his son to appease his anger. This primitive, monstrous interpretation does no justice to the depths of love in either Old or New Testament. But for many Christians, it's what they've grown up with.

The whole notion of atonement presented in this fashion of course makes a complete mockery of kenosis and cancels out Jesus's own understanding of what he was about. Ward Bauman grasps this point precisely when he writes: "His death, rather than being a sacrificial offering to appease an angry God, as the church would later articulate it, was the result of his personal dying to self, as he himself taught it."[8] The only way to approach this sacrifice in a way that does not violate Jesus's own integrity is through substituted love; it is the only backdrop against which his actions make sense. Jesus the lover willingly lays down his life for the beloved, humankind. There is no sacrificial appeasement, only the sheer, transforming force of true love followed all the way to its end, and thus revealing itself as "the birth-pangs of union on a higher plane."

Charles Williams also knew this intuitively. That is why he titled his grand exploration of the work of Messias (as he called Christ) "The Theology of Romantic Love." He understood that the "mystery ingredient" that gave direct access to the heart of Christ was that fragrance of transfigured eros. But steeped in the template of celibate theology, he assumed that eros is transfigured by being allegorized. Thus he approached his topic through a series of great allegorical novels, many of them set within the shadow realms of fantasy and sacred magic. He did not try to ground-truth his intuition in the life of Jesus himself.

But our explorations of the Fifth Way and the bridal mysticism of the Gospel of Philip allow us another option: that human spousal love is the "image" of the bridal chamber, an authentic reflection of what divine love is itself like. True, the image is vulnerable and subject to distortion, but when image and archetype have been brought together, then our human romantic love becomes not only a reflection but actually a sacrament of the divine communion.

However awkward and difficult it may be to imagine Jesus as a lover, it is far more difficult—in fact, flat-out impossible— to imagine him as a great high priest. The image has no basis whatsoever in his life. He never was; he eschewed the cultic, sacrificial dimensions of his Jewish faith and hung out, as the gospels themselves attest, as far away as possible from the temple precincts, with sinners and tax collectors, gentiles and women. The high priestly image is a reconstructed, intellectualized symbol coming from a male and sacerdotal tradition. And of course, it is ubiquitous. In basilica after basilica throughout Christendom, wherever one passes beneath the tympanum of those great western doors or gazes up at the high altar to behold the image of the Christus Pantocrator clad in great priestly or kingly robes (the two become easily intertwined), exercising his solitary dominion over all things, one is actually looking straight into the face of the dysfunction pressed so close to the heart of Christianity.

Conversely, whenever Mary Magdalene enters the picture—which she does rarely enough, sad to say—it is fascinating how the energy changes. Atonement theology softens, and with the same breath as she enters, a new warmth seems to blow. With her come the cadences of gentleness and forgiveness, the sounding of that core vibration of love.

I noted that configuration (although only in passing) all the way back in chapter 7 in regard to the passage from John Climacus, where the very mention of redeemed eros leads him immediately to "the woman who had been a sinner," as though the two are inseparably linked in his mind.[9] The quintessential expression of this linking comes in *The Cloud of Unknowing*, still to my mind the most mature mystical commentary in all of Christian tradition on Mary Magdalene's real gift to the world. In nine inspired chapters (chapters 15 through 23) the author brings her into the very center of the Christian Mystery and speaks the message contemporary Christians so desperately need to hear:

> When our Lord spoke to Mary as a representative of all sinners who are called to the contemplative life and he said, "Thy sins be forgiven thee," it was not only because of her great sorrow, nor because of her remembering of her sins, nor even because of the meekness with which she regarded her sinfulness. Why then? It was surely because she loved much.[10]

For what it's worth, we should also note that this unknown fourteenth-century monk does not shy away from the volatile issue that we like to think we have exposed only in our own era. His chapter 22, both forthright and uncannily timely, is well worth quoting at some length as we near the end of this section of our exploration. Here is his solution to the Jesus/Mary Magdalene koan:

> Sweet was the love between our Lord and Mary. She had much love for Him. He had more for her. Whoever would know thoroughly all that took place between Him and her, not as a gossiper would tell it but as the story of the gospel bears witness—which cannot possibly be false—he would find that she was so completely desirous of loving Him that nothing less than He could comfort her . . .
>
> And if a man should desire to see written in the gospel the wonderful and special love that our Lord bore to her . . . he will find that our Lord would not permit any man or woman—yes, not even her own sister—to speak a word against her without answering for her Himself. Yes, and what more? He blamed Simon Leprous in his own house for what he thought about her. This was great love. This was surpassing love.[11]

THE IMAGE OF REDEEMED LOVE

I have not yet made a systematic investigation of the foregoing point; I have merely noted the pattern. But I am willing to make you a wager, which you can check out more thoroughly on your own if you wish. The wager is this: that for the Christian mystical imagination, Mary Magdalene is archetypally linked to the qualities of forgiveness, tenderness, and longing. When her name is invoked in a theological text, the theology moves more into the ballpark of substituted love; in her absence, atonement theology becomes stronger. The linkage also works in the opposite direction: wherever the notes of forgiveness and love are sounded, her image comes readily to hand; when judgment and control are in ascendancy, her name is nowhere to be found.

My own familiarity with the Christian inner tradition suggests that this synchronicity is not coincidental. For it is in fact the abler soul that resonates through her, as the "body" of the love that she and Jesus share. Energetically it is attuned to these particular frequencies and brings a wisdom of inner softening and tenderness to all who open themselves to it. This is in fact, I believe, the sacramental role she still holds today and will be central to our exploration in part 3, where we will consider her crucial importance as a wisdom-bearer and catalytic agent for our own times.

But if even this sounds too esoteric, the plain and simple version is that we need her there at the foot of the cross, for her human heart is an arrow pointing straight to the Mystery of substituted love at the heart of the Passion.

PART THREE

MARY MAGDALENE
AS UNITIVE WISDOM

13

FIRST APOSTLE

⊙ ⊙ ⊙ ⊙ ⊙

Now
his body writhes
in pain:

once it was
my delight,
now it is
my sorrow.

Blood drains
from arms that
held me close.
now they are fixed
and life has fled
from flesh and bone.

As we take him from
wood to earth,
all is silent,
empty—

passion
surrenders
to another love
　　that is not here
　　or there
but rides the breath
of a greater mystery

confounding
the finite corpus
of my desires.

No longer the object
of my affections,
he has become the
subject of my truth.

The memory of
his love
no longer clings to
the skin of my life,
He has
dissolved
the mirage
of separation
and pours
the pure wine of
his presence into
the waiting
chalice of my heart.

　　　　　　　　　　　—ROBERT T. PYNN

PART 3 OF THIS book begins exactly where we left off in part 2: at the foot of the cross. Alone again, in an alchemy of grief so exquisitely caught by my friend Robert Pynn's poem,[1] Mary Magdalene undergoes her own version of the journey to the underworld. During those three days of anguished vigil, absence is gradually transmuted into a new kind of presence forged from the wreckage of her human hopes and desires. The fullness of that presence will suddenly announce itself in the garden on Easter morning, when she hears her name spoken—"Mary!"—and responds with the astonished, "Rabboni! My beloved Master!" From here on "the pure wine" of that presence will become the meeting ground, and she will by necessity bear witness to its reality.

In the terminology of the Gospel of Philip, that thunderclap speaking of her name announces her "restoration to fullness of being," or initiation into the state of singleness. From there, the bridal chamber follows directly in its dual aspects of freedom-in-unity and cosmic service. With a gentle "do not cling to me . . . but go, tell the others that I have arisen," Jesus sends her forth to bear witness to a unity of hearts that is stronger than the grave. Her apostolic commissioning is identical with the consummation of their Fifth Way union.

Now this is really quite an extraordinary realization, once you begin to think of it in these terms—and it relativizes a good deal of the discomfort and even scandal that people may feel around the idea of a possible romantic involvement between them. However Jesus and Mary Magdalene got to where they got—as intimate companions, teacher and student, fellow initiates, soul mates—the essence of her apostolic vocation is to live and minister out of that realm that comes fully into being only when the physically enfleshed phase of their journey is over, when "the object of my desire has become the subject of my truth." It is as if this is where things had been headed all along, as if those first baby steps at Jesus's human side were all along intended to catapult her into a kingdom in which very few of us have learned to walk. Through love, she has become the apostle of the imaginal.

On this point, at least, both the canonical and wisdom gospels are in agreement. The story of Mary Magdalene really begins at the moment of Jesus's physical death, and its epicenter is always in the profound transition point between dying to human love and awakening to a new reality. The difference between the two streams is that for the canonical gospels (at least in their orthodox interpretation)[2] Jesus returns from the dead in a fully resuscitated human body. In the wisdom stream, by contrast, Mary Magdalene is the one who crosses over, and their meeting takes place in the imaginal realm. It may also be unfolding simultaneously in the physical realm, but in any case this is not the main point. Her recognition of him is not simply a raw human response to a stupendous miracle; it reflects a transformed consciousness that allows her to match him at his own density. Her full emergence into spiritual mastery takes place in liminal space, in the imaginal meeting place between the realms, because, in point of fact, that is the only place where mastery *can* be conferred.

Imaginal, you recall, does not mean *imaginary.* This is the mistake made by early Christian Orthodoxy in its insistence upon the physical resuscitation of a corpse as the "meaning" of the resurrection: a tail-wagging-the-dog kind of literal-mindedness that in fact wound up obscuring the very point that Jesus was trying to make. Our hope for continuance lies in the fact that our home is in the imaginal. From our earlier discussion in part 1, we saw how Leloup describes this as "an ontological reality entirely superior to that of mere possibility."[3] It is a realm that objectively exists (one might think of it as an enveloping matrix of meaning around our own space-time dimension), and it is from this realm that our human sense of identity and direction ultimately derive. Within the wisdom stream Jesus himself clearly belonged to, it is that elusive "origin" or "source" that the Gospel of Thomas insistently points toward, and which the Gospel of Philip names as "the Aion," the fullness beyond time.[4]

However one names it, the point to keep uppermost in mind is that it designates a sphere that is not less real but *more* real than our so-called objective reality and whose generative energy can change the course of events in this world. As the contemporary theologian Walter Wink recently observed (and I am delighted that an acknowledgment of imaginal reality has finally begun to percolate into the theological mainstream):

It is a prejudice of modern thought that events happen only in the outer world. What Christians regard as the most significant event in human history happened, according to the gospels, in the psychic realm, and it altered external history irrevocably. Ascension was an "objective" event, if you will, but it took place in the imaginal realm, at the substratum of human existence where the most fundamental changes in consciousness take place . . . The ascension was a "fact" on the imaginal plane, not just an assertion of faith. It irreversibly altered the nature of the disciples' consciousness.[5]

One need only read the book of Acts to sense the breadth and power of this change of consciousness and to understand the truth of what Wink is saying here. But the book of Acts makes no mention of Mary Magdalene, and that is unfortunate because what is true for the disciples as a whole is true in spades on a path of intimate love. It is as if eros is born for this transformation, and all the currents within it set toward its ultimate transfiguration. If you recall the quote from that anonymous mystic I referred to in part 2—"True love demands sacrifice because true love is a transforming force and is really the birth-pangs of union on a higher plane"—the alchemical transformation of eros in the passage through death produces a particularly intense and powerful sphere of imaginal reality, which becomes essentially a bridge between the realms. This, in the remarkable words of Jean-Yves Leloup, is the real meaning of the resurrection from a Fifth Way standpoint: it is ". . . not merely an event of the past, *but the imaginal, transhistorical symbol of all love that is linked with a body of flesh and blood, and that is victorious over the space-time by which it was believed to have been limited.*"[6] In other words, it is not something that happened only once, to Jesus, but is the living reality and meeting ground of all who have traveled to the endpoint with a beloved and discovered there that "the object of their affection has become the subject of their truth," the very matrix in which they now swim. People can make of this teaching what they want, but it is extensively documented within the Fifth Way path as well as in the lives of innumerable widows and widowers who find themselves similarly (and equally unexpectedly) thrust into the role of apostles of the resurrection upon discovering, in the words of *The Cloud of Unknowing*, that "the soul is as truly there [in Heaven] when its love is as it is in the body which lives by means of it and to which it gives life."[7] The intensity of love transformed becomes a clear window into imaginal reality and a covenant to live by its truth.

This recognition of Mary Magdalene's unique positioning will be crucially important to our work in part 3, as we explore the kind of apostleship she was fundamentally commissioned to—and which, I shall suggest, she continues to exercise today. To be tethered between two realms, mediating the invisible to the visible, is supremely a wisdom function; in fact, as we will see shortly, it is the quintessential description of Holy Wisdom herself. And it is as a wisdom bearer that we most need to meet her today. To reclaim her legitimate historical role as a teacher and spiritual leader of early Christianity is an important first step, but in and of itself it is not enough. For we still need to account for her pervasive influence throughout the Christian centuries and her even more striking reemergence into public awareness today. What is it that she is bringing to us—that she has always brought to us—and how do we listen today? To answer these questions we need to move beyond the historical to the transhistorical (as Leloup terms it), to see how the reverberating impact of her presence between the realms continues to shape the heart of Christianity. In this last section of my book I will be following three strands of this wisdom presence: spiritual transformation, healing, and creativity.

14

THE ALCHEMICAL FEMININE

☉   ☉   ☉   ☉   ☉

IN OUR OWN times it has become widely obvious that Christianity is suffering, perhaps in extremis, from its lack of what is typically called "the feminine dimension." This situation has been the subject of scholarship and intense conversation in the church for at least four decades now, ever since the rise of feminism in the 1960s gave a language for addressing imbalances too long and silently suffered under. This conversation resumed with even greater vigor during the first decade of the twenty-first century in the wake of an epidemic of sexual abuse scandals and subsequent cover-ups within the Roman Catholic Church, exposing the increasingly dark and dangerous side of an impacted patriarchal consciousness.

But on what level is this problem to be addressed? For a first generation of woman warriors in the Christian church—and still very much a live strategy—the solution was essentially political. Feminine equated to "female," and the remedy for the imbalance was to increase the number of women holding visible leadership positions in the church as pastors, priests, scholars, and administrators. Mainline Protestant denominations got right on board with the program, opening their doors to women to such a degree that the balance has tipped in the opposite direction, with seminaries and pastoral posts now largely filled by women. The Roman Catholic and Orthodox churches, by contrast, have refused to open the doors even a notch.

Whatever success (or lack thereof) this corrective may have brought to the gender imbalances of institutional Christianity, one thing it has also clearly demonstrated is that "feminine" and "female" are not synonymous. Forty years of increasingly high-profile female church leadership have not yielded any commensurate increase in those qualities popularly thought of as "feminine": gentleness, receptivity, intuitive modes of thinking, and nonhierarchical ways of doing business. If anything, the gap has widened in the opposite direction as many women placed in positions of authority formerly occupied by males simply internalize those same old patriarchal values. The "political feminine" may be a necessary first step, but it is clearly no panacea.

This growing realization has added weight to a more psychological approach to the question of Christianity's missing feminine dimension: the quest for the "archetypal feminine." Working from primarily Jungian reference points, this approach seeks to identify a set of characteristics that can be seen as intrinsically feminine (the list generally includes: "intuitive," "relational," "sensitive," "receptive," "nurturing," "nonhierarchical") and to redress the imbalances in the Christian institutional psyche primarily at this level. The root problem is seen to be Christianity's unintegrated anima, and the solution thus entails a vigorous reclamation of this feminine dimension, not only in the political structure of the church but in its liturgical, symbolic, and language structures as well (in these latter capacities it is often referred to as reclaiming "the feminine dimension of God").[1]

It is the qualities themselves that are feminine, this approach emphasizes, not the individual woman or man who bears them. But this distinction is hard to maintain in real life, and practically speaking, most feminists I have encountered automatically assume that being a female gives one a leg up on those feminine qualities. When this happens, of course, the archetypal feminine collapses into the political feminine, and we are right back where we started.

Aside from this ongoing operational hazard, however, there are two serious difficulties with this "archetypal feminine" approach, particularly insofar as the stream of unitive wisdom we have been working in throughout this book is concerned. First, the criteria by which these categories are assigned are to a considerable degree arbitrary and culturally conditioned. Who decides that one quality is "feminine" and another "masculine?" Based on what objective evidence? Within our own cultural stream we tend to think of the feminine as intuitive and nonreflective, given to immediate empathetic response rather than intellection. Yet Valentin Tomberg argues the case persuasively in his *Meditations on the Tarot* that it is in fact the other way around: in the primordial creation mythologies at the root of our Western civilization, it is the feminine that holds the reflective and intellective posts; the masculine is all about doing.[2] And the kabbalah, that great masterpiece of Jewish medieval mysticism, blows our cultural stereotypes out of the water in its portrait of the twin pillars of the tree of life. Here it is the *male* pillar that is equated with the expansive, creative, and nurturing while the feminine principle is associated with constriction, winnowing, and judgment. To top it off, wisdom "herself" (*hochmah* in Hebrew) is assigned to the male column. Go figger! Might one dare argue that we are really dealing here with yet another variation on what Ken Wilber calls "the myth of the given"[3]—that is, the tendency to absolutize our own viewing platform? The qualities commonly identified as masculine and feminine are neither preordained nor universal, as so much of modern sophianic and Jungian literature is wont to assume, but are largely situational and sociological.

The second problem is that such an approach tends to ontologize gender, carrying it into the very essence of divinity itself. A Divine Father must be counterbalanced by a Divine Mother—and this is indeed the wild goose chase that so much of contemporary pop spirituality has set out upon, with the Blessed Virgin and Mary Magdalene/Sophia in a dead heat to claim the goddess title.

But if we pay careful attention to the wisdom stream that Mary Magdalene actually emerges out of, and the teachings by which she wields her apostleship, we see just how impossible this is.

Remember logion 114 in the Gospel of Thomas? When Peter complains, "Mary should leave us, for women are not worthy of this life," Jesus replies:

> Then I myself will lead her, making her male if she must become worthy like you males! I will transform her into a living spirit because any woman changed in this way will enter the divine realm.[4]

We have spoken of this passage already in part 1, and in my earlier analysis I called attention to Jesus's well-developed sense of irony, which essentially dismisses the entire level from which Peter is asking his question (and from which most readers will hear it). It is not a matter of females becoming male or of males becoming female; it is a matter of moving beyond the opposites to become a "living spirit." The inexorable unitive thrust of Jesus's teachings leaves no place for dualism, let alone cosmic dualism, and the "singleness" he seems to have in mind involves nothing short of a radical collapse of the binary mind with its insistence on paired opposites as its fundamental interpretive category. As he states categorically in the justly famous logion 22:

> When you are able to make two become one, the inside like the outside, and the outside like the inside, the higher like the lower, so that a man is no longer male and a woman female, but male and female become a single whole . . . then you will enter in.[5]

The Gospel of Philip reiterates this teaching and takes it even a step farther:

> The embrace of opposites occurs in this world: masculine and feminine, strength and weakness. In the Great Age—the *Aion*—something similar to what we call embrace occurs as

well, but though we use the same name for it, forms of union there transcend what can be described here. For in that place . . . Reality is One and Whole.[6]

Whatever this indescribable union might be, it is clear that Jesus lived it fully and transmitted it as his legacy to Mary Magdalene. Thus, to constrain her within an "archetypal feminine" scenario, even if for very good reasons, is essentially going backward. Not only does it separate her from the context in which her apostleship was originally conferred; it obscures the key element of what this apostleship actually comprises.

THE ALCHEMICAL FEMININE

There is a third possibility, however, hidden beneath the play of opposites, which has been there all along but has been almost entirely overlooked. I call it the "*alchemical* feminine," for alchemy is about a change in state, and a change of state is exactly what I am talking about. To make "two become one, the inside like the outside" implies some sort of metamorphosis; a transforming of the "lead" of egoic perception into the "gold" of unitive awareness. It announces the entry into a more spacious mind, into what the texts we have been working with call a state of oneness or "singleness."

I call it the "alchemical *feminine*" because when this idea first presents itself in the wisdom literature of ancient Israel—and in virtually all renditions thereafter—its personification is clearly female.

The classic job description of this alchemical feminine is laid out in several passages of stunning beauty and profundity in the Old Testament book known as the Wisdom of Solomon.[7] The exposition begins with a list of those qualities associated with wisdom. I quote here from the elegant contemporary translation by Rami Shapiro[8]:

What is Wisdom?
She is intelligent, holy, unique, subtle,

flowing, transparent, and pure;
She is distinct, invulnerable, good,
keen, irresistible, and gracious;
She is humane, faithful, sure, calm,
all-powerful, all-seeing, and
available to all who are intelligent, pure,
and altogether simple. (Wisdom of Solomon 7:22–23)

To my mind the most striking feature about this list is that these characteristics are first and foremost qualities belonging to the unitive or spacious mind. These traits belong neither to the archetypal male nor the archetypal feminine, but to the "living spirit": the transformed human being. While wisdom is portrayed here as female (since this text was originally composed in Greek, her name is literally as well as functionally Sophia), the qualities can be represented in either gender; they are androgynous. In the gospel portrayals of Jesus, we certainly see them in male form. In dialogues 2 and 4 of the Gospel of Mary Magdalene, one might argue that we see them equally clearly in female form.

With this list of qualities in place, the writer goes on to describe the primary function of wisdom: a seamless, transparent creativity that is both intimate and effortless:

She is the mobility of all movement;
She is the transparent nothing that pervades all things.
She is the breath of God,
A clear emanation of Divine Glory,
No impurity can stain Her.

She is God's spotless mirror
reflecting eternal light
and the image of divine goodness.
Although she is one,
She does all things.
Without leaving Herself
She renews all things.
Generation after generation She slips into holy souls,

Making them friends of God and prophets . . .
(Wisdom of Solomon 7:24–27)

This remarkable passage envisions wisdom as the primordial reflective principle, simultaneously creating and created in a seamless dance of divine becoming. There is a goddess aspect to her portrayal, to be sure—the hint of a divine co-creator—but the important thing to keep in mind is that Sophia/wisdom is presented not as a divinity to be worshipped but as *a transformational force to be actualized*. She is pure action, and as, through her invisible influence, "holy souls" become "friends of God and prophets," the meaning of her divinity is made manifest. Wisdom is about transformation and transformation is about creativity; the three form an unbroken circle.

The importance of this passage to our consideration of Mary Magdalene cannot be overstated. It furnishes a powerful new scriptural access point from which to approach her, a context in which her unique qualities come most fully into focus. It does indeed allow us to make that link between Mary Magdalene and the Sophia archetype—but not simply on the grounds that she is woman; rather, because she is a *transformed* woman, a living spirit. And just as Sophia/wisdom herself exercises her powers on unitive ground, from that imaginal space between the realms, so, too, does Mary Magdalene as she walks forth from the garden on Easter morning to become the first witness to the resurrection. The aspect of the divine Sophia that Magdalene most fully incarnates is not simply her femininity, but a particular kind of femininity: initiated into "singleness," consecrated to a love that now spans the realms, and exercising her ministry through a spontaneous and seamless creativity that is really, when viewed from the inside, simply an extension of her unbroken intimacy with Jesus back into the world of space and time.

LOGOS AND SOPHIA REVISITED

"In the beginning was the Word, and the Word was with God, and the Word was God," the prologue to the Gospel of John sonorously intones. And most people know that the word being translated as "Word" is in fact the Greek *logos*. In traditional theological reflection the *logos* has been identified with Jesus ("The Word became flesh and dwelled among us," as the prologue concludes) as an intrinsically masculine expression of the divine ordering principle. More recently, at least partially in recognition of this woeful lack of feminine representation in the Christian symbolic imagination, it has become fashionable in some theological circles to think of *logos* and *sophia* as the masculine and feminine dimensions of God, the former represented by the maleness of Jesus and the latter by the femaleness of the Holy Spirit.

This alternative roadmap forms the basis for much of contemporary gnostic and sophianic theology, for the profound mystical explorations of Father Bruno Barnhart, and for the current liberal/progressive groundswell toward feminizing the Holy Trinity. I have my own serious reservations about these efforts, which I have spoken about elsewhere.[9] But since Mary Magdalene is now being widely identified with Sophia (and I do so myself), it is important to be very clear about what this identification entails. What I mean by Mary Magdalene as a sophianic presence is, I suspect, quite different from what others may assume I mean.

Tidy as this *logos/sophia* parallel may be, Rami Shapiro comes close to pulling the rug out from beneath this entire symbolic castle when he suggests, with persuasive evidence behind him, that *logos* is merely the grammatically masculine synonym for exactly the same job description as has already been ascribed to Sophia in the Wisdom of Solomon; or in other words, it is wisdom minus the feminine personification.[10] Functionally, the terms are equivalent, and the gospel text could just as easily have begun, "In the beginning was the *Wisdom*, and the *Wisdom* was with God, and the *Wisdom* was God . . . and the *Wisdom* became flesh and dwelled among us." In so doing, it might better have conveyed the context and mystical lineage out of which this insight actually emerges. There is no "male" ordering principle counterbalancing a "female" ordering principle—only grammatically masculine and feminine synonyms for a single ordering principle.

Rabbi Rami's clarification certainly helps us to cut through at least one layer of this current fashionable silliness. But another, more insidious layer still remains. For even if there were a "male" ordering principle and a "female" ordering principle authentically differentiatable in these terms *logos* and *sophia*, it is clear that the usual way in which they are being juxtaposed nowadays does not work; it is off by one realm. The logos, the "masculine" equivalent of the Holy Spirit, is not the human Jesus but the divine Christos (or "Christosophia," as the medieval mystic Jacob Boehme androgynously labels it). These terms belong to the imaginal plane. And the "feminine" equivalent of the *human* Jesus is not the divine Sophia, but the human Mary Magdalene.

This is exactly the mistake, in my opinion, that Bruno Barnhart makes in his otherwise magnificent exposition of sophianic presence in *The Good Wine*, his commentary on the Gospel of John.[11] Remember my earlier dialogue with him from part 1, when I asked him about the various Marys in the gospel narratives and he replied, "They're all one woman"? This is his basic premise in *The Good Wine*. In a powerfully original way (which I will describe more thoroughly in appendix 2), he traces the women who interact with Jesus throughout this gospel and weaves them into a single presence captured in four crucial episodes: the wedding at Cana (John 2:1–11), the Samaritan woman at the well (John 4:1–41), the anointing at Bethany (John 12:1–8), and the garden of the resurrection (John 20:1–18). He concludes that the imagery is overwhelmingly nuptial in each of these episodes and that they all point to the same woman. But as a true son of the monastic tradition, he cannot bring himself to identify this woman as Mary Magdalene. Instead, he leaps to the next level and identifies Jesus's bride as Holy Sophia herself, apples to oranges.

It is an expedient save, and one which many nowadays are adopting. Within the confines of monastic spirituality it allows one to have one's cake and eat it, too, affirming bridal mysticism while eschewing sexual intimacy (and thus, narrowly remaining within the bounds of orthodoxy). But at the same time it violates an essential incarnational principle at the heart of Christianity: the unbreakable continuity between the divine archetype and its human embodiment. As interest in Mary Magdalene continues to grow, along with an increasing appreciation of her extraordinary spiritual gifts, this "expedient save" can land us in very hot water. We have made this mistake before. We cannot afford to do it again.

Angels and Icons

"Come bind our angels to our icons!" exclaims the Gospel of Philip (analogue 14). Throughout the entire wisdom stream we have been considering in this book, the emphasis has consistently been on the conjunction of "angel and icon" (or "icon and image" or "image and analogue" in the alternative version of the gospels of Thomas and Mary Magdalene). And appropriately so: for only in this alignment can the realms come into a creative reciprocity. Icon without angel is rudderless, adrift in the cosmos, as all three gospels insist. But angel without icon is equally stranded: like the peak of a triangle cut off from its base, it has no way to touch the ground. For the real work of divine self-communication to go on, there must be traffic between the realms.

In exactly this same vein (and for the same reason) Christian tradition has unwaveringly affirmed that there is a continuity between the human Jesus and the cosmic Christ. It's not a question of the earthly Jesus having merely been some kind of celestial booster rocket, eclipsed and redundant now that the cosmic Christ has been launched into orbit. The human Jesus is the access point. From our human standpoint he furnishes the model for what a completed human being—a true "son of humanity" or "living spirit"—looks like. And his very humanness keeps us honest in walking the path. While there has always been a certain tendency in Christian theology toward a more docetic version of Christ— a god man merely "appearing" to be human—orthodoxy has always, correctly, resisted this notion. For as Leloup points out (in that passage we looked at in part 2), "That which is not lived is not redeemed."[12] Only insofar as Jesus begins in the same place as we do can he take us where he is going.

When it comes to feminine models of wholeness, however, this same rule does not seem to apply. In fact, I would argue that our biggest challenge for a full reappropriation of the feminine dimension of Christianity is not that we lack models, but that we lack *believable* models. We are like angels without their icons: floating in outer space.

In this regard, a telling incident happened to me a few summers ago on the Greek island of Patmos. Like so many other pilgrims, I made my way up the hill to the celebrated Orthodox monastery of St. John the Divine, towering both literally and figuratively above the island it guards. Wandering through the treasure trove of icons in its church and museum, I understandably had my eyes peeled for Mary Magdalene, but no such icon could I find. In the end, I asked the monk on host duty whether there might indeed be a Mary Magdalene icon I had somehow missed. He looked at me archly and responded, "This is a *men's* monastery. We have no icons of women."

I don't know which flabbergasted me more: the blatant misogyny of his remark or the fact that the church was indeed heavily laden with images of the Blessed Virgin, which he had somehow failed to register as "woman." His remark was sad but telling. For if the church struggles against its tendency toward a docetic Christ, before a docetic Mary it caves in instantly. Whatever the mystical meaning of "virgin motherhood" may be, in practical terms it leaves us with no handholds; no starting points in recognizable human experience.[13] In the words of that old Maine quip, "You can't get there from here."

With Mary Magdalene it is different. While she has often been sentimentalized or sexualized, there has not until recently been the slightest threat of her being divinized, and her intact humanness is her saving grace. Now that a new generation of Bible scholarship has corrected the glaring inaccuracy of her earlier portrayal as a prostitute and is steadily laying the groundwork by which we will sooner or later be able to fully reclaim her role as Jesus's spiritual partner and lineage bearer, what presents itself to us is an accessible and entirely believable portrait of "one who got there." Applying the teachings that Jesus showed her, she did her inner work and emerged through the eye of the needle into singleness. If Jesus shows us what the completed human being looks like in male form, she models it for us in its female version; together they become the Christosophia, the androgynous archetype of human wholeness. And because her human heart and lover's passion are so central to this transformation, she teaches us that we need not be afraid of these things in our own spiritual striving; the path to the fullness of being lies *through* human intimacy, not away from it. She binds the icon of the human heart to the angel of Holy Sophia.

15

ANOINTING AND ANOINTED

⊙ ⊙ ⊙ ⊙ ⊙

CHRIST IS NOT Jesus's last name—an obvious but so-often-overlooked truism. It means "the anointed one." And however much his followers may have wished for the ceremonial anointing that would have proclaimed him the Davidic Messiah, the fact is that he became "the Anointed One" at the hands of an unidentified woman who appeared out of nowhere at a private dinner bearing a jar of precious perfume and sealed him with the unction of her love.

Traditionally this woman is remembered to have been Mary Magdalene. Together with that other stable feature of her portrait (her presumed prostitution), her identity as "the woman with the alabaster jar" has been a core element in the mythological Mary Magdalene of Western Christendom.

Today, with the best of intentions, Bible scholars have been hard at work to disassemble that conflated portrait, put together largely by Pope Gregory I. With the prostitution issue now laid to rest, attention has focused on the question of disentangling the anointing piece and reallocating it to its proper owner—which, according to the Gospel of John, is Mary of Bethany. If in medieval times the women surrounding Jesus rolled a bit too easily

into one, the thrust of modern scholarship has been to differenti-
ate them and to acknowledge very different personality types and
relationships with Jesus. In recent years Mary of Bethany has
definitely come into her own as a concrete historical figure—to
such an extent that in certain circles the balance has now tipped
in the opposite direction and Mary Magdalene is being conflated
into her![1]

As I mentioned in part 1, I myself initially sat on the fence
about this issue. If one takes the Gospel of John at face value,
"Mary M" and "Mary B" assuredly cannot be the same person,
since John so clearly distinguishes between their personalities
and specifies their roles, and Mary Magdalene does not even enter
the text until John 19:25, well into the crucifixion narrative.

The question is: is it safe to take John at face value?

My own conclusion, after several years of further pondering,
is "no." I have come to believe that much of this modern thrust
toward disentangling Mary M and Mary B is yet another case of
"doing the wrong thing for the right reasons," based on a serious
misconstrual of John's purposes and the rather naive assumption
that he is writing a factual biography according to contemporary
standards of historicity. This assumption simply cannot bear the
weight of literary analysis. While Mary of Bethany may indeed
have existed historically, her function within the Gospel of John
is primarily rhetorical, determined by literary and thematic concerns. The support for this conclusion is somewhat technical; for
those interested, I have laid out the evidence in appendix 2. The
bottom line is that she—together with several other of the women
in this gospel—serves as what literary critics call a "foil" for Mary
Magdalene, highlighting certain aspects of the Magdalenic personality while holding a space for her presence. Mary Magdalene
is indeed discreetly present throughout the entire Gospel of John,
and both her presence and the discretion surrounding it are part
of John's subtle artistry.

Assuming I have done my homework correctly, my purpose
here and now is to deal with the implications of the evidence I
have assembled in appendix 2. I believe that the traditional memory of Mary Magdalene as Jesus's anointer is substantially accu-

rate and that there are valid and in fact urgent reasons for keeping this part of her portrait intact. It holds the key to the Fifth Way understanding of the Passion as an act of substituted love. It also captures the very essence of the alchemical feminine I spoke of in the last chapter and offers a powerful ritual access point to the Christian pathway toward singleness and "restoration to fullness of being." If we are fully to avail ourselves of Mary Magdalene's wisdom presence today, it will be, I believe, primarily through recovering a wisdom relationship with the ritual of anointing—that is, coming to understand it once again as she herself understood it, as an act of conscious love marking the passageway into both physical and spiritual wholeness.

HEAL THE SICK, CAST OUT DEMONS . . .

One of the most immediate and cogent reasons for keeping Mary Magdalene linked to sacramental anointing is that there is considerable circumstantial evidence to suggest that she and Jesus actually practiced it on many occasions—perhaps even as a shared ministry. While the anointing at Bethany, taken in isolation, may strike the modern reader as an exceptional and even exotic event, it has a context both culturally and personally in which it becomes much more understandable. We know that in his own time Jesus made his reputation as a healer and exorcist and that ritual anointing figured prominently in this work. In fact, anointing seems to be the ritual with which he is most consistently identified. While the gospels give no evidence of his ever having baptized anyone, they do record several incidents of his practice of anointing. In the healings of both the deaf man in Mark 7:33 and the blind man in John 9:6, he is depicted as performing this anointing using his own spittle—a distinctly shamanic detail that tends to make modern-day Christians a bit nervous.[2] If scriptural tradition remembers correctly that Mary Magdalene received a healing at his hands, it is likely that anointing figured in this as well.

In fact, claims the historian Bruce Chilton, Jesus may actually have learned the art of ritual anointing from Mary Magdalene! In his remarkable book *Mary Magdalene: A Biography*, Chilton speculates that her struggles with demons may have brought her into the healing and shamanic circles for which her region of Galilee was well known.[3] Anointing may have been a core piece of the healing arts with which she gifted him, accounting for his increasing divergence from the Nazirite path to which he was originally consecrated.

While there is clearly some circular logic at work (and quite a few eggs in the basket of Luke's brief comment in 8:2, "Mary called Magdalene had been freed of seven demons"), I believe that Chilton is genuinely onto something here. Less important than the bottom line of who-taught-whom the actual spiritual skill in question is his implicit understanding that Jesus may have learned from Mary Magdalene as much as he taught her. I have myself raised this possibility in part 2 of this book. We know that during the course of his brief public career Jesus diverged significantly from his original spiritual trajectory. From an interior stance based initially on judgment and renunciation, he threw himself headlong in the direction of inclusivity and wholeness: toward a purity of heart that comes not from withholding, but from letting everything flow. The fact that he may have discovered this truth in the context of a deeply flowing and intimate relationship with the person whom biblical tradition overwhelmingly remembers as his *koinonos*, his companion, makes a good deal of sense—at least, to anyone who has ever been in love.[4]

For we know that that's what real love does: it changes outcomes and creates whole new people. Whether or not Mary Magdalene and Jesus shared an outward ministry of anointing (and there is a good likelihood that they did), inwardly their life together was a continuous, mutual anointing. The specific incident at Bethany when she ritually bathed his head and feet in perfume was merely the outer sign of the inner fragrance of their love. "Set me as a seal upon your heart," that extraordinary line from the Old Testament Song of Songs (and we will be looking at the Song of Songs shortly), is the charter of all Fifth Way anointing. In this mutual sealing of love, the two become a new reality, and old habits and self-definitions are sprung loose. For Magdalene, the anointing of Jesus's love freed her from "seven demons" and launched her on the path toward inner integration. For Jesus, the anointing of Mary Magdalene's love freed him from his self-identification with the Nazirite role and allowed him to trust his heart. She is, I believe, the principal human agent in the course deviation of his ministry, away from exo-piety and toward kenotic love. Symbolically this is the meaning of the anointing at Bethany understood as a sacrament of Fifth Way love, and the reason that it appropriately belongs to her, and her alone.

DYING AND RISING

The second reason for keeping Mary Magdalene closely linked to anointing is that it provides a powerful ritual access point to Christianity's own deepest transformative wisdom. To begin with, it makes it virtually impossible to experience the Paschal Mystery in any other way than as an act of redemptive love. When Mary Magdalene is returned to her traditional role as the anointer of Jesus, a very important symmetry is also restored. We see that Jesus's passage through death is framed on either side by her parallel acts of anointing. At Bethany she sends him forth to the cross wearing the unction of her love. And on Easter morning he awakens to that same fragrance of love as she arrives at the tomb with her spices and perfumes, expecting to anoint his body for death. He has been held in love throughout his entire passage.

As Bruce Chilton succinctly summarizes: "She connects his death and Resurrection."[5] And she accomplishes this precisely by bracketing the entire experience in the parallel rituals of anointing. In so doing, Chilton adds, "Mary Magdalene established the place of anointing as the central ritual in Christianity, recollecting Jesus's death and pointing forward to his resurrection."

But what is it that she is actually pointing forward to? What *is* this Paschal journey from a wisdom standpoint? In the common understanding, Christianity has tended to view the resurrection as Jesus's triumph over physical death. But for Christians in the wisdom tradition (who include among their ranks the very earliest witnesses to the resurrection)[6] its meaning lies in something far deeper than merely the resuscitation of a corpse. Jesus's real purpose in this sacrifice was to wager his own life against his core conviction that love is stronger than death, and that the laying down of self which is the essence of this love leads not to death, but to life. He was not about proving that a body lives forever, but rather that *the spiritual identity forged through kenotic self-surrender survives the grave and can never be taken away.* Thus, the real domain of the Paschal Mystery is not dying but dying-to-self. It serves as the archetype for all of our personal experiences of dying and rising to new life along the pathway of kenotic transformation, reminding us that it is not only possible but *imperative* to fall through fear into love because that is the only way we will ever truly know what it means to be alive.

Within the context of the resurrection, then, anointing becomes the ritual most closely associated with the passage from death of self to fullness of life, from egoic alienation to "union on a higher plane." As such, it conveys the very essence of Christianity's transformative wisdom.

And its gatekeeper is Mary Magdalene.

TOO HOT TO HANDLE?

This image of a single sacramental action, performed by a single woman (not two separate women), and a woman who is remembered as Jesus's apostolic companion and at the same time his beloved *koinonos*, carries great spiritual power—perhaps *too* much power for the comfort zone of the early church! That may well have been one of the earliest *un*-doings of primitive Christianity, argues Bruce Chilton: to obscure the original unbroken connection between Mary Magdalene's presence at Bethany and her presence in the garden of the resurrection, for it gave both her and the ritual of anointing with which she was so closely associated far too much spiritual authority. In a brilliant and fascinating argument he makes his case that the early gospel writers knew full well that the woman who anointed Jesus at Bethany was Mary Magdalene, but deliberately chose to obfuscate this point so as to sabotage her claim to apostolic legitimacy and the basis on which this claim rested. Inadvertently they also sabotaged most of original Christianity's powerful knowledge of the healing arts, as well as the transformational wisdom at its very core.[7]

Today, within the mainstream of Christian sacramental practice we have indeed forgotten much of what our wisdom forebears once knew. Most Christians are still familiar with anointing only in its most stark and literal form, as the sacrament of extreme unction, administered shortly before physical death. While the ceremonial use of anointing for healing is on the increase (and this is a positive trend), even within these healing circles most people are unaware of the tightly interwoven threads that connect this action, through Mary Magdalene, to redemptive love and rebirth into fullness of being. They would be astonished to discover that anointing has not only something but *everything* to do with bridal mysticism and that it is not physical death but "dying before you die" that is its primary field of reference. To reclaim anointing in its original context would make it the sacramental centerpiece of a whole new vision of Christianity based on spiritual transformation and the alchemy of love.

This dovetails beautifully, of course, with the schematic we have seen in the Gospel of Philip, in which the five sacraments—baptism, anointing, eucharist, restoration to fullness of being, and the bridal chamber—work together to bring a person to that state of enlightened singleness that wisdom Christianity recognizes as "the completed human being." It gives us a new and wider understanding of anointing—not even just for healing, but as the sacrament par excellence of that sacred passage through the eye of the needle of kenotic love. To see it and reclaim it that way in contemporary Christianity would create powerful new momentum toward the transformative vision to which Christianity originally aspired, but which stalled out along the way in the heavy hand of dogma and church authority. Meanwhile, sacramentally and historically anchored in Mary Magdalene, it creates

a powerful niche for honoring her presence and accessing her alchemical feminine in a twenty-first-century Christianity recalled
once again to its wisdom roots.

A HEART OF FLESH

The final reason for moving in this direction is an entirely practical one. Because anointing is still the most underdeveloped of the
Christian rituals, it is also the most open-ended. It comes without
that huge weight of theological and sacramental baggage attached
to the more familiar rituals of baptism and eucharist, and without
the heavy backload of male and priestly stereotypes that are immediately triggered in the other two (unlike the eucharist, anointing for healing has never been officially closed to lay officiants,
and some of its most powerful practitioners have traditionally
been women). In other words, it has fewer negative associations
and tends to allow for fresh experiences. The fact that it is intrinsically connected to the feminine is yet another factor working in
its favor. If baptism and eucharist come with heavy doctrinal safe-
guards around them and well-defined roles and response patterns,
anointing is still a marvelously understated ritual, less defended
theologically and with natural associations with Mary Magdalene.
It is an obvious window of opportunity.

I saw for myself how powerfully this could all come together
during the spring 2009 session of the Nine Gates Mystery School
in Southern California. I have been associated with this Mystery
school for a number of years now, and it is certainly one of the
most rewarding teaching assignments I have ever taken on. Interspiritual and completely "hands on," it tends to attract some of
the keenest spiritual seekers I have ever met. Many of these come
from the ranks of what I call "heartbroken Christians": people
whose early religious training was in Christianity, but who for
various reasons became turned off by the church and fled to other
paths, or no path at all.

My assignment as the Christian faculty member is to hold
down what Nine Gates calls the "high heart" passage: the move-

ment from the heart understood as the seat of one's personal emotions to the heart as an organ of cosmic perception. The fact that the spring Mystery school nearly always coincides with the Christian Holy Week adds to the intensity. For years I had tried to build the concluding ritual for this high heart passage around the eucharist, but it always backfired. Perhaps it was too identified in people's minds with old, Pavlovian responses. Or perhaps it was not the right ritual for the occasion.[8] Either way, it threw people into heaviness and anger.

For the 2009 season I decided to try a different approach. From one of my Mary Magdalene research trips to France I had brought home a liturgy called "The Unction at Bethany," created by the Commuauté de l'Agneau, which I had seen performed in Paris on the Monday of Holy Week. In an ornate and beautiful ceremony, it liturgically reenacted Mary Magdalene's anointing of Jesus, with members of this mixed monastic community playing the respective parts. For our Nine Gates version, we simplified the text but preserved the liturgy's basic contours and allowed the momentum to build steadily toward the moment when our designated Mary Magdalene knelt before our designated Jesus and anointed his feet. Departing from the text, we then had Jesus kneel before Mary Magdalene and anoint her feet. Then, working in pairs, the entire group did likewise.

To call the impact wrenching would be an understatement. People were blown wide open, then put back together in a space that most had never encountered before, at least in a Christian context. From my earlier work with this same ceremony in a more traditional Christian environment (the Aspen Chapel, where I am a clergy associate), I knew already that it could be powerfully effective. The liturgical enactment of the woman anointing the feet of Jesus offers the perfect mirror image to the traditional foot-washing service of Maundy Thursday and came as a welcome surprise to my congregation, beautifully counterbalancing the predominantly male energy of the Holy Week liturgy. But here, within the experiential and totally transformation-focused context of the Mystery school, the impact was particularly compelling. The mutual anointing reverberated powerfully with all we have been speaking of in this book: love, healing, dying before you die, the reconciliation of the feminine, rebirth into wholeness, the tenderness that a kenotically transformed eros has to bring to Christianity's hardened institutional heart. The moment I had been waiting for over the course of more than thirty years in Christian ministry had finally come to pass as I watched "heartbroken Christians" taste the miracle that Christianity is, after all, a religion of love.

In the liturgy for the great vigil of Easter, one of the readings comes from the Old Testament book of Ezekiel: "I will remove from your body the heart of stone and give you a heart of flesh" (Ezekiel 36:26). It seems to me that this promise captures the essence of Mary Magdalene's healing vocation to contemporary Christianity, and anointing offers the means by which she can most powerfully accomplish it. As we explore the various interwoven aspects of this sacrament—for healing of illness, marking the passage through death and ego-death, celebrating the mystical union of the bridal chamber in which "the two become one"—we will once again discover the ritual expressions that best embody our renewed understanding of this sacrament of wholeness. And our Christianity will be the stronger for it.

16

WHY FRANCE?

☉ ☉ ☉ ☉ ☉

ONE OF THE KEY pieces in *The Da Vinci Code* mythology (in fact, the linchpin of the whole argument) is the assertion that after the crucifixion Mary Magdalene fled to France bearing a child who was Jesus's lineal descendent. The Holy Grail that she did indeed bear with her was not the *sainte grail*, or chalice from which Jesus drank at the Last Supper,[1] but the *sang réal*, or royal bloodline that flowed through their biological progeny. The child allegedly intermarried into the Frankish tribes, and the fruit of this union eventually emerged as the Merovingian dynasty of French kings.

This hypothesis—which was lifted more or less lock, stock, and barrel from the earlier "bloodline conspiracy theory" of the British journalists Michael Baigent, Richard Leigh, and Henry Lincoln—has intrigued millions and infuriated nearly as many. Part of its appeal is that it offers a fabulous cloak-and-dagger explanation for many of the otherwise inexplicable enigmas of medieval European history. Its weak link is that it depends on genealogies that are highly speculative and perhaps fraudulent—although defenders deny this accusation roundly. And of course, to those who insist on the celibacy of Jesus (in other words, most of traditional Christianity), it is a red flag waved in the face of a bull.

Is it a standoff, then, with traditional Christians sticking to their guns on the traditional story and neo-gnostics creating an entire new mythology out of what many would claim to be thin air? Did Mary Magdalene go to France or not? Did she and Jesus have children or not? Logically, it seems as if you can't have it both ways. Either *The Da Vinci Code* craze is completely barking up the wrong tree, or else the church is so deep into denial that it has (as the present grassroots rebellion implies) essentially relinquished the right to be the custodian of its own history.

My suggestion, however, is that neither of these extremes is true and that there is a way of bringing these alternative scenarios together—or at least substantially together. Having by now spent nearly forty years of my life investigating Mary Magdalene's alleged apostolic activities in France, I am inclined to believe that she did touch down on French soil as Jesus's authentic lineage bearer, and she did indeed succeed in planting a seed there that carries the unmistakable signature of their intertwined lives. But this does not necessarily lead to the conclusion that she bore Jesus's literal progeny, or that their physical bloodline is intermingled with the Merovingian dynasty. As my spiritual teacher Rafe used to say, "There's more than one way to have a child." The problem with *The Da Vinci Code* hypothesis is not that it's wrong but that it's looking for results in the wrong place. From the fruit of their love, Mary Magdalene and Jesus assuredly bore progeny, and they continue to do so. But this procreation is according to the ways of wisdom, not according to the ways of bloodline conspiracy. Theirs is an imaginal lineage, and it is on the imaginal plane that we need to be looking to find it. In this regard, the persistent rumors of Mary Magdalene's continuing involvement with France offer a textbook case for how wisdom transmission actually works.

CULTURAL MEMORY

While it cannot be categorically proven that Mary Magdalene actually lived in France, the *conviction* that she did so is an indelible part of the French cultural memory. According to the ancient folk traditions of the Camargue, the swampy coastal land south of Arles, in about the year 42 C.E. Mary Magdalene came ashore in what is now the tiny village of Les-Saintes-Maries-de-la-Mer, accompanied by Mary Jacoby, Mary Salome, and a young dark-skinned girl named Sarah traditionally presumed to be her servant.[2] As this local folk memory blended seamlessly into the more dominant version of the legend circulating throughout Provence,[3] Mary's companions became Martha and Lazarus and the scene shifted from the Camargue to the countryside around Marseille, but the testimony to her presence in southern France remained unequivocal. It is said that after performing many miracles, she retired to a cave near Baume, where she finished out her days in hermit's seclusion. Her relics are claimed by the basilicas built in her honor in both Baume and Vézelay, and each of these sites is a powerful Magdalenic shrine and a popular pilgrimage destination.

Now there is something to be said for cultural memory. The energy behind it comes from *somewhere*, and in the imaginal realm it is a well-attested phenomenon that characters can become linked to a geographical place with a "truth" that transcends literal facticity—and can work either forward or backward in time from its causal epicenter. Just as the Virgin Mary has come to be associated with Ephesus to such a degree that one can palpably feel her presence there—whether she ever actually lived there or not—so too, the pervasive linking of Mary Magdalene and France has a psychic truthfulness to it that is well worth taking seriously. The fact that both the memory and the energy of her presence seems so to haunt this country of love is by no means coincidental.

BEGOTTEN OR CREATED?

From the description of Sophia/Wisdom we looked at in the preceding chapter, we can see that an invisible, seamless creativity is the very essence of her presence: "She is the transparent nothing that pervades all things . . . Although she is one, she does all things without leaving herself." From the mystical standpoint, she seems to specialize in what would today be called "nonlocalized action": the ability to bring about results in the physical world without recourse to the physical mechanisms that normally convey these results.

This insight invites us to return to that cryptic set of teachings in the Gospel of Philip concerning the distinction between "begotten" and "created." This topic surfaces in many of the analogues, since spiritual procreation is one of Philip's major themes. In essence, he draws a distinction between being "created," which is simply a mechanical reproductive act, and "begotten," which involves the active engendering of the Holy Spirit. In analogue 57 he writes:

> Horses naturally give birth to horses, humans to humans, and God gives birth to God. That is the way that sons and daughters are born from Lover and the Beloved in the Bridal Chamber. Jews did not come into being from Greeks, and Christians came into being not from Jews, but from other anointed ones.[4]

His most extended discussion of spiritual procreation is in analogue 66, a passage well worth quoting in its entirety:

> The Son of Humanity exists, as do the children of the Son. The Son of Humanity is the Master who has brought the children into created being. The Son of Humanity, therefore, has received the power to both create and beget. That which he creates, is, of course, a finite object—a creature, but what he begets, however, is a "child"—or offspring. Created objects are not able to conceive, but what has been conceived and born can create. Some will say, "Well, human creatures of course do conceive and give birth." True, but their progeny are in fact creatures, and what they give birth to are not "theirs," but sons and daughters of God.
>
> The one who creates objects works outwardly in the external world.
>
> The one who labors in secret, however, works within the icon, hidden inwardly from others. The one who creates

makes objects visible to the world. The one who conceives gives birth to children in the Realm of the Unseen.[5]

In this complex distinction (traces of which show up in the Nicene Creed—"begotten, not made, one in being with the Father"), Philip insists that begetting must come "from above"—exactly the same teaching that we find in John 3, in Jesus's cryptic exchange with Nicodemus. It requires a free and conscious regeneration in the Spirit. "Begotten" is an alchemy in which spirit actively participates, and its fruit is the anthropos, or completed human being.

From Philip's point of view, then, lineal descendents of Jesus, even if they existed, would not be "anointed ones," unless this claim were to be validated by their own spiritual transformation. The kingdom over which the Anointed One reigns is beyond the space/time continuum and cannot be inherited lineally (that technicality consistently overlooked in the literal-mindedness of *The Da Vinci Code*); it can be entered only by becoming a new kind of human being—what Philip actually describes as "a new *race* of human beings."[6] "Only true sons and daughters can gain immortality," he writes in analogue 56, "and no one can gain it without becoming a true son and daughter." Progeny cannot be fashioned out of flesh and blood; they are the fruit of an alchemy of consciousness.

Philip makes it clear that *this* is the kind of spiritual procreation that Mary Magdalene and Jesus were chiefly about. As we discussed in chapter 10, his symbol for this type of richly engendering spiritual love is the kiss, which (as is universally the case throughout the Near Eastern culture) is seen as a sign not of sexual attraction but of spiritual begetting. When he indicates in analogue 37 that "the Master loved her more than the other students and many times would kiss her on the mouth," he is not describing an illicit romance but rather a sacred exchange of their deeply commingled beings. The spiritual kiss is the symbol par excellence of Fifth Way love.

From a Fifth Way standpoint, this kind of intense and transforming love, "which is really the birth-pangs of union at a higher plane," will indeed bear fruit. But the fruit may not be human children so much as an energetic sphere of pure creativity, in which reality is touched at the core and love itself is the progeny.

As analogue 66 points out, "The one who creates objects [i.e., literal offspring] works outwardly in the external world. The one who labors in secret, however, works within the icon, hidden inwardly from others." In other words, the work goes on at the imaginal (or causal) level, and its potency is made manifest not by producing new people but by engendering *transformed* people—giving birth to children "in the Realm of the Unseen," in the words of the text.

Interchangeability

The poet Rilke takes Philip's insights a step further in his powerful fourth letter in *Letters to a Young Poet*, where he grasps the utter interchangeability of physical and imaginal love: "In one creative thought a thousand forgotten nights of love come to life again and fill it with majesty and exaltation. And those who come together in the nights and are entwined in rocking delight perform a solemn task and gather sweetness, depth, and strength for the songs of some future poet."[7] Rilke is not talking about sublimation here in the usual platonic way; he is not saying that sexual abstinence will express itself in a heightened artistic creativity. Rather—and astonishingly—he is saying that the passionate act of lovemaking engenders its progeny in many realms. "For mental creation too arises from the physical, is of one nature with it, and only like a softer, more enraptured, and more eternal repetition of bodily delight."[8]

I mention this point to emphasize yet again that when I speak of Jesus and Mary Magdalene as Fifth Way beloveds, I am not necessarily implying that their spiritual procreativity depended on their sexual abstinence. There are schools of Fifth Way love that teach this, certainly (we will be encountering one of them shortly). But there are opposite and equal schools that suggest, quite to the contrary, that the sphere of intimacy accessed in the totally transparent lovemaking of Fifth Way partners becomes itself a dynamo of creativity and establishes the vibrational field in which they will continue to stay connected when one of them is no longer in the physical flesh.

While the couple is in the asymmetrical arrangement—one in human flesh and the other beyond—the sphere of engendering becomes very powerful between them, as transforming wisdom pours through the crack between the realms. As we have seen already, this is the configuration in which virtually all of Mary Magdalene's apostolic work is done. Whether its human underpinnings included or denied sexual expression we cannot say with certainty, but in its transfigured form a "softer, more enraptured, and more eternal" cosmic intimacy is both the medium and the message, and the fecundity fans out in all directions.

If this "asymmetrical apostleship" is exercised with sufficient force and spiritual prowess, then, when the other party has also left the flesh, the imaginal sphere that has been brought into being between them will continue to reverberate in alignment with their realized oneness and will become its own localized agent of "the engendering spirit." It will continue to beget its "children in the Realm of the Unseen," since its presence has become a crystallized energy field of creative love.

These teachings from the Christian esoteric tradition help shed light on the places I believe we need to be looking in order to spot the presence of Mary Magdalene in France and to sense her hand at work in several Fifth Way progeny that I would like to comment on briefly. Whether or not she and Jesus had human heirs is so much a nonissue that it is hardly worth spending time on. (If they did, judging from the way their traces disappeared from the physical planet, these children were merely "created," not begotten.) In any case, the real legacy of Mary Magdalene and Jesus lies in the way that over and over in this French soil, the path of Fifth Way love keeps spontaneously reinventing itself. Let me call attention to just a few fascinating examples.

THE *VISITATIO SEPULCHRI*

In the second half of the tenth century, in a Benedictine abbey most likely in France,[9] an event took place that would quietly change the course of cultural history. As the monks gathered at first light on Easter morning to chant the traditional liturgical office of vigils, the dramatic tension inherent in the gospel account of the three Marys at the tomb erupted into staged dialogue.

ANGELS: Whom do you seek in the sepulcher, O followers of Christ?

MARYS: Jesus of Nazareth who was crucified, O heavenly ones.

ANGELS: He is not here; he is risen as he foretold; go, announce that he is risen from the sepulcher.

Called the *Quem Quaeritis* trope (the Latin words for "Whom do you seek?"), it is the earliest specimen of drama in Europe, heralding a rebirth of the dramatic art form in the West after more than eight centuries of sleep.

Within a few centuries that first proto-drama had emerged into the full *Visitatio Sepulchri* (*The Visit to the Sepulcher*), a beautiful play—or *opera*, actually, since it is sung entirely in Gregorian chant—depicting the encounter between Mary Magdalene and Jesus at the tomb. It is filled with human emotion and a sense of mounting tension that is both dramatically and theologically sophisticated. While numerous versions of this play survive (attesting to its "blockbuster" status on the medieval monastery circuit), the twelfth-century version from the Benedictine abbey of St. Benoit-Sur-Loire, preserved in the celebrated Fleury Playbook, is by far the most subtle and beautiful. I have myself directed this play, and it is in fact through my work with it as a performing medievalist during the early 1970s that I was first exposed to the powerful energy field connecting the hearts of Jesus and Mary Magdalene. I find it fascinating that the intense drama of Mary Magdalene's own "bridal chamber" experience on Easter morning should be the viaduct by which the theater arts return to the West; it is quite extraordinary to find the Magdalenic energy at the epicenter of this cultural reawakening. Drama is reborn in the West in the eye of the needle of Fifth Way love.

THE CATHARS AND COURTLY LOVE

It is difficult to make a valid assessment of the Cathars, since most of the primary evidence has been destroyed and the vast majority of commentaries merely recycle the standard clichés applied to Gnosticism. I have read in any number of books about the Cathari (or Albigensians, as they are alternatively known) that they were radically dualistic, hated the body, renounced sexuality, aspired to an elite form of spiritual perfection, and considered all matter to be intrinsically evil. On the basis of this caricature (and of course, with the usual intermingling of political agendas), they were judged to be a heretical sect and brutally exterminated by the Catholic Church in a series of campaigns beginning in 1209.

What we do know is that throughout southern France, then known as the Kingdom of Languedoc—not far from the multicultural influence of Spain and very much within the legendary domain of Mary Magdalene—there emerged during the eleventh and twelfth centuries two remarkable and, I suspect, interrelated movements: the religious sect known as the Cathars and the phenomenon of courtly love. This latter made its presence known in an extraordinary outflowing of love poetry (the troubadour songs) and in the emergence of the principles of chivalry, which subjected aspiring warriors to a rigorous code of honor and transformed knighthood into a spiritual path. Under these two mitigating influences, the culture of Languedoc reached a pinnacle of civilization heretofore unknown in medieval Europe. When the church's invading armies entered, they succeeded in reducing to rubble a culture that had arguably been the most advanced and sophisticated in Christendom.

"By their fruits you shall know them" is still a good adage, and the portrait of the Cathars as radical ascetics despising everything the world has to offer simply does not fit with the gentle and sophisticated culture that came into being around them.

If we take a closer look at the troubadour songs and courtly romances (which *did* survive the Albigensian crusades), my suspicion is that we will find we actually have a good deal more information on hand about the Cathars than has been previously reckoned; we have simply missed the connecting link. What scholars have consistently failed to spot is that Catharism and courtly love are interlocking pieces; fit them together, and you are staring at a school of Fifth Way love! Far from renouncing the world and human sexuality, these early Cathari adepts were exploring the terrain of spiritual procreativity in much the way we have just seen it laid out in the Gospel of Philip. How does love become "a transforming force and the birth-pangs of union on a higher plane"? The answers are there to be discovered in the culture and spirituality of Languedoc.

Boris Mouravieff, whom we met earlier, is one of the few who early on grasped this connection, and his extensive discussions of the Fifth Way path in his three-volume *Gnosis* rely heavily on his knowledge of the traditions of courtly love. In essence, he considers the whole phenomenon of courtly love to be a loosely disguised esoteric pathway based on the transformation of eros. In keeping with the classic understanding of this tradition, he maintained that sexual passion must be sublimated in order to ignite the heavenly fire that will fuse two human beloveds into one immortal soul, and he saw courtly love as an early and brave attempt to provide guidance for those spiritual warriors about to enter the all-consuming fires of love.

As I have mentioned before, Fifth Way tradition diverges on this point. And there is strong evidence that the Cathars did as well, with some opting to practice physical procreation for the continuity of biological life, while others committed to sexual abstinence in order to dedicate themselves entirely to spiritual begetting. But they made these choices in solidarity with each other, as a single community of believers, and the "hidden ground of love" at the base of their experiments validated itself in the astonishing cultural fecundity and spiritual civility for which the region is still justly famous. If such is indeed the case, then we have sorely misunderstood the real treasure that lies in wait for us in the Languedoc of the Cathars: an integral and nearly unique expression of Christianity as a Fifth Way path, together with a practical path for the transformation of eros equally suitable for celibates and for couples working together in the world.[10]

Again, the signature of Mary Magdalene is hard to miss.

MONASTIC LOVE MYSTICISM

Directly across from the statue of Mary Magdalene in the basilica at Vézelay stands the statue of St. Bernard of Clairvaux. And this placement is a fitting one, for while the two of them are indeed in many ways mirror opposites, their paths are also deeply intertwined. The specific reason for Bernard's commemoration at Vézelay is that it was from there that he preached the sermon which launched the Second Crusade.[11] But his true gift to the world was his sublime articulation of what has come to be known as "monastic love mysticism": the monastic version of the Fifth Way path. The Cistercian Order, which he founded in 1098, to this day describes itself as a "school of love," and Bernard's extraordinary sermons and commentaries continue to furnish the core of the curriculum.

His magnum opus is undoubtedly his magnificent commentary on the Old Testament Song of Songs, a commentary comprising eighty-six sermons and conferences delivered over the course of his long monastic career. In his memorable words from sermon 79, we can taste both his wisdom methodology and the passion of his heart:

> If anyone desires to grasp these writings, let him love! For anyone who does not love, it is vain to listen to this song of Love—or to read it, for a cold heart cannot catch fire from its eloquence. The one who does not know Greek cannot understand Greek, nor can one ignorant of Latin understand one speaking Latin. So, too, the language of love will be a meaningless jangle, like sounding brass or tinkling cymbal, to anyone who does not love.[12]

Now this is really quite significant, because the Song of Songs is supremely Mary Magdalene's song. Not officially, of course. This short, unabashedly sensuous Old Testament love song found its way into the Hebrew Bible and later into the Christian scriptures by virtue of being heavily allegorized. For the early Jewish commentators it stood for God's love for Israel. For Christians, it was variously interpreted as symbolizing Christ's love for the church or God's love for the human soul. But "unofficially" its imagery has been applied to Mary Magdalene beginning as early as the Gospel of John and continuing in a series of commentators including Origen, Gregory, Bernard, and, right down into our own times, Bruno Barnhart.[13] And with good reason. For the Song is in essence a prototypic Fifth Way romance, singing the passion, desolation, and, ultimately, triumphant victory of a love that, frustrated at one level, seeks its consummation at another.

It would take us far beyond the scope of this chapter to substantiate all the details of this assertion. (For those interested, I have included some of the most pertinent evidence as appendix 1.) One of the most intriguing current theories about the Song is that it is based on the story of Abishag the Shulammite, as recorded in 1 Kings 2:13–25. When Adonijah, King Solomon's older half-brother, asks for Abishag's hand in marriage, Solomon perceives a threat to his kingship and has Adonijah executed. This hypothesis clears up many of the traditional mysteries enshrouding the Song: its traditional association with King Solomon; the persistent confusion between the apparently *two* male suitors, one of whom appears to be Solomon and the other her true beloved; and above all, the woman lover's designation in Song 7:1 as "The Shunammite," a plausible enough variant of "Shulammite."[14] Moreover, it accounts for the otherwise unexplainable mounting of emotional intensity in a poem that on the surface appears to be largely static: the lovers' inevitable tragic separation creates the urgency behind their fleeting ecstatic trysts.

Suffice it to say that the Song's stunning lyrics, particularly its description of the woman lover's vigil (Song 3:1–4) and its triumphant final proclamation in Song 8:6–7—"Love is as strong as death"—mirror with such accuracy Mary Magdalene's own emotional journey that they essentially place in her mouth the words that tradition has never allowed her speak directly (you'll find these texts quoted in full in appendix 1). Meanwhile, the actions and motifs with which she has traditionally been associated—anointing, perfumes, the "garden enclosed" in which she and Jesus are reunited on Easter morning—all come straight out of the Song of Songs.

Drawn to the Song like a bee to honey, Bernard maintains the official decorum: Mary Magdalene appears in the pages of his commentary only in the role of penitent sinner, while love itself is consummated allegorically. But he does succeed brilliantly in making his case that eros is the touchstone of all spiritual transformation; monastic celibacy is no excuse for the failure to fully engage love's transfiguring fires. Bernard's language is sensuous, daring, and risqué—not for those whose vision of spiritual purity lies in distancing themselves from their sexuality—for in his own words, "a cold heart cannot catch fire." As one of the most powerful spiritual and political figures of his time, he offered an illumined mystical exegesis that called Christianity squarely back to a path of love and opened the way toward engaging love's alchemical fires within the context of the celibate monasticism, which by that time had become the only authorized expression of Christianity's transformative wisdom.

The Underground River

It is both striking and mysterious that these three great expressions of French Fifth Way mysticism all came to their peak in the twelfth century. After that—perhaps because of the brutal suppression of the Cathars, or the rise of scholasticism in the thirteenth century as the dominant intellectual modality—the trail goes cold for several centuries. While there are signs of life beneath the surface, there are no more what I would call recognizable Magdalenic phenomena until our own time. Perhaps, as Margaret Starbird and others have suggested, the memory of her presence was kept alive in art, in secret societies, and in fairy tales.

The river was still flowing, but underground; the surface was too inhospitable.[15]

In our own times, however, the signs of a new upwelling are unmistakable, and once again France is at the heart of the action. As harbingers of this new emergence, one might point to the powerful revisioning, in the work of the contemporary French Jesuit Pierre Teilhard de Chardin, of the sacred heart of Jesus as the driving force of cosmic evolution. When we collectively learn to harness the energies of this love, he avers, "on that day, for the second time in the history of the world, human beings will have discovered fire."[16] Or one can hear the voice of the troubadour rising again in prolific outflowing of spiritual love songs from the monastic community of Taizé, touching the heart of the world as they renew the call to Christian gentleness and love. Or yet again, one can point to the astonishing growth of the new French monastic order, Les Fraternités monastiques de Jérusalem, where men and women monks work side by side to create the gorgeous liturgy and mystical prayer at the heart of the community's charism. This was the group I encountered at Vézelay in 2005, whose sublime rendition of Mary Magdalene's vigil at the tomb changed my understanding of Christianity.[17]

But the most obvious sign is right under our noses. We have been staring at it throughout this entire book.

FULL CIRCLE

In earlier centuries, pilgrims in search of Mary Magdalene would make their way to Vézelay or Baume, to kneel in prayer before her relics. Since the publication of *The Da Vinci Code* in 2003, a third shrine has emerged for her pilgrimage (also laying cryptic claim to her relics): the glass obelisk marking the entrance to the newly refurbished Louvre Galleries in Paris. And the pilgrims indeed pour in, standing in long lines to visit the scenes made famous in the movie version of *The Da Vinci Code*. If in former days these worshippers lit candles, today they don interpretive headsets. But no matter: the sense of excitement, and sometimes even a hushed reverence, is still just as palpable as they stand before the artifacts of her revisioned story.

That story, of course, has some major flaws in it. Yet there is an authenticity to *The Da Vinci Code* phenomenon itself that confirms the underlying principle I have been trying to explore in this chapter. Whatever one may think of the literal truth of its argument, the *psychic* truth of its intuition about where the blockage has lain all along in Christianity is right on target, and the grassroots revolution it has touched off is no less than extraordinary. The voice of Mary Magdalene has again spoken loud and clear, calling Christianity back into accountability for the love story at the heart of its theology and to a responsible revisioning of human sexuality and feminine wisdom.

If I am right, then, the true progeny of Mary Magdalene and Jesus is the path of Fifth Way love itself. Their intertwined hearts bear fruit in a distinctive flavor of love that is visionary, transformative, inclusive, and ubiquitously creative. It is France that most consistently claims the living memory of Mary Magdalene. And it is France where this work of recalling Christianity to the path of love has most consistently gone on. To me, these facts cannot possibly be coincidental, and they are more than enough to validate, at the imaginal level, her claim to being Jesus's rightful lineage bearer. The *sang réal* is true, but it is the same *sang* as flows in the communion cup, uniting the two worlds in one love.

17

THE WISDOM
MARY MAGDALENE

⊙　⊙　⊙　⊙　⊙

EIGHT CENTURIES after its brutal suppression in Languedoc, the Magdalenic energy has again awakened in the cradle of France, inviting the church to rediscover the love song at its heart. This time, are we ready to listen?

In this final chapter I would like to lay out five concrete tasks, all growing out of issues we have explored in this book, that would go a long way toward maintaining the momentum of the Magdalenic awakening that *The Da Vinci Code* craze has set in motion. Never before in the history of Christianity have the tools and insights been so readily at hand to address the areas of dysfunction and to begin to rebuild the church from the ground up on its authentic foundations in imaginal wisdom and mystical love. New scriptural texts, new scholarly approaches, a growing worldwide interspiritual community that understands what *unitive* means: all of these create a marvelously hospitable climate for new beginning; the only question is whether the church will have the courage to rise to the occasion and reinvent itself. The suggestions I am proposing below may at first seem drastic; they would certainly change the face of Christianity as we are used to it. But my sense is that in the end, like pruning an apple tree, they would create a far more robust and sweet-tasting fruit. I will list them in ascending order of difficulty, that is, beginning with the easiest.

As I have made clear throughout this book, by far my own first choice is to accommodate this resurgence of Mary Magdalene within the institutional church and allow her energy to heal it rather than further divide it. But I know that for many of my readers (those "heartbroken Christians" I was referring to earlier), the church is no longer an option, while for still others Mary Magdalene belongs to the great worldwide stream of spiritual awakening and has nothing whatsoever to do with organized religion. Since within every institution reform tends to emerge from the bottom up rather than the top down, it seems that the real task at hand for all of us—whether churchgoing Christians or not—is to create those "new wineskins" to hold the new wine of Magdalenic presence, work that will more likely go on in smaller, grassroots circles. Acknowledging this reality, I have tried to offer two versions of each task, one more institutionally oriented and the other more individual and personal.

1. Update the Holy Week Liturgy

If we are serious about activating Mary Magdalene's wisdom presence within contemporary Christianity, the first step is to increase her visibility within the liturgy, particularly during Holy Week, where her presence is so crucial to understanding the Paschal Mystery as an act of redemptive love.

This is an easy task, relatively speaking, because it does not necessarily require a single excursion beyond the boundaries of the canonical New Testament. At the simplest, all that needs to happen is to reinsert those authentic parts of the Passion story that tradition has conveniently excised, such as John 19:25: "Near the cross of Jesus stood his mother, his mother's sister Mary, who was the wife of Cleophas, *and Mary of Magdala*"; or from Matthew 27:61: "*Mary Magdalene and the other Mary remained seated in front of the tomb.*" To hear Mary Magdalene's name explicitly mentioned as part of the Passion narrative would make a huge difference to how we envision the story. Never again would we be able to picture Jesus on the cross alone—or accompanied by only his mother and the disciple John (as it is so pervasively portrayed in the iconography of the West). We couldn't look right through her anymore. We would have to start looking *at* her.

Moving still more boldly toward enhancing that Magdalenic presence, the next step would be to begin to develop a whole new set of ceremonies, in which the role of the feminine in general and Mary Magdalene in specific can receive greater prominence. The simple ceremonial enactment of the burial of Jesus that Good Friday at Vézelay changed my vision of Christianity forever; as did our enactment of the "Unction at Bethany" ceremony at the Aspen Chapel and the Nine Gates Mystery School. The symbolism of the woman anointing the man's feet perfectly counterbalanced the symbolism of Jesus washing the disciples' feet in the Maundy Thursday service of Holy Week and allowed people to experience these two symmetrical actions as a deeply satisfying reintegration of masculine and feminine polarities within the Holy Week liturgy.

Ideally, of course, I would like to see the entire Holy Week liturgy reframed around those two parallel anointings—at Bethany and in the garden of the resurrection—which so powerfully convey the energy of transformative love. And accomplishing this shift is actually easier than it looks. All it takes is: *first*, to create a contemplative service of anointing (built on the anointing at Bethany) for one of the early days of Holy Week; then *second*, on Easter morning, to ceremonially enact (rather than merely read) the gospel account of Mary Magdalene's visit to the tomb. The basic ceremony, the *Visitatio Sepulchri*, has, as we have seen, been around since the tenth century; it merely needs to be returned to active duty.

Ideally, this kind of liturgical overhaul is a win-win situation, for it invites us to address a problem area through creativity, not contraction. New theological understandings invite new liturgical expressions, and as Christianity's spiritual imagination rises to the challenge, the result could be a whole new flow of energy toward the sacred arts: new chants, antiphons, choral works, drama, sculpture, and iconography: a whole new mirror in which the Christian Mystery can find itself reflected. And this, in turn, would free us from an overdependence on earlier artistic forms, reflecting an earlier mode of theological understanding.

I had the opportunity to participate in some of this cross-pollination myself a few years ago with a Passion libretto I created for the Aspen Choral Society. The Society's composer-in-residence, Ray Adams, had asked me for a new text to work with that would eliminate the scapegoating and vindictiveness of the traditional accounts and set the Paschal Mystery within a context of universal love. The task turned out to be fairly straightforward. I simply went to the Farewell Discourses of John 13–17 and framed the traditional Gethsemane and crucifixion scenes within those sublime Johannine passages emphasizing Jesus's voluntary sacrifice and the continuing presence of his love: "I will not leave you orphans"; "I am the vine, you are the branches: abide in me as I in you"; "Behold, I give you a new commandment: to love one another as I have loved you." Then, in a moment of inspiration—I was literally awakened out of my sleep in the middle of the night!—I brought the libretto to its close by placing in the mouth of Mary Magdalene those powerful words from the Song of Songs:

All night I lay on my bed;
I searched for the one my heart loves.
I searched for him, but I did not find him.
I will arise now and go about the city,
Among its streets and squares I will search.
I will search for the one my heart loves . . .
For love is as strong as death,
Its fire a mighty flame.
Waters cannot quench love;
Rivers cannot quench it, waters cannot wash it away.[1]

My composer friend turned these words into a beautiful aria for soprano soloist, and its impact left the audience visibly moved.

If I had ever had any doubt that Mary Magdalene belongs at the very center of the Passion story, they vanished in that moment. She carries both the symbolism and the symbolic weight of the Paschal Mystery understood not as an expiation for sin but as an act of conscious love. Until Christianity can recover this fundamental inner understanding, it cannot heal itself.

This concert version of this Passion was a big project, involving a full orchestra and some sixty singers. (It was later adapted to liturgical format by the Episcopal Order of Saint Helena and is now available online.[2]) Mindful, however, of my earlier observation that most liturgical work with Mary Magdalene is going to be carried out in much smaller circles or even in private meditation, I would like to offer you here a simple ceremony put together by another member of our Calgary wisdom group, Betsy Young. It was created for a contemplative service during our July 2007 Wisdom School in Telephone, Texas, and has been used widely since, both for private meditation and for small group gatherings. Without ever straying beyond the canonical gospels, it moves Mary Magdalene's Holy Week presence front and center. You will find it as appendix 3, page 241.

2. RECLAIM THE WISDOM GOSPELS

The second task involves more of a challenge because it does, in fact, push us beyond the comfort zone of Christian orthodoxy. The basic outlines of the canonical New Testament were established by 367, and when a Christian affirms that "scripture contains all things necessary to salvation," it is *this* scripture that he or she has in mind. As a spiritual tradition, we are heirs to a sixteen-hundred-year legacy of knee-jerk and phobic reactions to texts that have been demonized as "gnostic." But unless we get over these attitudes, we are never going to be able to move beyond first base in healing Christianity's deeply repressed and wounded feminine.

Feminist scholars have been hard at work for several decades now, revisioning the role of women in the early church and attempting to make the case for female leadership and for the full reclamation of Mary Magdalene as "apostle to the apostles." But to do so on the basis only of the canonical New Testament scriptures is a bit like squeezing water from a rock, for the gospels, as we have seen, in many cases already bear a distinctly anti-Magdalene bias. Just beneath the surface it is easy enough to spot a deliberate agenda to minimize Mary Magdalene's role and isolate her from the group, casting her as a mercurial devotee or a wealthy camp follower rather than a full member of Jesus's inner circle.

The wisdom gospels, particularly Thomas and Mary Magdalene, allow us to see more of the full picture, and to understand why these early repressive tendencies set in. And in and of themselves they allow contemporary Christianity to move out from under the long shadow cast by the "master story" and recognize that the actual beginnings of Christianity lie in diversity and fluidity rather than uniformity of belief and practice. What we today experience as "orthodoxy" is merely the successful competitor in an originally diverse field of local options, and we are much more likely to find authentic early models of women's leadership "outside the box" than inside it! These texts give us a much wider resource pool to draw on as we begin to confront the question of what went off track in early Christianity and how the errors can be corrected.

But the real reason that these texts are so important is that they create the context out of which Mary Magdalene operates and in which her apostolic leadership makes sense. And this is a wisdom context: exactly the context that most Christians do not know about. The wisdom trilogy of Thomas, Mary Magdalene, and Philip together lay out the conceptual framework for Jesus's vision of "singleness" as a state of enlightened being, and they allow us to see that the recovery of Mary Magdalene's voice within contemporary Christianity has nothing to do with a "feminine dimension of God," but rather it has to do with the "singleness" that moves us into nondual perception. To reclaim her simply as a female role model without also reclaiming the wisdom she is modeling is a waste of her resources; we cannot in good conscience acknowledge her apostolic authority without also recognizing wherein its charter lies.

My own sense is that the single most important thing Christianity could do to completely renew itself would be to reclaim the Gospel of Thomas on an equal footing with the present canonical gospels for liturgical use, study, and sacred proclamation. It would completely revolutionize our understanding of the religion we think we know so well and make inescapably clear the real and imperative reasons why the male-dominated versions of Christianity are a luxury the world can no longer afford. Again, if such a vision seems like a pipe dream, the place to begin is in a smaller wisdom circle. I personally know of more than a hundred such circles across North America, where people gather, lectio divina style, to read, reflect, and share insights emerging out of a deep heart-immersion in this incomparable wisdom text. Individually, each of these groups may feel like a pebble tossed into the ocean, but the ripples extend widely and are already beginning to have a significant impact on the consciousness of the whole.

3. Recover the Centrality of Anointing

I have already laid the groundwork for this third task in chapter 15, when we looked at the closely interwoven threads of healing, spiritual transformation, erotic love, and kenotic surrender that were once powerfully conveyed in the act of sacramental anointing. Jesus himself made clear use of this practice in his healing ministry, and we see him receiving it as well at the hands of the woman whom tradition remembers as his *koinonos*, his partner. Thus, by all accounts anointing is a core piece of what Jesus was about, and recovering its centrality today is not a matter of inventing something new, but of restoring what originally was. Bruce Chilton speaks movingly of the "scar" on the face of Christianity when, in its effort to distance itself from the uncomfortable erotic and shamanic aspects of Jesus's and Mary Magdalene's dual involvement in anointing, the church wound up excising as well most of what it knew of the healing arts and of the integral relationship between physical healing and kenotic surrender.[3] To return this missing piece is not only a matter of historical accuracy, but gives a much firmer platform from which to address the thrust of our own times toward holistic healing and the inseparable connection between physical, emotional, and spiritual wellness. In this new/old vision, anointing is not simply for the moment of death, or even just for physical healing. Its primary reference point is spiritual transformation: the "dying before you die" that inaugurates the passage into "singleness" or unity of being. For a wisdom Christianity, it is supremely the sacrament of wholeness.

How might this new understanding play out? Aside from restoring the anointing ceremonies to the Holy Week liturgy, I would encourage the growing use of anointing for healing and introduce the practice of anointing at times of intentional spiritual passage, particularly through those classic "dark nights" of the spiritual journey. And of course, to incorporate it into a wedding ceremony as a symbol of the couple's commitment to mutual transformation along a Fifth Way path seems like an opportunity not to be missed.

For the full impact to register, of course, it is helpful to specifically reinforce the connection between anointing and Mary Magdalene. But even this is not really necessary if one merely trusts in her imaginal presence; "bidden or unbidden" she shows up. Through her very essence Mary Magdalene weaves into one whole cloth those strands that have traditionally been kept so stringently separated: conscious love, healing, kenotic surrender, the feminine, singleness, transformation. To touch any part of this hologram is to invoke all the rest.

4. End the Hegemony of Celibacy

At first this task looks so gargantuan as to be almost inconceivable. How does one begin to take apart two thousand years of Christian sexual conditioning identifying celibacy with purity,

monasticism with the royal road to God, women with temptation, and lovemaking with "concupiscence"? How does one begin
to heal that squeamishness around human eros and sexuality that
has so dominated the Christian mindscape even into our own
times? While attitudes around these issues are finally beginning
to soften in the pastoral arena, the imprint of the old mythology
is still theologically pervasive.

The challenge is indeed monumental, but if I have done my
work well in this book, I have at least laid out the beginnings of a
trajectory that could eventually lead to a genuine reconciliation of
Christianity with human sexuality and free both celibacy and conjugal love to be the transformative pathways that they truly are. At
the same time, this trajectory provides the theological basis on
which it becomes possible even to *begin* to entertain the notion
that Mary Magdalene and Jesus might have been human beloveds.

The first step is to remember very clearly that the "singleness"
Jesus has in mind *is a state of unitive being, not a state of celibacy.*
He may or may not have been celibate himself, but in any case,
this was not the bottom line. And here is where we so need the
Gospel of Thomas to call us back to those core teachings on nonduality that are unmistakably the framework out of which Jesus is
operating but that tend to get blunted in the canonical texts.
"When you are able to make two become one . . . then you will
enter in" (logion 22); so teaches the Master whose first title among
his Aramaic-speaking followers was Ihidaya, "the Single One."
But the decisive element in this singleness—as we explored in
detail in part 2 of this book—is not celibacy, but kenotic surrender. It is not obligatory for Jesus to be celibate in order for the
path he teaches to hold integrity.

The second step, then, is to name the Christian path for what
it actually is: a path of kenotic love. I have borrowed the term
Fifth Way from Boris Mouravieff, and in that sense, the nomen-
clature is modern. But the idea itself goes right back to Jesus and
is in essence found in these words: "There is no greater love than
this, to give one's life for one's friends" (John 15:13). I have depicted it in the simple formula $A = E \times K$, where A is *agape* (trans-

figured love), E is *eros* (passion) and K is *kenosis*. According to this particular alchemy of transformation, the unitive point (or "singleness") is attained not through renunciation and sexual abstinence but rather through the willing surrender of attachment to the very thing(s) one holds most precious. Wherever Jesus began in his lifetime, this is where he ended up, and the gospel he teaches is pure Fifth Way.

Now it is quite true that this kenotic surrender can be done in two modes: celibate and noncelibate. Let me be very clear here: when I call for "ending the hegemony of celibacy," I am not in the least implying any disrespect for Christianity's rich monastic tradition, in which I have myself been deeply spiritually nurtured. Kenosis is powerfully authentic in celibate form, and within the conditions of cloistered monasticism it can attain an intensity and luminous beauty unparalleled in the more fragmented conditions of daily life in the world. One need only stand with the Cistercian monks at the close of each day and sing the exquisite Gregorian "Salve Regina" before the stained glass window of the Blessed Virgin to know that monastic love mysticism is profoundly real. But what connects the celibate and noncelibate versions is greater than what separates them, and without the presence of an illumined kenosis at the core, neither version will work.

Hopefully, a recognition of that underlying unity of the kenotic path would allow us finally to break through the barrier and acknowledge openly the most likely explanation of Mary Magdalene's anomalous circumstances: that she may indeed have been Jesus's beloved partner, perhaps even his sexual partner. And there is no cause to feel embarrassed or betrayed by this, because once we grasp what kenotic love is all about, this open admission creates a new beginning for everyone. Right at the heart of the faith we discover Christianity's long missing archetype of relational wholeness. This discovery allows us to claim Mary Magdalene in *all* of her roles, not just some of them (OK to keep apostle and wounded healer, but not beloved), and to see that these roles are inextricably connected and work together to create the fullness that she is. It allows us to finally quit allegorizing the

Song of Songs and experience its sacred beauty through concrete human reference points. It allows us to realize that bridal mysticism is not about sex but about transformation—or more radical still, that sex itself can be about transformation! Or in other words, to help us quit being afraid of human intimacy and start learning how to handle it better.

"What is not lived cannot be redeemed," says Jean-Yves Leloup. Our willingness to entertain the possibility that Jesus, too, may have lived the experience of sexual intimacy allows us to reclaim this experience as sacred and holy—and to treat it that way. It holds beloveds accountable to one another for their spiritual transformation. In a celibate-dominated Christianity whose theology of partnership still overwhelmingly echoes St. Paul's infamous "Better to marry than to burn," little wonder there has been so little understanding of, let alone training in, the fine points of mystical commingling, shadow work, and mutual servanthood that are all part of the territory along the Fifth Way path of erotic transformation. A reclaimed vision of Jesus and Mary Magdalene walking this same Fifth Way allows us to honor and accept human intimate partnership as the very crucible of transformation—but obliges us to apply the kenotic principles that will bring this transformation to its fruition. It breaks the centuries of denial and doubletalk and allows us to begin to reappropriate the Christian story in terms of human love and even human lovemaking. Relationship as a sacred path . . . what a novel idea!

5. REAWAKEN TO THE POWER OF THE IMAGINAL

In a way this final task may seem esoteric, but for me it is really at the heart of everything. For so many of its centuries Christianity has lived in a diminished cosmos, a sense of exile or separation weighing heavily on its heart, with a tacit understanding that its Risen Lord is in actuality an "absentee landlord." The church's eucharistic liturgy forlornly announces, "When we eat this bread and drink this cup, we proclaim your death, Lord Jesus, until you come again in glory." We talk of his "coming again" only in terms of a final judgment or a deathbed encounter. For the most part, our Christian path encourages us to "meet" him in the sacraments, to live ethically in this world, and to await a mystical reunion in the next.

But that is not what Jesus himself proclaims, or what the earliest Christians experienced. They experienced Jesus as *present*: alive, palpable, vibrantly connected; their experience was that the walls between the realms are paper thin and that our embodiment is no obstacle to the full and intimate participation in relationship with him here and now. The kingdom of heaven is not later, it is *lighter*: it exists right here, right beneath our noses, in a more subtle but expansive presence that is ours the moment we move beyond our egoically generated space-time continuum (what Jesus calls "the world") and directly encounter the Source. From this imaginal plane of reality, reality floods back into our own world and fills us with grace, presence, and creativity. Here we discover that God is not only for us, but *with* us.

The earliest Christians awakened to this reality at the resurrection; this was in fact the *real* resurrection—not the resuscitation of a body that later tradition would come to set such store by, but the unmistakable certainty that Jesus was present and that their hearts now knew their way to him. Some of those earliest gospel accounts involve no resurrection appearance at all—as for the Marys in the Gospel of Mark, who encounter only an empty tomb, or the "beloved disciple" in the Gospel of John who enters this tomb and immediately deduces the presence from the absence. And as the Gospel of Mary Magdalene makes clear, whether this encounter takes the form of a vision, an intuition, or a physical reunion, the real meeting ground is in the imaginal.

While all Christians are called to discover the reality of this realm, still, it seems that Fifth Way lovers get there particularly powerfully and swiftly—because, as Ladislaus Boros and others have pointed out, love is itself already a kind of death: the death of the separated ego self. In and of itself it catapults the beloveds into that new sphere of encounter that T. S. Eliot describes in *The*

Four Quartets as "neither here nor there . . . but moving toward a further union, a deeper communion."[4] I myself became a full believer in the resurrection (not just an intellectual believer) when my own Fifth Way teacher Rafe died fifteen years ago, and I discovered that far from being gone, he was still present, just as he assured me he would be, and continues to be to this day. We meet in that realm of oneness that was already coming into being between us before his death, in a cascade of continuing intimacy and insight.

It is clear that Mary Magdalene knew a good deal about that realm. At that spiritual tipping point where "no longer the object of my affection, he has become the subject of my truth," a new energy emerges: pure creativity and effortless action. This is the "spiritual procreativity" described by both the Gospel of Philip and the poet Rilke. As the "singleness" of the bridal chamber becomes a lived reality, it creates a continuous and effortless immediacy between the realms, and confers the ability to live and minister out of that imaginal ground. It is in this that Mary Magdalene's apostolacy chiefly consists. Whatever she knew before Jesus's death was sealed in his resurrection—as indeed it was for all of his apostles. But the fact that her transformation took place in the domain of love, with transfigured eros as its quicksilver, brings a particular fragrance of sweetness to the alchemical agape.

We do not know for certain what happened to Mary Magdalene after the resurrection. The gospel bearing her name confirms that her spiritual leadership was honored in at least some circles of early Christianity. She may well have sojourned in France. What we do know for certain is that the fragrance of her presence did not disappear from Christianity. In mysticism and allegory, in art and folklore, in esoteric circles—all veiled, but pointing like a finger at the moon—her mysterious alchemical feminine was kept alive. Until at last, in our own times, it comes above ground again, asking us to awaken yet again to the morning of the resurrection and find ourselves in the garden, awaiting the encounter that can change our institutional hearts.

The Risen Lord is indeed risen. Present, intimate, creative, "closer than your own heartbeat," accessed through your vulnerability, your capacity for intimacy. The imaginal realm is real, and through it you will never be separated from any one or anything you have ever loved, for love is the ground in which you live and move and have your being. This is the message that Mary Magdalene has perennially to bring. This is the message we most need to hear.

APPENDIX I

Mary Magdalene and the Song of Songs

Like Mary Magdalene herself, the Song of Songs has had a long history of both admirers and detractors. It has been called, with some justification, "the most unbiblical book in the whole Bible," and there are those who feel that its inclusion in among the wisdom writings of the Old Testament was a grand mistake. But others see it as nothing short of scripture's mystical highpoint, an inexhaustible fountainhead of beauty and spiritual wisdom. Among this latter group was Rabbi Aqiba (d. 135), one of the most influential of the early rabbinic commentators, whose celebrated words eventually carried the day: "All the ages are not worth the day on which it was written for all the writings are holy, but the Song is the Holy of Holies."[1]

At the heart of all this consternation, as you might expect, is the fact that this text is a love song—and not just a mild-mannered, "spiritual" love song, but an unabashed celebration of erotic pleasure. From its opening salvo, "Let him kiss me with the kisses of his mouth," to its parting affirmation, "Love is as strong as death," it never breaks stride. In eight canticles of stunningly evocative imagery, it sings the glories of carnal desire in exquisite and scintillating detail.

Aside from its traditional association with King Solomon (it is in fact more commonly known in Protestant circles as "The Song of Solomon"), the only reason that such a clear-cut piece of erotica could be considered suitable material for canonization is that almost from the first it was viewed as an elaborate spiritual allegory. For the early rabbinical commentators it spoke of the love between God and Israel. The third-century Christian teacher Origen *did* raise the possibility that the Song of Songs might have something to do with Mary Magdalene, but like many of his other bold intuitions, this one was quickly swept under the rug. For succeeding generations of Christian monastics, the

Song spoke of the mystical union between the bridegroom (Christ, the divine *logos*) and a bride who was variously seen as the church, the mother of Jesus, and the individual human soul.

In our own times, allegorical exegesis has fallen decisively out of favor, leaving contemporary Bible scholars again somewhat at a loss to account for any plausible reason why the Song of Songs should be considered a sacred text. There are those who simply want to revel in the unadulterated naturalism of the text, savoring the delicious irony that a collection of ancient erotica should somehow wind up in the Bible. Others view the Song as primarily satiric in its intent, while still others are struck by its distinctly feminist leanings and even conjecture that it may have been composed by a woman.[2] Practically all commentators are charmed by the saucy energy of the woman lover who is the Song's protagonist and driving force, and by the mutuality and genuine caring that seems to exist between the Song's pair of lovers.

Stripped of its allegorical superstructure, the Song seems impressively in tune with modernity. It accommodates itself as gracefully to the deconstructionist temperament of our own times as it did to the lofty mysticism of an age gone by. Yet even here the Song refuses to stay put. There is something about this text that intrinsically points beyond itself; it keeps jumping the fence and winding up back in those familiar mystical pastures in spite of itself.

"Let it be said from the outset that there is indeed a bridge between the naturalistic reading of the Canticle and its mystical reading," writes André LaCocque, one of the Song's most respected contemporary commentators.[3] In part, this bridge can be attributed to the Song's unusually vivid imagery, which serves as a magnet for the archetypal imagination. But to an even greater degree, as LaCocque clearly recognizes, it resides in the quality of the love itself; while unabashedly erotic, it has a deeper and more compelling dimension that touches the holy, despite itself. Respect, fondness, and fidelity are the cornerstones of this relationship—"to the point that it becomes paradigmatic for all authentic love."[4]

THE FIFTH WAY?

Now when I hear a statement such as this, what immediately comes to my mind is, "Ah, yes, he is describing a Fifth Way text!" One of the reasons the Song has been so notoriously difficult to pin down (as either a spiritual allegory or a specimen of biblical erotica) is that it intrinsically holds the tension between these two realms. In fact, what

LaCocque correctly intuits as the "bridge" is none other than the trajectory of Fifth Way love following its own intrinsic dynamism. The reason this rather obvious explanation for the Song's mysterious self-transcending quality is not more widely recognized is that the concept of Fifth Way love is still largely unknown outside of esoteric circles.

But for confirmation that we are at least in the right ballpark, we need go no further than that list of criteria set forth by Vladimir Solovyov, which I have already laid out in chapter 9 (page 120). The particular type of love suitable for this path of spiritual transformation, according to Solovyov,

> is distinguished from other types of love by a greater intensity, by a more engrossing character, and by the possibility of a more complete overall reciprocity. Only this love can lead to the real and indissoluble union of two lives into one.

In other words, the raw material of the Fifth Way is an eros characterized by (1) unusual intensity; (2) unusual reciprocity; and (3) a capacity for self-transcendence that may eventually, with commitment and dedicated spiritual work, transform the lead of human passion into the gold of holy union. From our earlier investigations, we learned that this alchemy is usually set in motion when the lovers submit to a path of kenosis, or laying down of self for the other.

The lovers in the Song are young at their game, and there is no indication that the idea of spiritual transformation has yet occurred to them. But in prototypic form, all three of these core elements are present in the text, the first two manifestly so and the third in a more latent form.

Of the intensity of the lovers' passion there can be no doubt. The woman herself unabashedly proclaims (5:8): "I am sick with love!"— and not only sick, but alternately delirious, distraught, and mad with desire. The whole Song unfolds in a kind of hyperrealism; the highs are ecstatic, the losses devastating. The Technicolor visuals, the lavish metaphors, and the delicate fragrances all heighten the already full-to-bursting intensity of the lovers' desire. The ardor of their longing engulfs the entire poem.

Equally, as we have seen, scholars are struck by the reciprocity of this love. While the woman is clearly the sparkplug in the relationship, the mutuality of their lovers' attraction is never in question. Like good dancing partners, they take turns leading and following, and their delight in each other is obviously mutual. An even more telling sign is the terms of endearment they use for each other. For her, he is "the one whom my soul loves" (1:7, 3:1). For him, she is "my sister, bride" (4:12, 5:1)—a term that comes about as close as possible to conveying that sense of *koinoinos* we spoke of earlier: soul mate, or intimate companion. While the physical passion between them runs strong, what gives the Song its real staying power is the deep emotional intimacy and trust between the two, all the more striking for the era in which the poem was written.[5]

PRESENCE AND ABSENCE

But what of the third point, the capacity for transformation or self-transcendence? While less fully developed in the Song, I think it is also present. But we have to look for it in a different place: not in plot or characterization, but in a subtly gathering emotional momentum that is built into the structure of the poem itself.

Like many sacred texts, the Song proves on closer examination to be loosely chiastic; basically this means that that the text has a "mirror imaging" structure, with parallel episodes fanning out from a central dramatic core. In the Song, this core proves to be 4:12–5:2, the poem's exquisite invitation to the "garden enclosed" where the two lovers will consummate their passion (we will be discussing this celebrated passage just ahead). But on either side of this vignette of pure communion are symmetrical vignettes of absence, and it is these that are chiefly responsible for the poem's elusive but clearly building emotional intensity.[6]

For some reason the male lover vanishes in canticle 3, and the anguish of the woman is unbearable. In defiance of both social convention and her personal safety, she goes out searching for him and does indeed manage to locate him, to her ecstatic relief. But in canticle 5 he disappears again, this time more permanently. When she again takes to the streets to search for him, she is beaten up by the watchmen (who mistake her for a prostitute), and she does not by her own power succeed in finding him again; she must wait, "sick with love," until he appears on his own terms. In the meantime, she must learn to find comfort, no matter what the external circumstances may be, in her inner assurance that "I am my lover's and he is mine" (6:3).

While the circumstances of loss and absence are never fully explained, they do tend to push the text forward emotionally and create a deepening and maturation of love's intensity. As Roland Murphy, another distinguished contemporary scholar, comments: "If the beloved other's absence is intolerable, it is also creative of more intense emotions: the ardent yearning to reunite, a compulsive seeking that is not satisfied until the other is found again, and the 'sickness of love' that paradoxically, the lover's physical presence will only deepen, never cure."[7] In other words, there is a gathering emotional momentum that builds steadily and relentlessly toward the poem's dramatic climax in 8:6–7, when suddenly, out of nowhere, the woman proclaims:

> Place me as a seal on your heart,
> as a seal on your arm.
> Strong as Death is love;
> intense as Sheol is its ardor.
> Its shafts are shafts of fire,
> flames of Yah.
> Deep waters cannot quench love,
> nor rivers sweep it away.[8]

Love and death—how did we get here? Not only is this stunningly strong poetry, it is sheer alchemy as well, as fire and water, life and death wrestle, and the seal upon the heart is forged in the flames of Yah (Yahweh): Holy love. One cannot help but think back to those remarkable lines by the anonymous contemporary mystic cited in chapter 12: "True love demands sacrifice because true love is a transforming force and is really the birth-pangs of a union on a higher plane." Suddenly the Song has jumped levels. Out of the sacrifice of many partings and returns, of longing stretched to the breaking point, something has galvanized within this thoroughly secular love song that resonates with divine longing itself.

Within the terms of the Song itself this sudden quantum leap in spiritual intensity makes no real sense. But from a Fifth Way perspective, it makes perfect sense, for what we are witnessing here is the pure dynamism of love itself, floating a bit mirage-like above any firm moorings in plot and character, but following its own pure imperative toward self-transcendence. It is surely this quality that Rabbi Aqiba was sensing when he proclaimed the Song of Songs "the holy of holies"—and from the intensity of his language we can safely infer that he was not experiencing this love through any allegorical filter but rather in its own direct reality.

As I mentioned in chapter 16, one of the more intriguing current theories about the Song is that it may be based on the true story of Abishag the Shulammite, as recorded in 1 Kings 2:13–25. Abishag has been brought to the royal court of Israel to care for King David in his dotage. When Adonijah, Solomon's older half-brother, asks for her hand in marriage, Solomon perceives a threat to his kingship and has Adonijah executed. While this theory, set forth by the British genealogist Sir Laurence Gardner, has yet to win widespread scholarly approval, it does clear up many of the mysteries long associated with the Song and suggests that it comes by its Fifth Way ambience honestly. We might be well advised to pay closer attention to the mounting emotional intensity in a poem that on the surface appears to be largely static.

MAGDALENIC RESONANCES

Once this implicit Fifth Way character of the Song is recognized, the deck is indeed cleared for a rich conversation with Mary Magdalene. Indeed, it almost seems as if the Song had been lying in wait all those centuries for Mary Magdalene to step into it. While I know that such a statement can only be made with extreme caution,[9] the correspondences are simply too powerful to ignore. In particular, embedded within the Song are several shorter poems—and a few dazzling one-liners—which in the precision of their emotional mirroring literally give voice to the crucial pieces of the Mary Magdalene story that have gone missing in the mainstream of Christian tradition. They have long furnished the symbolic building blocks for her underground presence in the spiritual imagination of Christianity. And they are still the obvious starting points for reclaiming her voice today. Let's look at each of these in turn.

1. "Black am I, and beautiful, O Daughters of Jerusalem . . ." (Song 1:5–6)

As I have mentioned already, virtually all commentators on the Song are immediately drawn to the decidedly unconventional and spunky woman who is the poem's protagonist (and according to some, its author). Her unabashed desire and determination create one of the most powerful yet economically designed characters in all of biblical literature.

Unlike her lover, who remains discreetly in the background, we learn quite a bit in this poem about her character and circumstances. In this first canticle she describes herself in striking detail:

> Black am I, and beautiful, O Daughters of Jerusalem,
>   like the tents of Quedar,
>   like the pavilions of Solomon.
> Do not stare at me because I am blackish,
>   for the sun has burned me.
> The sons of my mother were angry with me;
>   they assigned me as the keeper of the vineyards—
> my own vineyard I have not kept. (1:5–6)

These verses furnish us with a powerful image ("Black am I, and beautiful") and also an important piece of information. Her darkened skin is literally due to her having been forced to tend the vineyards of her brothers in the scorching heat. Symbolically, however, her "blackness" also suggests something a little "off" in her character or history, and this suspicion is borne out in the skimpy details of her life that the text furnishes. We know that she is at odds with her brothers and seems to live on her own (not in her father's house, as would be expected of an unmarried Jewish woman of her times); she comes and goes as she pleases. We know as well that she has a passionate temperament, which on more than one occasion lands her in trouble. On the up side, the fruit of her "blackness" is a feisty independence that makes its presence felt throughout the poem. She tends her own garden, has her own freedom, and makes her own choices. In a world geared toward the silencing of women's voices, her own voice speaks loud and clear.

More than a few commentators have noted the similarities between the woman portrayed here and the Samaritan woman who meets Jesus at the well in John 4 and whose conversation with him amounts to a virtual textbook account of a Fifth Way lovers' first meeting. In later Christian tradition this passage (known in Latin as the beautiful canticle, "Nigra sum sed pulchra") would come to be applied to the Virgin Mary, spawning a veritable cult of black Madonnas.[10] But if we look at the text more closely, the obvious primary field of resonance is with Mary Magdalene. We can see that throughout Christian tradition this same aura of "blackness" has followed her, and for the same reason: that telltale combination of unabashed, passionate devotion and spunky independence that becomes the classic "Magdalenic signature." As we see in the gospels (particularly Thomas and Mary Magdalene), she, too, is at odds with her "brothers," who simply cannot handle her intensity and try (as do the brothers in the final canticle of the Song), to confine her by various methods: shutting her out, locking her in, silencing her voice. But both this unknown lover and Mary Magdalene simply go about their business, serenely wielding an identical trump card: the sure and certain knowledge that love is, indeed, as strong as death, and as irrepressible as freedom itself.

2: "All night I lay on my bed . . ." (Song 3:1–4)

This is the passage, as you will recall from my concluding chapter, that roused me out of deep sleep to offer itself as the conclusion for my Passion libretto. I quoted it earlier from the New Revised Standard Version of the Bible, but Murphy's translation is very close:

> Upon my bed at night
>   I sought him whom my soul loves,
>   I sought him, but I did not find him.
> "I will rise and make the rounds of the city,
>   in the streets and crossings
>   I will seek him whom my soul loves."

With good reason was I drawn to this passage, for its description of the search for the missing beloved captures with excruciating poignancy and beauty the feeling tone of Mary Magdalene's own vigil at the foot of the cross and beside the tomb. When confronted by devastating loss, the Song's lover is distraught but not incapacitated. Rather than simply suffering on her bed, she resolves to "rise and make the rounds of the city"—at considerable risk to her own safety and reputation—to "seek him whom my soul loves." The emotional resonance is palpable between this passage and the simple statement in Matthew 27:61: "And Mary Magdalene and the other Mary remained standing there before the tomb." Once again we see foreshadowed here that striking Magdalenic configuration of passionate longing, but expressed in determined witness rather than hysterical grief.

3. "A garden enclosed, my sister, my bride . . ." (4:12–5:1)

This passage has always been perceived as nuptial in character, symbolically if not in fact literally. Located at the Song's epicenter, it is an invitation to the consummation of love, couched in images of unsurpassed sensuous beauty. As the currents of passion all set toward this consummation, the two beloveds call and answer one another, and the male lover addresses his partner as "my sister, my bride." That "complete overall reciprocity" of Fifth Way love shines forth gently and

tenderly. While the passage is too long to quote in full here, I will
share some of its highlights (the M and W in the left margin stand for
"man" and "woman," respectively).

M   A garden enclosed, my sister, bride
        a (garden) enclosed, a fountain sealed!
    Your shoots, a paradise of pomegranates,
        with choice fruits:
    Henna with nard,
        nard and saffron,
    Cane and cinnamon,
        with all scented woods;
    Myrrh and aloes,
        with all finest spices.
    A garden fountain,
        a well of fresh water,
        flowing from Lebanon! [. . .]

W   Let my lover come to his garden
        and eat its choice fruits.

M   I have come to my garden, my sister, bride!
        I gather my myrrh with my spices.
    I eat my honeycomb with my honey;
        I drink my wine with my milk.

    Eat, friends, drink!
        Drink deeply of love!

The link between this passage and the story of Mary Magdalene
is provided largely through the Gospel of John. Just as this "garden
enclosed" furnishes the epicenter of the Song, so too, does it furnish
the epicenter of John's telling of the Paschal Mystery. Significantly, he
is the only one of the four evangelists to locate the resurrection drama
within a garden (Matthew and Luke merely place it tombside), and his
intention here is clearly symbolic. While this garden may also evoke
the primordial Eden from which Adam and Eve were expelled,[11] the
olfactory trail linking it to the Song of Songs is far more obvious.
Nard, myrrh, aloes: all of these fragrances wafting forth from the garden in the Song figure prominently in the anointing and burial of
Jesus, and the links between these scents and Mary Magdalene have

been commented on extensively in monastic allegorical criticism, from Origen, Gregory, and Bernard of Clairvaux right down to Bruno Barnhart in our own times. In fact, when Barnhart comes to this section of his discussion in his commentary on the fourth gospel, he begins quoting repeatedly from the Song of Songs, following a well-trod symbolic trail to its inevitable conclusion: "The meeting between Magdalene and Jesus here will be implicitly a nuptial meeting."[12] We will have more to say about the Gospel of John in appendix 2, but the bottom line seems to be that John has deliberately constructed his resurrection drama around the Song of Songs, in such a way as to emphasize not only the kerygmatic character—the apostolic commissioning—but also the distinctly nuptial character of the reunion taking place. The "garden enclosed" is John's symbol for the bridal chamber, and the sending forth shortly to ensue is "the birth-pangs of union on a higher plane."

4. "Set me as a seal upon your heart." (Song 8:6–7)

When I quoted this passage earlier in the text, I mentioned that its stunning emotional impact seems to arise out of nowhere. Most commentators experience it as the dramatic climax of the entire Song, as the text suddenly leaps levels from the particular to the universal and from the erotic to mystical. Viewing this text through a Fifth Way lens allows us to see much more clearly where this impact comes from: this quantum leap in intensity encapsulates that "alchemical moment" when eros does, indeed turn itself inside out and become the "beginning of the union of the higher level."

Again, additional perspective on this passage is provided through our continuing conversation with the Gospel of John. In broad contour as well as specific detail, John's depiction of the resurrection drama curiously mirrors the chiasm of the Song of Songs. In both texts, that central scene of reunion and bliss in the garden (Song 4:12–5:2; John 20:11–16) is flanked by two absences, and in each case the nature of the absences is similar. If Song 3:1–4 essentially furnishes the libretto for Mary Magdalene's vigil at the tomb, Song 6:1–3 mirrors the second and more consequential lover's departure in John 20, as Jesus gently but firmly reminds the ecstatic Magdalene that his return to human flesh will be brief.

In Song 3:4, the lover triumphantly proclaims, "I found my love and clung to him." Jesus's cryptic instructions in John 20:16—"Do not cling to me, for I have not yet ascended to the father"—seem to re-echo this passage, while pointing to its resolution at an entirely different level: "But go! Tell my brothers that I have risen!" Like the lover in Song 6:3, she must henceforth find her bearings entirely by the light of her inward recognition that "I am my lover's and he is mine." Love is always there in the eternity of their hearts, but the time for clinging is over and the time for proclamation has begun.

Thus, Jesus sends her forth from the bridal chamber to announce the good news to the disciples—exactly as our discussion of the bridal chamber in part 2 would lead us to expect. The sacramental "single-ness" of the bridal chamber entails by necessity that component of "go forth . . . proclaim . . . serve." Thus, in this final resonance with the Song of Songs, the Gospel of John is able to represent Mary Magdalene's apostolic commissioning as identical with the consummation of her Fifth Way union. "Love is as strong as death" becomes the Easter kerygma she is sent forth to proclaim.

APPENDIX 2

The Anointing according to John

The case for Mary of Bethany as the anointer of Jesus rests exclusively on the testimony of the Gospel of John. The other three gospels leave undisclosed the identity of the woman who dramatically invades a private dinner party to perform her singular act of devotion (although Matthew and Mark concur that it takes place in Bethany shortly before the crucifixion). John appears to furnish the missing detail: the anointer is Mary of Bethany, sister of Martha and Lazarus, that mysterious threesome whom John expressly designates as the "friends" of Jesus.

This is another of the many places in which John threads his independent way through the Passion narrative, diverging significantly from the Synoptic accounts. While the two sisters do make a brief appearance in the Gospel of Luke (Luke 10:38–41),[1] the "Lazarus family" is known only in John, and the special status attributed to this family has fueled a good deal of speculation among those wanting to "crack the code" of John, including the hypothesis that these people are not just "friends" but Jesus's *in-laws*, related to him through his secret marriage to Mary of Bethany. The underlying assumption, of course, is Mary, Martha, and Lazarus are concrete historical characters, and the task at hand is to discover their "true" identity.

While this assumption may be understandable in the light of our modern notions of historicity, it can lead us down the primrose path when we try to retroject it onto an earlier era. It is simply not accurate to read John—or for that matter, any of the gospels—as a historical biography of Jesus. Historical biography as we know it today did not exist before the eighteenth century. All ancient and medieval biography is primarily rhetorical in intent, written to inspire and encourage. One need only recall Athanasius's gilded biography of the life of Saint Anthony or Pope Gregory's equally gilded reconstruction of the life of

St. Benedict to see how fact and fiction flow together seamlessly in the service of the work's overarching thematic design. There is indeed a "code" to be cracked in John, but it can be done without recourse to secret genealogies, simply by paying close attention to the way the text works as a piece of literature.

Remember chiasm from our earlier discussion of the Song of Songs? It means, essentially, that rather than following linear chronology, events fan out symmetrically from a thematic epicenter according to the basic pattern A-B-C-B-A. It will perhaps come as no surprise, given the highly orchestrated nature of this gospel, that scholars have recently discovered the presence of a complex and rigorous chiasm as its core structural principle. I will discuss this in greater detail shortly, for it has considerable bearing upon the question we will soon be exploring—that is, Mary Magdalene's subterranean involvement throughout the entire gospel. For now, suffice it to say that the presence of this highly ornate literary device at the heart of John's compositional strategy should be a huge red flag warning us that he cannot possibly be presenting a "factual" account. If we are to follow what he is up to, we need to stay with his underlying purpose. Beneath the narrative surface John is unfolding his own version of bridal mysticism, and as we pay attention to how the individual pieces of the text work together, we will have a better sense of the fundamental truthfulness underlying his artful deceptions.

DRESS REHEARSAL FOR GETHSEMANE

From a textual standpoint, the anointing scene in John (John 12:1–8) really belongs to a single unbroken episode beginning in chapter 11 with the raising of Lazarus. This is where the "Lazarus family" makes its debut in the narrative, and all three characters remain onstage until the conclusion of the anointing, at which point they permanently disappear.

The dramatic Lazarus episode, another event found only in John, clearly seems intended in some way to prefigure Jesus's own death and resurrection. The two incidents are connected not only by their overall similarity but by a number of specific details, such as the burial cave "with a stone laid across" it (11:38); the instruction to "roll away the stone" (11:39), and the mention of the burial cloths, which are prominent visuals in both episodes. The parallelism is too striking to be anything other than intentional, so what is the intention? It would seem that Lazarus is taking on the role of Jesus here, and the whole scene functions as a deeply emotional dress rehearsal for the crucifixion itself, whose thematic purpose is to explore unflinchingly Jesus's own human vulnerability and the painful inner landscape he must come to terms with before being able to meet his own death with stoic composure. Both structurally and emotionally, this is John's version of Gethsemane.

At the actual foot of the cross the two sisters will be replaced by a single Mary Magdalene. For now, at the dress rehearsal, we can begin merely by noting that each of these two sisters seems to carry a part of her personality—almost as if, for the purposes of this psychological exploration, she has been split in two.

Surprisingly, perhaps, it is Martha who actually carries more of the classic Magdalenic energy. Like the spunky lover in the Song of Songs, she does not abide her grief patiently, but boldly "rises and makes the rounds of the city" to intercept Jesus en route. Once face to face, she confronts and challenges him—"If you had been here, my brother would not have died"—and keeps upping the ante of her questioning until at last (exactly as in the dialogue with that other spunky woman, in John 4), Jesus is moved to a stunning spiritual confession: "I am the Resurrection and the life; whoever believes in me, though he die, shall live, and whoever lives and believes in me will never die" (John 11:25). The Good News that Mary Magdalene will be sent forth to proclaim on Easter Sunday is here first announced to Martha.

Mary, by contrast, remains at home until she is sent for: a fact often set forth within the "bloodline conspiracy" school as further evidence that she is Jesus's wife.[2] Whether or not this is true, it is clear that her relationship to Jesus has an entirely different quality to it from her sister's. If Martha carries the "apostolic gene," Mary carries the devotional one. If Martha's spirited energy evokes in response an equally spirited declaration of Jesus's spiritual powers, Mary's vulnerability evokes in response a deep soul-love and reciprocal vulnerability. Although her words to him are identical to her sister's—"If you had been here, my brother would not have died"—they call forth in him a very different reaction: "When Jesus saw her weeping, he was moved in the depth of the spirit" (John 11:33). Stung into action, he asks roughly, "Where have you laid him?"—followed in the text by that most excruciating of all two-word sentences, "Jesus wept." If his exchange with Martha was spirit to spirit, this one is soul to soul, revealing an emotional entrainment that is tender and mutual.

So what is the point here? My sense is that this division of the

Magdalenic character into its two most prominent strands is indeed deliberate, for John's purpose here is to place under the microscope, so to speak, the two core components of her personality that must come together as one to create the "singleness" that he will only finally name as Mary Magdalene. Here he is deliberately separating out the strands of her love in order to be able to weave them back together in a new and powerful way. Both the apostolic side—the bursting, courageous, "yang" energy"—and the vigiling side, the more traditionally receptive, vulnerable, "yin" energy, will have their role to play as "two become one" in the bridal chamber on Easter morning.

THE GOSPEL OF LOVE

True, Mary Magdalene does not actually enter the action by name until John 19:25, when we meet her standing beneath the foot of the cross. But can we really presume that she has been absent up to this point? Not if we understand the deep structure of the text.

A few pages ago I mentioned the literary device of chiasm. The rigorous chiasm of John was first described by the scholar Peter Ellis in his 1984 book *The Genius of John*.[3] Building on this lead in his 1999 commentary *The Good Wine*, Bruno Barnhart manages to delineate yet two more layers of structural complexity within this basic chiastic pattern: a mandalic pattern, which draws the symmetrical episodes into circle form, and a secondary overlay, based on the biblical seven days of creation, which further divides this circle into seven concentric rings. This complex diagram forms the working roadmap for Barnhart's intricate exposition of the gospel text.[4]

The scope of Barnhart's magisterial work is far beyond anything that concerns us here, but I mention it because it provides the springboard from which I will launch my own investigation. When Barnhart has finished applying his calculations, he winds up with a "sixth day" ring, which collects under one roof four key encounters, all of them unique to the Gospel of John and all of them involving women. Most of these we have encountered already and flagged as having special bearing on our study of Mary Magdalene. They are:

1. The wedding at Cana (John 2:1–12)
2. The Samaritan woman at the well (John 4:4–42)
3. The anointing at Bethany (John 12:1–8)
4. Mary Magdalene and Jesus in the garden (John 20:1–18)

These texts form part of a single structural unit. By leveraging them against each other, we can begin to fill in the missing pieces, as we see how each text contributes a vital key to the others' interpretation. Let's look at this process more closely.

THE WEDDING AT CANA

We met up with this section briefly in part 2 in the course of our discussion of the core issue in Jesus's own psychological development: his "separation" from the Mother and emergence into his own person. According to the Gnostic legend I cited in chapter 9, at exactly the time that this celebration at Cana is taking place, Mary Magdalene is crossing the Jordan into Judea, making her way to her as yet unbeknownst beloved. As a text, this vignette exudes a mysterious power far beyond its brief narrative contours. Small wonder that Dostoyevsky alights on it in *The Brothers Karamazov* as the backdrop for Alyosha's mystical breakthrough following the death of his teacher Father Zossima. For there is indeed a great beauty that emanates from this text, a lingering fragrance of an indescribable sense of felt significance, as if some great event is happening.

On the surface, however, this episode is really a nonevent—or at least an outer shell of an event—for the two principals, the bride and bridegroom, do not actually appear in the text at all. Some writers like to speculate that Jesus is himself the bridegroom (and the passage therefore another allusion to his "secret" marriage to Mary Magdalene), but this interpretation has always struck me as overly literal and forced, doing violence to the clearly symbolic intentions of the text. The episode *is* curious: a wedding scene with its epicenter missing. But as it turns out, this is all part of John's artistry, for the missing bride and groom will be provided by segment four, when we enter the garden on Easter morning.

THE WOMAN AT THE WELL

Again, this is an event from which the fragrance of Fifth Way love emanates. We have seen in our earlier discussion of this passage in chapter 9 that it carries all the intimacy and mysterious familiarity characteristic of a Fifth Way lovers' first meeting, and any number of writers have commented on its distinctly nuptial ambience. The unknown Samaritan woman clearly bears the energy signature we have identified as Magdalenic: spunky, outspoken, and honest, and with an independence bespeaking a somewhat maverick personal history. In appendix 1 I laid out the evidence linking this woman to Mary Magdalene through the Song of Songs, thus again evoking the erotic nature of the meeting and furnishing additional evidence that John is well aware of the Song of Songs and deliberately works with it throughout his gospel to imply the Magdalenic presence.

MARY MAGDALENE AND JESUS IN THE GARDEN

In this fourth segment (and yes, I know I have skipped over the third; we will return to it shortly), Mary Magdalene, at last designated by name, takes her full and rightful place. Once again, the influence of the Song of Songs is pervasive, providing both the setting for the encounter and its unmistakably nuptial ambience. This is clearly John's "bridal chamber" moment, when all the seeds he has carefully planted throughout the text finally bear fruit. In chiastic dialogue with its symmetrical opposite (the wedding at Cana), it supplies the missing bride and bridegroom for the feast—but not until, as at Cana, water has been turned into wine.

THE ANOINTING AT BETHANY

With these three other pieces in place, we are now able to return to the Lazarus/anointing at Bethany sequence and fill in the missing terms of the equation. Yes, there is a hidden teaching about love going on, but it is not an encrypted history of Jesus's "secret" dynastic marriage. John is up to a much more noble challenge: to explore the transfiguration of love itself. How does the "water" of eros become the "wine" of agape? How does the "twoness" of the human personality become the singleness of the transfigured heart?

When John splits the Magdalenic personality into two parts, he is portraying her symbolically in an as yet untransformed state. We know by plugging the information from the parallel chiastic segment (the woman at the well) into the equation that it is indeed Mary Magdalene under discussion here. But the allusion is deliberately veiled because John, unlike the more salacious temperaments of our own time, is interested in the process of transformation, not in the personal romance. In his woman at the well vignette he created an evocative portrait of Fifth Way love at its headwaters. In the Lazarus/anointing scene he gives us a "freeze frame" of this same love just before it goes over the waterfall. He is focused not so much on the personal drama of Mary Magdalene, but on how the separate elements of her character, accentuated so powerfully in the Mary and Martha story, will be drawn back together in the alchemy of the cross. The portrayal is intentionally stylized because that is the way in which the elements themselves come into clearest focus.

It is fascinating to follow his equation to its conclusion as we return to the anointing scene. Contrary to what we might expect, it is the "Mary" side of the Magdalene character that does the anointing, not the "Martha" side. The same side that at Lazarus's tomb reached out to touch Jesus's own human vulnerability—to send her arrow straight to his heart—is the side that now approaches him on this last private evening of their human life. That tells us something about the anointing itself, and it tells us something very important about the alchemy of love.

The touchstone is devotion, not detachment.

Yes, kenosis will be invoked shortly and will do its own transfiguring work. But it cannot create its divine agape out of thin air, or even out of a serene nonattachment or equanimity; it must work directly with the heart's deepest yearning. This is the great secret of kenotic love that so few Christians truly understand.

My own hunch is that the author of John was well aware of the traditions testifying to a deep romantic love between Jesus and Mary Magdalene. But because this love may not have taken the form of a traditional marriage, respect and delicacy were necessary in its presentation. Far more challenging than a "secret" dynastic marriage (which in any case would have created no scandal) is the paradox of a Fifth Way union which, for reasons known only to the lovers themselves, can neither be legitimized nor denied. John rises to the challenge brilliantly, creating what amounts to a mystical typology of Fifth Way love without ever exposing the players or calling into question the spiritual integrity of their relationship. By keeping his eyes focused on the imaginal—the alchemy of love itself—he is able to make the link, so rarely sustained in Christian theology, between the profound agape of Jesus's Farewell Discourses—"Behold, I give you a new commandment: to love one another as I have loved you"—and its underpinnings in human eros and intimacy.

APPENDIX 3

The Passion of Mary Magdalene

Created by Betsey Young, Wisdom Academy, 2007,
Telephone, Texas.

John 14:1a John 19:25–26a	Let not your heart be troubled . . . By the cross of Jesus stood Mary his mother; and his mother's sister, Mary the wife of Cleophas; and Mary Magdalene. And Jesus saw his mother and the disciple he loved standing by . . .
Mark 15:37, 40	Jesus gave a loud cry and breathed his last . . . And the women looking on from a distance included Mary Magdalene and Mary, the mother of James . . .
Matthew 27:59–64	Joseph of Arimathea took down the body, wrapped it in clean linen cloth, and laid it in a tomb. He rolled a great stone to the door of the sepulcher and departed. Mary Magdalene and the other Mary saw where the body was laid and sat against the sepulcher.
Matthew 28:1–9 Luke 24:1–3	On the first day of the week, when it was still dark, Mary Magdalene and the other Mary brought spices to anoint Jesus. But the stone was gone and he was not there. An angel of the Lord said, "Do not be afraid. I know you are looking for Jesus. He is not here. He has been raised from death, as he told you. Come and see! Go and tell the others.

John 20:14–18   Jesus himself appeared first to Mary Magdalene,
                     but she did not recognize him.
                             "Woman, why do you weep?"
                             "Sir, if you have taken him, tell me . . ."
                             "Mary . . ."
                             "Rabboni!"
                             "Mary, do not cling to me . . . Go and tell
                     the others."
                             Mary Magdalene went and announced to
                     the disciples, "I have seen the Lord!"

Mark 14:9   Wherever the good news is proclaimed in the
                     whole world, what she has done will be told in
                     remembrance of her.

NOTES

CHAPTER 1:
MARY MAGDALENE IN
THE CANONICAL GOSPELS

1. Ira Progoff, ed., *The Cloud of Unknowing* (New York: Delta Books, 1957), p. 99.
2. *The Book of Common Prayer* (New York: Church Hymnal Corporation, 1979), p. 242.
3. This otherwise unnamed disciple is traditionally—though probably incorrectly—assumed to be John himself. More recent speculation has suggested it might be Lazarus, or even Mary Magdalene. See Michael Baigent, Richard Leigh, and Henry Lincoln, *Holy Blood, Holy Grail* (New York: Delacorte, 1982), pp. 310–16.
4. And these, in turn, have already been introduced in Luke 8:2, with Mary Magdalene at the head of the list. See ahead in this chapter, page 11.
5. *"And their companions"*? This word is sometimes more innocuously translated as "the others." At very least these "others" implies "a specific group of people, a gathering of disciples among whom were a sizable number of women," according to the contemporary Catholic scholar Mary R. Thompson in her *Mary of Magdala* (Mahwah, N.J.: Paulist Press, 2006), p. 59. But the word *companion* (which we will see used in the Gospel of Philip to describe Mary Magdalene's relationship to Jesus) more commonly designates exactly what it sounds like: a partner or spouse. For the alert reader, this seemingly harmless phrase effectively shatters one or both of the two most sacred cows of traditional apostolic Christianity: that Jesus had only male disciples, and that they were celibate. See ahead in this chapter, pages 14–15.

6. In traditional Christian symbology, which assigns a historical identity and character to each of the four evangelists, Luke is classically described as a healer, and there are many "Saint Luke guilds" dedicated to the healing ministries.

7. Jean-Yves Leloup, *The Gospel of Mary Magdalene* (Rochester, Vt.: Inner Traditions, 2002), pp. 106–9.

CHAPTER 2:
THE WOMAN WITH THE ALABASTER JAR

1. In Luke 10:38–42, the well-known story of Mary and her sister Martha hosting a dinner for Jesus. Martha overburdens herself with the duties of preparing and serving the meal, while Mary merely sits rapt at the foot of Jesus, absorbing his teachings. According to the gospel, it is Mary who has "chosen the better part."

2. Quoted from Karen King, *The Gospel of Mary of Magdala* (Santa Rosa, Calif.: Polebridge Press, 2003), p. 151.

3. Among the most prominent of these: (1) For John, the Last Supper is not a Passover celebration, but takes place the day before the Passover. (2) There is no mention of the institution of the eucharist (the memorial meal of bread and wine); instead, Jesus washes the disciples' feet and gives them the New Commandment: "to love one another, as I have loved you" (John 13:35). (3) It is immediately preceded by the raising of Lazarus and anointing at Bethany rather than by throwing the money changers out of the Temple (as in the three Synoptic accounts).

4. See Michael Baigent, Richard Leigh, and Henry Lincoln, *Holy Blood, Holy Grail* (New York: Delacorte, 1982), pp. 240–46 and 316–19.

5. Margaret Starbird, *The Woman with the Alabaster Jar* (Santa Fe, N.Mex.: Bear and Company, 1993), pp. 50–51.

6. This exchange took place during a private conversation at New Camaldoli Hermitage, March 17, 2006.

7. See Mary R. Thompson, *Mary of Magdala* (Mahwah, N.J.: Paulist Press, 2006), pp. 47–48; also King, pp. 149–51.

8. For an excellent introduction to this fascinating genre, see Benedicta Ward, S.L.G., *Harlots of the Desert* (Kalamazoo, Mich.: Cistercian Publications, 1987).

9. Ira Progoff, ed., *The Cloud of Unknowing* (New York: Delta Books, 1957), pp. 100–102.

CHAPTER 3:
THE "GNOSTIC" GOSPELS

1. Karen King, *The Gospel of Mary of Magdala* (Santa Rosa, Calif.: Polebridge Press, 2003), p. 159.
2. King, p. 159.
3. King, p. 156. Just before this, on p. 155, she explains that these two camps "can be established only by hindsight, and even then they are not real entities, but only academic constructs. All the texts and persons grouped under these categories did exist in antiquity, but they never understood themselves to be Gnostics or Jewish Christians, let alone heretics." As a result of this initial oversimplification, "the enormous theological variety of literature characterized as Gnostic gets harmonized into an overly simplified and monolithic ideology" (p. 156).
4. A recent influential example of this sort of thinking is Richard Smoley, *Forbidden Faith: The Gnostic Legacy from the Gospels to* The Da Vinci Code (San Francisco: HarperCollins, 2006). While Smoley, the former coeditor of *Gnosis* magazine, assembles much useful information here, his tendency to view Gnosticism as a monolith (like the Roman Catholic Church, only with a different theology) dangerously conflates several wisdom streams that need to be clearly differentiated. He is correct, for example, that most Gnostic movements prize visionary seeing. But this does not necessarily imply that one must buy into the whole complex metaphysics of archons and demiurges, which in fact belongs only to a later, specifically Greek subset of the greater sophianic stream. In these overly hasty associations, he actually winds up doing damage to the cause of reclaiming the wisdom stream within Christianity itself.
5. *Logion* is the Greek word for a saying or short teaching. The Gospel of Thomas consists of 114 of these sayings of Jesus. By far my favorite edition of this text is Lynn Bauman's *The Gospel of Thomas: The Wisdom of the Twin* (Ashland, Ore.: White Cloud, 2002).
6. In his teachings (as yet unpublished) Lynn Bauman makes the intriguing suggestion that we think of the Gospel of Thomas as parallel (in date and genre) to the Gospel of Mark, the Gospel of Mary Magdalene to Acts, and the Gospel of Philip to John. They comprise essentially a "Semitic" equivalent to the Greek telling of the same story familiar to us from the Bible. He is using the word "Semitic" here to describe not the language the text was written in (all these texts are Coptic versions of a presumed Greek

original), but rather the cultural stream or flavor. See ahead in my text, pages 127–28.

7. I am quoting here from Jean-Yves Leloup, *The Sacred Embrace of Jesus and Mary: The Sexual Mystery at the Heart of the Christian Tradition* (Rochester, Vt.: Inner Traditions, 2006), p. 85.

8. King, p. 184.

9. For more on cosmovisions, and a sense of the usefulness of this term in interreligious dialogue, see Raimon Panikkar, *Christophany* (Maryknoll, N.Y.: Orbis Books, 2004), p. 19.

10. Ken Wilber, *Integral Spirituality* (Boston: Shambhala Publications, 2006), pp. 10–11.

11. Rami Shapiro, *The Divine Feminine in Biblical Wisdom Literature* (Woodstock, Vt.: Skylight Paths, 2005), p. xvii.

12. Even here, however, scholars are beginning to rethink traditionally ironclad definitions of Gnosticism. These definitions were basically the work of nineteenth- and early-twentieth-century biblical typologists, based on the only resource material available to them at the time: the pejorative descriptions of "heresy" (as it was called at the time) mounted by the early Christian polemicists such as Irenaeus and Tertullian—clearly men with an ax to grind! When the real primary source material was recovered at Nag Hammadi in 1945, scholars were in for a huge surprise: not a single one of the so-called gnostic materials bore all of the classic typological characteristics of Gnosticism, and some bore none of them at all! Gnosticism itself, even more restrictively defined as a late Greek heresy, is proving more and more to be a mirage. On this subject, see Karen King's exhaustive study *What Is Gnosticism?* (Cambridge, Mass.: Harvard University Press, Belknap Press, 2003).

CHAPTER 4:
THE GOSPEL OF MARY MAGDALENE

1. For more on this point, see Karen King, *The Gospel of Mary of Magdala* (Santa Rosa, Calif.: Polebridge Press, 2003), p. 184.

2. We in fact did exactly this as a project of the Aspen Wisdom School during the winter of 2008 and in Collegeville, Minnesota, the following summer. The results were rewarding and in some cases enlightening, clarifying interpretive difficulties that could not be resolved by textual analysis alone. I will explore a specific instance of this in chapter 5.

3. It is more typical of modern editors (including Lynn Bauman) to

extend dialogue 2 to include all the text up to the second set of missing pages. But Mary Magdalene's opening words about meeting Jesus in a vision seem so clearly to belong to the third dialogue—in fact, they furnish its underlying theme—that I have divided the sections accordingly. The advantages of arranging things this way will become clear in chapter 5.

4. Lynn Bauman, Ward Bauman, and Cynthia Bourgeault, *The Luminous Gospels* (Telephone, Tex.: Praxis Institute Publishing, 2008).

5. These appearances take place immediately after the resurrection and are recorded in John 20:19–29 and Luke 24:36–43.

6. In this idea of the "interwoven" material world unraveling at the end of its term into its elemental components, there are fascinating resonances with the teachings of Empedocles and Parmenides as laid out by Peter Kingsley in his remarkable book *Reality* (Inverness, Calif.: Golden Sufi Center, 2005). Kingsley proposes a radical revisioning of the origins of Western philosophy as lying not in intellectual speculation, but rather in the sacred practices of a long wisdom lineage of shamanic healing. There are distinctive overlaps between this tradition and the teachings and spiritual practices of Jesus. While it is risky to push too hard on such slender threads of synchronicity, it does offer additional confirmation of Jesus's wide-ranging familiarity with the Near Eastern wisdom traditions and his ability to synthesize from a variety of sources.

7. Jean-Yves Leloup perceptively paraphrases: "when you act according to the habits of your corrupted nature." In his *The Gospel of Mary Magdalene* (Rochester, Vt.: Inner Traditions, 2002), p. 25.

8. Jacob Boehme, *Confessions* (Kila, Mont.: Kessinger, n.d.), p. 41.

9. I say "cautiously" because within the Jungian categories that influence our use of the term today, an archetype suggests something deeply interior and "subjective," arising from the primordial ground of the collective unconscious and needing to be consciously integrated within one's psyche. In traditional metaphysics, the archetypal realm is objective and transconscious; it is "higher" than our own realm and generates the images that arise here on this earth. The integration of an archetype, then, does not occur within the personal psyche; it is always an objective union of two different realms of being—a *syzygy* ("not one, not two, but both one and two") of the finite and infinite.

10. Again, the brief reference in this gospel does not allow this distinction to become fully evident, but you will find it spelled out in greater detail in the Gospel of Thomas.

11. Lynn C. Bauman, *The Gospel of Thomas: The Wisdom of the Twin* (Ashland, Ore.: White Cloud, 2002), p. 120.
12. For more on the great chain of being, see Ken Wilber's voluminous writings, particularly *The Eye of the Spirit* (Boston, Mass.: Shambhala Publications, 1997), pp. 39–40.
13. This instruction is repeated almost verbatim in the Gospel of Thomas, logion 3. See Bauman, *The Gospel of Thomas*, p. 10.
14. Lynn Bauman, ed., *The Gospel of Thomas: The Wisdom of the Twin* (Ashland, Ore.: White Cloud Press, 2002), p. 51–52.
15. That is why one is able to make "one image supercede another": because one has accessed the level from which the images originally arise. Jesus is most likely alluding to this same accessing of the causal level in his popular teaching in the canonical gospels, "If you but had faith so much as a grain of mustard, you would be able to speak to the mountain and it would topple into the sea" (Matthew 17:20). A modern-day mystic, Jacques Lusseyran, speaks of his own experience of this causal place. Blinded as a child, he miraculously learned to "see" again by discovering the light at its place of arising and following the same direction of flow: from the causal template into the particular form. When it came to listening to music, he discovered

> that there is nothing in the world which cannot be replaced with something else; that sounds and colors are being exchanged endlessly, like the air we breathe and the life it gives us; that nothing is ever lost; that everything comes from God and returns to God along all the roadways of the world, and that the most beautiful music is still only a path. (Lusseyran, *And There Was Light*, New York: Parabola Books, 1998, p. 95.)

CHAPTER 5:
DYING AND RISING

1. Moreover, her words make very clear that she is talking about a *vision*, not simply a dream. While our modern, "vertically challenged" era tends to lump these two modes of inner communication together, the ancient world was very clear about their differences in origin and import. Both visions and dreams are seen in the ancient wisdom traditions as authentic forms of "inter-realmic" communication—that is, along the vertical axis. But a dream tends to "come from" another realm while its recipient is

in a state of sleep; a vision comes in waking consciousness and essentially "transports" its recipient to the realm from which it emerges.

2. As we will discover later in this book, resurrection appearances and visions are in fact more similar than dissimilar, for they both originate in the imaginal realm (that place of "Origin") and represent a meeting ground between the worlds. A resurrection appearance is also an imaginal encounter; it is simply more "substantially" enfleshed than a vision. We will see in part 3 how the earliest Christian understanding of Resurrection as an imaginal encounter was eventually displaced by an emphasis on Jesus's literal return to the physical flesh.

3. This phrase itself is from the Apostles' Creed, the earliest of the Christian creeds. Jesus himself is said to have predicted this descent to the underworld in Matthew 12:40, when he says, "As Jonah spent three days in the belly of the world, so the son of man will spend three days in the heart of the earth."

4. Ira Progoff, ed., *The Cloud of Unknowing* (New York: Delta Books, 1957), p. 204.

5. Thomas Merton, "A Member of the Human Race," in *A Merton Reader*, ed. Thomas P. McDonnell (New York: Image Books, 1989), p. 347; originally published as *Conjectures of a Guilty Bystander* (New York: Doubleday, 1966). Merton's understanding here was deeply influenced by his readings in Louis Massignon's translation of the work by the ninth-century Sufi master Al Hallaj known as "A Treatise on the Heart," in which the classic anthropology of the heart understood as an organ of spiritual perception is expounded.

6. Jean-Yves Leloup, *The Gospel of Mary Magdalene* (Rochester, Vt.: Inner Traditions, 2002), p. 153.

7. I am reminded here of a beautiful insight from the contemporary Native American mystic Black Elk: "I looked all around me and could see that what we were doing just then was like a shadow cast on earth from yonder vision in the heaven, so bright it was and clear. I could see that the real was yonder and the darkened dream of it was here." The quotation came to me in the form of a Christmas card that arrived in my mailbox in 1994, but it comes from John G. Neihardt, ed., *Black Elk Speaks* (Albany: State University of New York Press, 2008), p. 134. The quotation itself perfectly captures the wisdom sense of the visionary realm as being more real than the so-called objective reality that we normally inhabit.

That pungent sense of reversal, and the recognition that reality is of an incomparably higher order of luminosity than our usual take on it here is at the heart of all visionary revelation.

8. The term itself was coined by Henri Corbin in his extensive exploration of the metaphysics of Islamic mysticism, as evidenced particularly in the works of Ibn Arabi and the so-called Persian Platonists of the twelfth century. See particularly *Creative Imagination in the Sufism of Ibn Arabi* (Princeton, N.J.: Princeton University Press, 1969) and *Spiritual Body and Celestial Earth: From Mazdean Iran to Shiite Iran* (Princeton, N.J.: Princeton University Press, 1990).

9. Leloup, p. 153.

10. Leloup, p. 127.

11. As you will see just ahead in the encounter with wrath, this final realm recapitulates all the others, so it is easy enough to identify the missing first encounter with the help of this list.

12. I am quoting here from our earlier (pre-publication) translation of this passage, which I prefer. In the published version (page 68), *Craving* became *Desire;* "enslavement to the physical Body" became "the force of the physical Body"; and "the false peace of the Flesh" became "the foolish wisdom of the Flesh."

13. In Buddhist teaching, these comprise four of the six so-called *bardo* realms, through which the soul may travel in the interim between death and rebirth. The idea that these energies actually comprise "realms," distinct climates with their own gravitational fields, is an idea deeply embedded in universal sacred wisdom.

14. Father Keating's notion of the false self system and its healing through "the divine therapy" of centering prayer is the core conceptual piece in his prolific writings and teachings. The best starting place is his *Invitation to Love* (Rockport, Mass.: Element Books, 1992). I also give a basic overview of this teaching in my *Centering Prayer and Inner Awakening* (Cambridge, Mass.: Cowley Publications, 2004).

15. Lynn C. Bauman, ed., *The Gospel of Thomas: The Wisdom of the Twin* (Ashland, Ore.: White Cloud, 2002), p. 48.

16. This point, in fact, has considerable bearing on the soul's final comment in this exchange, which might otherwise seem to be a non sequitur: "Though they never recognized me, I now perceive that heaven and earth will pass away and all things composed shall be dissolved." What does this have to do with ignorance? This is a deep metaphysical question, later tackled by the kabbalah and still later by the German mystic Jacob Boehme. From both quar-

ters emerges the insight that judging (leading to a state of dualistic separation and hence ignorance) is one of those constituitive conditions that allows this realm to be; as ignorance and dualism pass away, so, in fact, does this earth plane. This deep insight is perhaps beyond the scope of this text. Closer to hand, though, it is interesting to note how this teaching reverberates with the very first response of Jesus with which this gospel opens: "all matter shall be dissolved, everything to its own root."

17. Thomas Merton, *The Asian Journal of Thomas Merton* (New York: New Directions, 1975), p. 233.

18. Leloup's translation here reads "a design was erased by virtue of a higher design" (p. 37): less technical and profoundly poetic, but also less accurate. Karen King translates, "In a world I was set loose from a world, and in a type from a type which is above" (*The Gospel of Mary of Magdala,* Santa Rosa, Calif.: Polebridge Press, 2003), p. 16. The metaphysics of image (type) and analog are clearly evident in this passage.

19. In Greek the word for truth is *alethia,* which means nonforgetfulness. You will see at the root of this word an allusion to Lethe, or the "river of forgetfulness" of Greek mythology, which separates the realms and causes travelers to fall into ignorance of their true nature and destiny. Truth—"a-Lethia"—thus amounts to "waking up" from this sleep of forgetfulness into remembrance of who one truly is: a fascinating insight into Jesus's celebrated comment in the Gospel of John, "You shall know the truth and the truth will set you free."

20. Ladislaus Boros, *The Mystery of Death* (New York: Seabury Press, 1973), pp. 148–49. Boros's book is itself the product of an extraordinary visionary revelation. He wrote the core of the manuscript in a single, uninterrupted "download" over the course of about three weeks, then added revisions and commentary. The vision also changed his life. Within short order he resigned the priesthood, married, and fathered four children before his death at the age of fifty-three.

21. Boros, p. 149.

22. Jacob Boehme, *The Way to Christ,* ed. Peter Erb (Mahwah, N.J.: Paulist Press, 1978).

23. For this insight I am indebted to Peter Kingsley, particularly his book *Reality* (Inverness, Calif.: Golden Sufi Center, 2005), which explores the beginnings of Western civilization in the Near Eastern traditions of shamanic healing.

24. This is the argument mounted by the historian Bruce Chilton in his book *Mary Magdalene: A Biography* (New York: Image/Doubleday, 2005). We will return to it in more detail in chapter 15 of this book.

CHAPTER 6:
WINNERS AND LOSERS

1. It is true, of course, that Acts records the tension between Peter and the Church of Jerusalem with regard to observance of the Jewish dietary laws, but the conflict is depicted as being quickly resolved. Similarly, the entrance of Paul into the ranks of the apostles is recorded as being seamless, and an alleged tension between the "Hellenists" and the "Hebrews" (Acts 6:1) is swiftly smoothed over through the appointment of "seven respected men full of wisdom and spirit" to be deacons. The real voices I am speaking of as silenced are those of Mary Magdalene and Thomas, who bear witness to an apostolacy comprising both men and women and to a teaching whose roots are to be found neither in the Hellenist nor Hebrew camps, but rather in the deeper wellsprings of universal sacred wisdom.

2. This would be the one piece of evidence that might cause me to question Karen King's assertion that the manuscript dates from the first half of the second century. King writes: "Because the Gospel of Mary defends the validity of Mary's revelation on the basis of her character, not by appeal to a fixed apostolic succession, a limited canon, or a rule of faith, it was probably written before these had been fully developed and were widely accepted" (*The Gospel of Mary of Magdala*, Santa Rosa, Calif.: Polebridge Press, 2003, p. 184). While her qualifiers *fully* and *widely* allow for a considerable "wiggle room," it does nonetheless appear that Andrew's response here indicates some sort of a dawning awareness of a "limited canon."

3. Jean-Yves Leloup makes the insightful observation: "There is a curious parallel between Peter's attitude toward Miriam and his attitude toward Yeshua himself" (*The Gospel of Mary Magdalene*, Rochester, Vt.: Inner Traditions, 2002, p. 170). Openness and rejection, insight and obtuseness alternate within him with terrifying regularity. At the core of this inner vacillation, Leloup suggests, is Peter's own unintegrated feminine. "Peter has not yet entered into the climate of the new wedding proposed by the

Teacher," he writes (p. 165). "The climate of jealousy still holds him back, and his consequent mistrust of the feminine prevents him from reclaiming the missing parts of his love."

4. Lynn C. Bauman, *The Gospel of Thomas: The Wisdom of the Twin* (Ashland, Ore.: White Cloud, 2002), p. 237.

CHAPTER 7:
RECLAIMING THE PATH
OF ROMANTIC LOVE

1. Margaret Starbird, *The Woman with the Alabaster Jar* (Santa Fe, N.Mex.: Bear and Company, 1993).

2. An excellent summary of the growing "sexual neurosis" of the early church can be found in the foreword to Starbird, *The Woman with the Alabaster Jar* (see preceding endnote), contributed by the Reverend Terrance A. Sweeny, PhD. See also Jean-Yves Leloup, *The Sacred Embrace of Jesus and Mary: The Sexual Mystery at the Heart of the Christian Tradition* (Rochester, Vt.: Inner Traditions, 2006).

3. See chapter 1, endnote 5, to refresh yourself on this point.

4. The Roman Catholic Church, that is. Married priesthood continues to be accepted in the Orthodox Church, but bishops, the significant players in the power structure, are drawn exclusively from the ranks of those vowed to celibacy

5. In his introduction to *The Gospel of Philip* (Rochester, Vt.: Inner Traditions, 2004), Jean-Yves Leloup quotes Pope Innocent III (d. 1216) as saying, "The sexual act is itself so shameful as to be intrinsically bad" (p. 30). Even between a husband and wife and for procreative purposes, it was considered to involve carnal sin. This conundrum delayed the church's official recognition of marriage as a sacrament until 1150. It took considerable theological maneuvering to iron out the wrinkle of how something could be a sacrament that also involved carnal sin. See Kenan B. Osborne, *Sacramental Guidelines* (Mahwah, N.J.: Paulist Press, 1995), p. 138.

6. Thomas Merton, *The Seven Storey Mountain* (New York: Harcourt Brace & Co., 1948), p. 366.

7. For a more detailed exploration of this point and the limits of what I call "the egoic operating system" as a tool for spiritual inquiry, see my book *The Wisdom Jesus* (Boston: Shambhala Publications, 2008), pp. 33–35.

8. John S. Dunne, *The Reasons of the Heart* (New York: Macmillan, 1978), p. 141.

9. Ken Wilber, *Grace and Grit* (Boston: Shambhala Publications, 1991), p. 405.

10. Anders Nygren's *Agape and Eros* was first published in London by the S.P.C.K. House: part 1 in 1932; part 2, vol. 1, in 1938; and part 2, vol. 2, in 1939. It was revised, retranslated, and published in one volume in 1953. The first U.S. paperback edition was by Harper & Row, 1969.

11. Quoted from Joseph Chu Cong, OCSO, *The Contemplative Experience* (New York: Crossroad, 1999), p. 27.

12. "The Divine Life: An Interview with Swami Chidananda," *What Is Enlightenment?*, no. 13 (spring–summer 1998), p. 106.

13. "The Divine Life: An Interview with Swami Chidananda," p. 106.

CHAPTER 8:
THE GREAT IDENTITY THEFT

1. Barbara Thierring, *Jesus the Man*, rev. ed. (New York: Atria Books, 2006), p. 19. From more than twenty years of meticulous study Thierring finds evidence of an anagram-style encoding at work (she calls it the "pesher technique"), which, when properly decoded, offers a highly politicized alternative version of the classic events of the Christian Holy Week narrative. While her findings are controversial (and in my opinion, uneven), much of her scholarship around the intertwining histories of the Essene community and early Christianity is sound and extremely helpful.

2. These beautiful words were not actually composed by Paul; he is quoting from an ancient Christian hymn, perhaps the earliest known to exist. The version of this text I am citing here is a translation by the monks of New Camaldoli Hermitage, Big Sur, California, in active use in their liturgical and devotional life. It was through many years of singing this hymn with the monks during Saturday night vespers that its deeper significance began to open to me.

3. Lynn Bauman, ed., *The Gospel of Thomas: The Wisdom of the Twin* (Ashland, Ore.: White Cloud, 2002), p. 48.

4. Helen Luke, *Old Age* (New York: Parabola Books, 1987), p. 84.

5. Michael Brown, *The Presence Process* (Vancouver, B.C.: Namaste Publishing, 2006), p. 246.

6. These and the following two citations from the Gospel of Thomas are all from the 2002 Bauman edition: logion 5, p. 15; logion 22, p. 51; logion 106, p. 221.

7. I discuss this point more thoroughly in my article "The Gift of Life: The Unified Solitude of the Desert Fathers," *Parabola* 14, no. 2 (summer 1989), pp. 27–35. The original research comes from Dr. Gabriele Winkler, "The Origins and Idiosyncrasies of the Earliest Form of Asceticism," in *The Continuing Quest for God: Monastic Spirituality in Tradition and Transition*, ed. William Skudlarek, O.S.B. (Collegeville, Minn.: Liturgical Press, 1981).

8. I am indebted to my friend the Islamic scholar Ibrahim Gamard for his insight (in a letter to me on July 18, 1998) that "in the Islamic tradition monasticism was disapproved of in the Qur'anic verse which states that the monasticism of the followers of Jesus was invented by them and was not something commanded by God."

9. The word commonly translated as "infidelity" is ambiguous and has been hotly debated by scholars. Many feel that this entire bracketed passage is a later insertion.

10. Here as throughout most of my text I am using the Christian Community Bible as the principle source for these translations of the New Testament scriptures. In this passage in particular, however, nuances of translation enter mightily into the end results, so by way of comparison I am laying out the somewhat different "take" on this passage implied in the New Revised Standard Version. Those readers fluent in ancient Greek are encouraged to consult the original.

> Some Pharisees came to him, and to test him they asked, "Is it lawful for a man to divorce his wife for any cause?" He answered, "Have you not read that the one who made them at the beginning 'made them male and female,' and said, 'For this reason a man shall leave his father and mother and be joined to his wife, and the two shall become one flesh'? So they are no longer two, but one flesh. Therefore what God has joined together, let no one separate." They said to him, "Why then did Moses command us to give a certificate of dismissal and to divorce her?" He said to them, "It was because you were so hardhearted that Moses allowed you to divorce your wives, but from the beginning it was not so. And I say to you, whoever divorces his wife, except for unchastity, and marries another commits adultery."
>
> His disciples said to him, "If such is the case of a man with his wife, it is better not to marry." But he said to them, "Not

everyone can accept this teaching, but only those to whom it is given. For there are eunuchs who have been so from birth, and there are eunuchs who have been made eunuchs by others, and there are eunuchs who have made themselves eunuchs for the sake of the kingdom of heaven. Let anyone accept this who can."

CHAPTER 9:
THE PATH OF CONSCIOUS LOVE

1. In fact, tantra is an ancient and authentic spiritual path, based on a comprehensive metaphysical system that survives today in its most subtle forms in the teachings of Tibetan Vajrayana Buddhism. I am indebted to my student Seonaigh MacPherson, an outstanding scholar and practitioner of this path of Buddhism, for her 2006 doctoral thesis "Mary Magdalene and the 'Return of the Repressed': A Tantric Reading of a Christian Trope," submitted in fulfillment of degree requirements at Vancouver School of Theology. Her paper clarifies many aspects of this practice and draws a deliberate parallel between the role of Mary Magdalene and the *dakini*, or "enlightened consort," in Vajrayana Buddhism. I will be referring to her work at many times during our exploration.
2. Tau Malachi, *Living Gnosis: A Practical Guide to Gnostic Christianity* (Woodbury, Minn.: Llewellyn Publications, 2005), pp. 52–56. I am indebted to my colleague Lynn Bauman for bringing this resource to my attention.
3. In the interest of brevity I am deliberately omitting here two details that are in fact of vivid dramatic and symbolic import. At the precise moment Mary Magdalene crosses the Jordan, Jesus is emerging from the waters of baptism. On the day she enters the Holy Land, he performs his first miracle, changing water into wine at the wedding feast in Cana. Malachi comments: "Thus, the great mystery of the Gospel was already transpiring between them before they ever met in the world." (p. 55).
4. Malachi, p. 55.
5. Jean-Yves Leloup, *The Gospel of Philip* (Rochester, Vt.: Inner Traditions, 2004), p. 65, plate III. In his translation of this same passage, Lynn Bauman also uses this same word, *companion*, to render the meaning of *koinonos*; see Lynn Bauman, Ward Bauman, and Cynthia Bourgeault, *The Luminous Gospels* (Telephone, Tex.: Praxis Publishing, 2008), p. 94.

6. Raimon Panikkar, *Christophany* (Maryknoll, N.Y.: Orbis, 2005), p. 115.

7. Boris Mouravieff, *Gnosis*, 3 vols., trans. S. A. Wissa and Robin Amis (Newburyport, Mass.: Praxis Institute Press, 1989–1993). Note that Praxis Institute Press, founded by the British esotericist Robin Amis, is not the same as Praxis Publishing, founded by Lynn Bauman, although both of these small presses are the publishing arm of organizations known identically as Praxis Institute.

8. In his own writings, Gurdjieff had enumerated the three traditional spiritual pathways as being the way of the fakir, of the monk, and of the yogi, then he proposed his own method as "the Fourth Way": "The Way of the Conscious Man."

9. John Welwood, *Journey of the Heart: The Path of Conscious Love* (Boston: Shambhala Publications, 1990), p. 13.

10. Eckhart Tolle, *The Power of Now* (Vancouver, B.C.: Namaste Publishing, 1997), p. 125.

11. Mouravieff, vol. 1, p. 244.

12. Vladimir Solovyov, *The Meaning of Love* (Hudson, N.Y.: Lindisfarne Press, 1985), p. 51.

13. Ken Wilber, *Grace and Grit* (Boston: Shambhala Publications, 1991), p. 405.

14. Welwood, p. 20.

15. Is there only one authentic soul partner, predestined, as it were, from all eternity, or are a number of combinations possible? Mouravieff was emphatically convinced that each soul was accorded only one authentic "polar being" and that finding this person was indispensable to spiritual completion: shades of the Platonic myth of the "bipolar soul" ("Men and women were once whole but were torn in two, and the pursuit and desire of that whole is what is called love"; quoted from Wilber, p. 405). While he may ultimately be correct, from the limited perspective of this planet such a stipulation runs the risk of diverting the Fifth Way journey into a quest for the perfect partner. My own sense is that a number of combinations are workable—at least at the outset—and if the path itself is engaged with sincerity, all will unfold rightly. For more on this point, see my book *Love Is Stronger than Death* (New York: Bell Tower, 1999; Telephone, Tex.: Praxis Publishing, 2008), pp. 151–52.

16. Welwood, p. 95.

17. Rainer Maria Rilke, *Letters to a Young Poet*, trans. Stephen Mitchell (Boston: Shambhala Publications, 1993), p. 101.

18. Maurice Nicoll, *The New Man* (New York: Penguin Books, 1972), pp. 32–43.
19. This evocative term comes from John Donne in his poem "A Valediction: Forbidding Mourning." For the full text of this poem, see ahead, chapter 12.

CHAPTER 10:
THE BRIDAL CHAMBER

1. Jean-Yves Leloup, *The Gospel of Philip: Jesus, Mary Magdalene, and the Gnosis of Sacred Union* (Rochester Vt.: Inner Traditions, 2004). Lynn C. Bauman, Ward J. Bauman, and Cynthia Bourgeault, *The Luminous Gospels* (Telephone, Tex.: Praxis Publishing, 2008). Lynn Bauman is the translator and overall editor; Ward Bauman and I each helped fine-tune the translations and contributed section introductions.
2. *Luminous Gospels*, p. xi.
3. *Luminous Gospels*, p. xi.
4. Valentinus was born in the Nile delta in the early second century and educated in Alexandria. In the rich spiritual and cultural mix of that city, he was exposed both to Hellenic Platonism and to the work of the great first-century Alexandrian Jewish philosopher, Philo of Alexandria. Valentinus's work thus features a unique synthesis of Hellenic and Semitic elements. According to church father Clement of Alexandria (ca. 150–215), Valentinus was a follower of Theudas, a disciple of Paul, and through this lineage Valentinus claimed to have directly received the "secret wisdom" that Paul had taught privately to his inner circle and mentioned publicly in connection with his visionary encounter with the risen Christ (Romans 16:25; 1 Corinthians 12:2–4; Acts 9:9–10). Valentinus taught first in Alexandria, then went to Rome about 136 C.E., where he became an influential teacher and shaper of early Christianity, narrowly missing election as pope. He died around 160 C.E.
5. *Luminous Gospels,* p. 76.
6. Leloup, p. 9.
7. Jacob Boehme, *Confessions*, quoted in Cynthia Bourgeault, *Love Is Stronger than Death* (New York: Bell Tower, 1999; Telephone Tex.: Praxis Publishing, 2008), p. 186.
8. Leloup, p. 16.
9. In Leloup's translation these three chambers are designated as

"Holy," "Holy of holiness," and "holy of holies." See Leloup, p. 107.

10. The actual Greek word being translated here is often translated simply as "salvation," but since this word can have such heavily loaded connotations for Christians, Lynn Bauman prefers to use the entire phrase "restoration to fullness of being" to express the real meaning intended here. For more on the difference between "salvation" and "restoration to fullness of being," see Cynthia Bourgeault, "The Gift of Life: The Unified Solitude of the Desert Fathers," *Parabola* 14, no. 2 (summer 1989), p. 27.

11. *Luminous Gospels*, p. 79.

12. T. S. Eliot, "East Coker," from *The Four Quartets*, collected in *The Complete Poems and Plays* (New York: Harcourt, Brace, and World, 1952), p. 129. The actual quotation runs, "we must be still and still moving into another intensity, for a further union, a deeper communion."

13. Raimon Panikkar, that brilliant contemporary Christian nondualist, clarifies this distinction in his *Christophany* (Maryknoll, N.Y.: Orbis Books, 2005), p. 81: "I have succeeded in experiencing the 'me' as the *you* of an I . . . I was able to notice that my so-called prayer was a letting myself be guided rather than a request for help, an answer to a solicitation to which I was subject rather than a request addressed to another. To call God a thou, it seemed to me, with all due respect, was not very convincing—and also egocentric. God is the I, if anything, and 'I' the you."

14. Leloup, p. 23.

15. T. S. Eliot, "Little Gidding," from *The Four Quartets*, p. 145.

16. Rainer Maria Rilke, *Letters to a Young Poet*, trans. Stephen Mitchell (Boston: Shambhala Publications, 1993), p. 81.

17. Boris Mouravieff, *Gnosis*, vol. 1, trans. S. A. Wissa and Robin Amis, 3 vols. (Newburyport, Mass.: Praxis Institute Press, 1989), p. 131.

18. This is in fact the esoteric meaning of Jesus's parable of the "wise and foolish bridesmaids" (Matthew 25:1–13), which is also, not coincidentally, set within a nuptial context. While traditional Christians are typically horrified that Jesus seems to approve of the five "wise" bridesmaids refusing to share their oil with their friends, from an esoteric standpoint such sharing would be impossible, since the oil represents their attained conscious awareness and cannot be given to another. For more on this subject see Maurice Nicoll, *The New Man* (New York: Penguin Books, 1972), pp. 79–86.

CHAPTER 11:
JESUS AND MARY MAGDALENE
IN THE BRIDAL CHAMBER

1. This is Lynn Bauman's reading, at any rate, based on his insight (which I believe is correct) that the line in the text stating "the Father of All came down and united with the virgin, and on that day made light shine forth from the fire" refers to the "virgin" place within Jesus's soul (a teaching we discussed in chapter 10) at the time of his baptism and not the Virgin Mary at the time of his conception. Thus, in Bauman's interpretation, the whole event being described in analogue 50 took place at Jesus's baptism, which was simultaneously his experience of the bridal chamber. See Lynn C. Bauman, Ward J. Bauman, and Cynthia Bourgeault, *The Luminous Gospels* (Telephone, Tex.: Praxis Publishing, 2008), p. 127, note 3. Jean-Yves Leloup's translation of this same passage in *The Gospel of Philip: Jesus, Mary Magdalene, and the Gnosis of Sacred Union* (Rochester, Vt.: Inner Traditions, 2004), pp. 113, is much more vague, moving quickly beyond the temporal link to baptism in favor of a more general and archetypal pronouncement:

> The Father of all united with the Silence
> of woman, and he illumined it.
> He manifested in the bridal chamber;
> His body was born on the day when he was witness to
>   the Union,
> Fruit of the merging of the Lover and Beloved.

   In this more spacious setting, Jesus's experience of the bridal chamber could have taken place under almost any circumstances, including in union with Mary Magdalene. But tempting as this option may be, it pushes the text a bit too far beyond its literal meaning.

2. The more I work with these texts, the more the feeling grows in me that her actual initiation into the bridal chamber does not take place until that first resurrection appearance on Easter morning. Before that time, her love for him is still marked by a yearning and clinging which to that degree prevents it from attaining the full "virginity" of the bridal chamber. The missing piece, then, or where her initiation took place, has actually been right there under

our noses all along! The downside to this interpretation, of course, would be that the koinonia between them during the time of their earthly walk together would have been of a human variety rather than a fully realized union of image and archetype.

3. Bauman's translation in *The Luminous Gospels* inserts the words "appeared to" into the text ("Jesus appeared to love Mary Magdalene more than the others"; p. 94) but he admits in the endnotes that this is an interpretive word added to clarify what he takes to be the meaning of the text. I prefer to allow the original ambiguity stand.

4. Leloup, p. 28.

5. Leloup, p. 29.

6. In this instance I am citing from Leloup, p. 63. Bauman's rendition of this text in analogue 17 is "Fully realized human beings are, thus, conceived through a kiss and then they are born" (p. 89).

7. Lynn Bauman, ed., *The Gospel of Thomas: The Wisdom of the Twin* (Ashland, Ore.: White Cloud, 2002), p. 225.

8. To refresh yourself on this point, see chapter 10, pp. 135–37

9. Boris Mouravieff, *Gnosis*, vol. 2, trans. S. A. Wissa and Robin Amis, 3 vols. (Newburyport, Mass.: Praxis Institute Press, 1992), p. 257.

10. Jean-Yves Leloup, *The Sacred Embrace of Jesus and Mary: The Sexual Mystery at the Heart of the Christian Tradition* (Rochester, Vt.: Inner Traditions, 2006), p. 13. As an epilogue, Leloup appends a "Confession of Faith," evidently requested of him by his monastic superiors. Here he writes (p. 138):

In spite of venerable traditions and the historical context, there is no evidence that permits me to claim that Jesus expressed his full sexuality (the latter of course not reducible to genitality) with Mary Magdalene or with any other woman. In all respect to the strictest orthodoxy and the doctrine of the Incarnation, there is also no evidence that permits me to claim he did not do so.

11. Leloup, *Gospel of Philip*, p. 27.

12. Leloup, *Gospel of Philip*, p. 27.

13. Leloup, *The Sacred Embrace of Jesus and Mary*, p. 13.

14. Caryll Houselander, *The Reed of God* (New York: Sheed & Ward, 1944), p. 84.

15. Coleman Barks, *The Essential Rumi* (San Francisco: HarperSanFrancisco, 1995), p. 106.

16. J. G. Bennett, *Sex* (York Beach, Maine: Samuel Weiser, 1981), p. 17. Bennett was a student of G. I. Gurdjieff, as well as having his own extensive knowledge of the esoteric traditions of the Near East and central Asia.

17. The most important analogues treating this theme are 9, 16, 17, 25, 52, 57, 62, 71, and 72. Leloup also considers this theme in some detail in his introduction to *The Gospel of Philip* (pp. 19–27).

CHAPTER 12:
SUBSTITUTED LOVE

1. The classic study of Charles Williams's theology is *The Theology of Romantic Love* by Mary McDermott Shideler (New York: Harper, 1962).

2. Ladislaus Boros, *The Mystery of Death* (New York: Seabury Press, 1963), p. 47. I referred to this book at the end of part 1 in regard to the Gospel of Mary. See chapter 5, pp. 69–70.

3. Ladislaus Boros, *God Is with Us* (New York: Herder and Herder: 1967), p. 5.

4. *The Recapitulation of the Lord's Prayer*, pp. 88–89. This mystical gem was written anonymously and published privately by a twentieth-century British contemplative. According to the story told me when a copy of it was gifted to me, the author had been a student of the Russian philosopher P. D. Ouspensky and in attendance at Mr. Ouspensky's death. He was so moved by what he experienced during that passage that he lived as a hermit in India for three years, seeking to go deeper into the mystery he had experienced.

5. John Donne, "A Valediction: Forbidding Mourning," in *The Complete Poems of John Donne*, ed. Roger E. Bennett (Chicago: Packard, 1942), pp. 32–33.

6. Donne, p. 33.

7. I am making this statement based on the witness of all four canonical gospels (most strongly in John) that she was right there at the foot of the cross, together with Mary, mother of Jesus, and "the beloved disciple" (traditionally thought to be John himself). While the gospels give her no speaking role, in the light of all we have seen so far about the quality of love between Jesus and Mary Magdalene, it seems virtually inevitable that their eyes would have met one final time.

8. Lynn Bauman, Ward Bauman, and Cynthia Bourgeault, *The Luminous Gospels* (Telephone, Tex.: Praxis Institute Publishing, 2008), p. 76.
9. See chapter 7, page 94.
10. Ira Progoff, ed., *The Cloud of Unknowing* (New York: Delta Books, 1957), p. 99.
11. Progoff, ed., pp. 114–15. "Simon Leprous" is Simon the Leper, the wealthy Pharisee at whose house the anointing is said to have occurred, according to Luke's account.

CHAPTER 13:
FIRST APOSTLE

1. The Very Reverend Robert Pynn is dean emeritus of the Anglican Cathedral in Calgary, Alberta, and a leading figure in the wisdom work in Canada. His poem "First Apostle" was written during a Mary Magdalene seminar I led at the Praxis Institute for Research and Learning in Elwood, Texas, during the summer of 2006. It was later published in *LifeLines*, his first volume of poetry (Calgary: CooperBlack Publishing, 2007).
2. Increasingly scholars are seeing that the insistence on Jesus's bodily resurrection as the linchpin of orthodoxy represents a later literalization of the meaning of resurrection, which is at variance not only with what would later be called "Gnostic" tradition, but with the earliest testimony of both the gospels themselves and of St. Paul. On this point, see particularly Elaine Pagels, *The Gnostic Gospels* (New York: Random House, 1979), pp. 3–27, and Bruce Chilton, *Mary Magdalene: A Biography* (New York: Doubleday/Image, 2005), pp. 88–90.
3. Jean-Yves Leloup, *The Gospel of Mary Magdalene*, p. 153. Our earlier discussion of this subject was in chapter 5, pages 61–62.
4. See, for example, analogue 3: "Those who sow in the winter reap in the summer. Winter symbolizes the world-system (the *kosmos*), and summer the Great Age (the Aion), the realm of transcendence" (Lynn Bauman, Ward Bauman, and Cynthia Bourgeault, *The Luminous Gospels* [Telephone, Tex.: Praxis Institute Publishing, 2008], p. 84); also analogue 58: "The embrace of opposites occurs in this world: masculine and feminine, strength and weakness. In the Great Age—the Aion—something similar to embrace occurs, but though we use the same name for it, forms of union

transcend what can be described here" (in *The Luminous Gospels*, p. 104). The same word occurs in the Gospel of Mary Magdalene, at the conclusion of dialogue 3: "From this moment onward, I go forward into the *Aion*, and there, where time rests in stillness in the eternity of time, I will repose in silence" (in *The Luminous Gospels*, p. 69). The key point in all cases is that the Aion is not an afterlife, another form of temporality that begins after we die, but the end (or "fullness") of time itself as a structuring dimension of reality.

5. Walter Wink, "Easter: What Happened to Jesus?" *Tikkun*, March–April 2008 (www.tikkun.org/article.php/MarchAprilTOC2008). *Tikkun* describes itself as "a Jewish and interfaith journal of politics, culture and society." In this article Wink uses the word "ascension" to designate what most Christians would call "resurrection," and he makes clear that he is doing so intentionally, in order to emphasize that he is not talking about the resuscitation of a corpse (the usual Christian understanding of resurrection), but "the entry of Christ into the archetypal realm," which occurred simultaneously with this bodily resurrection and was the real imaginal breakthrough.

6. Leloup, pp. 128–29.

7. Ira Progoff, ed., *The Cloud of Unknowing* (New York: Delta Books, 1957), p. 206.

CHAPTER 14:
THE ALCHEMICAL FEMININE

1. In his 1952 work *Answer to Job*, Carl Jung made a valiant offering on this behalf in his influential proposal that the Virgin Mary should be seen as Christianity's missing divinity and elevated to full membership in the Trinity—which would, thereby, turn it into a "quarternity," a configuration he felt to be intrinsically more stable and psychologically satisfying. More recently this role has been claimed on behalf of Sophia, or Holy Wisdom: the elusive feminine presence who first emerges in the wisdom literature of postexilic Judaism as a kind of feminine cocreator and has been weaving her way into the Trinity by a different route, as the feminine face of the Holy Spirit. We will be meeting her shortly.

2. Valentin Tomberg, *Meditations on the Tarot*, trans. Robert Powell (Rockport, Mass: Element, 1985), p. 39. This same primacy of the reflective and intellective principles will be seen in the description

of Sophia in the Wisdom of Solomon. See ahead in the text, pages 173–75.

3. For more on this notorious blind spot, affecting virtually all of traditional and modernist intellectual discourse (including theology, philosophy, and spiritual teaching), see Ken Wilber, *Integral Spirituality* (Boston: Shambhala Publications, 2006), pp. 175–78.

4. Lynn Bauman, Ward Bauman, and Cynthia Bourgeault, *The Luminous Gospels* (Telephone, Tex.: Praxis Institute Publishing, 2008), p. 41. Also in Lynn Bauman, ed. *The Gospel of Thomas: The Wisdom of the Twin* (Ashland, Ore.: White Cloud Press, 2002), p. 237.

5. *Luminous Gospels*, p. 17.

6. *Luminous Gospels*, p. 104 (analogue 58).

7. Those readers with traditional Protestant versions of the Bible may not find this book in their Old Testament, because it is part of the Apocrypha: Jewish writings from the intertestamental period (generally first century B.C.E.–first century C.E.) that are part of the Roman Catholic canon but not of the Jewish or Protestant ones. It is belongs to the canon of Jewish wisdom literature, which includes the books of Psalms, Proverbs, the Song of Songs, Ecclesiastes, the Wisdom of Solomon, and the Wisdom of Sirach. It was originally composed in Greek (not Hebrew), and while attributed to King Solomon, it is thought to be the work of an unknown Jewish sage writing in Alexandria during this intertestamental era. For a more comprehensive introduction, see Rami Shapiro, *The Divine Feminine in Biblical Wisdom Literature* (Woodstock, Vt.: Skylight Paths, 2005), particularly pages xxxvi–xxxvii.

8. Shapiro, p. 29.

9. See my "Why Feminizing the Trinity Will Not Work," *Sewanee Theological Review* 44, no. 1 (December 2000), pp. 27–35.

10. The term *logos* was first widely used by Philo, a Jewish philosopher writing in Alexandria in the first century C.E.; from there it was picked up by John.

11. Bruno Barnhart, *The Good Wine* (Mahwah, N.J.: Paulist Press, 1999). I will be discussing this book in greater detail in appendix 2.

12. Jean-Yves Leloup, *The Gospel of Philip: Jesus, Mary Magdalene, and the Gnosis of Sacred Union* (Rochester, Vt.: Inner Traditions, 2004), p. 27.

13. I realize that I may be opening a can of worms here and will state clearly that I mean no disrespect either to the traditional symbolic portrait of the Virgin Mary or the obviously deep and tender devotion in which untold thousands of Catholics have held her

throughout the ages. But the image itself, as many contemporary scholars and feminists have pointed out, is a mythological creation of early Christendom and bears even less grounding in historical time and place than most the other elements in the gospel narratives. As a mythological creation, it took root in an institutional soil in which celibacy was the ascendant spiritual climate and in which human sexuality, particularly genital sexuality, was phobically regarded. The archetype of "virgin motherhood" negates most aspects of a woman's lived experience and creates a celibate romanticism that becomes doubly punishing when, as is the case in much of Christian monasticism, particularly among the Orthodox, this fantasy is held up as the only acceptable standard of female purity.

CHAPTER 15:
ANOINTING AND ANOINTED

1. This is particularly the case in the various "bloodline conspiracy" schools of thought, in which Mary of Bethany has now eclipsed Mary Magdalene as the favored candidate for the mysterious "secret bride of Jesus." Rather imperiously (since there is not a scrap of supportive evidence), the British *Holy Blood, Holy Grail* team of Michael Baigent, Richard Leigh, and Henry Lincoln trace her lineage to the Benjaminite line of the twelve tribes of Israel, thus providing not only a context but a motive for her marriage to Jesus: to bring about a dynastic reunion between the tribes of Israel (Jesus belonged to the tribe of Judah) that would seal his claim to the throne and "reboot" a powerful Davidic bloodline (*Holy Blood, Holy Grail*, New York: Delacorte, 1982; pp. 307–10). Hopping right on this bandwagon, Margaret Starbird points out that Mary's anointing of Jesus at Bethany would in this case have political as well as personal significance: at the same time that she prepares her dying husband for burial, she is also performing the ceremonial ritual that proclaims him to be the Messiah, or "Anointed One," the true king of Israel. As to Mary Magdalene's traditional claim to this role, we have already in chapter 2 seen Starbird's ingenious solution: she proposes that "Magdalene" (which in Hebrew means "the tower") is Mary of Bethany's nickname, expressing the high regard in which the other disciples held her. See Starbird, *The Woman with the Alabaster Jar* (Santa Fe, N.Mex.: Bear and Company, 1993), pp. 49–51.

2. In his *Mary Magdalene: A Biography* (New York, Doubleday/ Image, 2005), the Bible historian Bruce Chilton writes: "This is a record of the magical dimensions of his practice, which the later Gospels preferred to repress" (p. 63). While the tendency of modern liberal and progressive scholarship is to discount still further Jesus's reputation as an exorcist and healer, treating these reports as legend and metaphor, others are beginning to acknowledge that Jesus's indebtedness to the ancient Greek and Near Eastern shamanic traditions may offer powerful new insight into what he was about. In addition to Chilton's work, shortly to be introduced into my discussion, see also Peter Kingsley, *In the Dark Places of Wisdom* (Inverness, Calif.: Golden Sufi Center, 1999), and Kyriacos Markides, *Fire in the Heart: Healers, Sages, and Mystics* (New York: Penguin Arkana, 1991).

3. Chilton, p. 63.

4. I am not saying here, of course, that scriptural tradition *officially* recognized her in this role. That is true only for the Gospel of Philip, and to a degree, for the gospels of Thomas and Mary Magdalene. But the long shadow of her presence casts itself over all four gospels, largely in their inability to write her out of the Passion narrative, much as they try to disguise or diminish her role. The memory of the sacred space she clearly held in Jesus's life is attested both directly and indirectly, but it was evidently too powerful to simply override.

5. Chilton, p. 52.

6. Both Chilton (pp. 71–80) and Elaine Pagels, in her classic *The Gnostic Gospels* (New York: Vintage Books, 1979, pp. 3–27), demonstrate convincingly that the belief in the literal resurrection of the body did not enter as a dictum of orthodoxy before the time of Tertullian (early third century) The earliest Christians experienced the resurrection as an event in the imaginal realm, which does not mean that it was unreal, but that it concerned itself with a more subtle level of reality.

7. Chilton builds his case over the course of several chapters, basically chapters 5 through 10, or pages 47–110. He also adds the important additional consideration that "Unction is inherently sensuous" (p. 68), and notes that an additional motivation in downplaying the role of anointing and separating it from Mary Magdalene is to weaken the already bubbling rumors that she and Jesus were romantically intimate. The connection of anointing with sensuous love—aside from the obvious physicality of the act

itself—comes largely through the Old Testament *Song of Songs*, particularly song 1:1–3:

> He shall kiss me with the kisses of his mouth;
> For thy caresses are better than wine,
> Because of the aroma of thy fine unctions
> Thy name is oil poured forth . . .

and song 4:10:

> How beautiful thy caresses, my sister, bride,
> How much better thy caresses than wine,
> and the smell of thine unctions than all spices.

From the Gospel of John right down into our own times commentators have interpreted the anointing at Bethany in terms of these two great erotic passages in the Song—and applied them both implicitly and explicitly to Mary Magdalene! For more on the Song of Songs, see ahead in the text, chapter 16 and appendix 1.

8. The Nine Gates Mystery School curriculum is based on an experiential journey through the chakra system—albeit a modified system in which there are nine chakras ("gates"), not the more usual seven. The "high heart" passage I referred to in the texts moves students from the fourth chakra, the heart, to the fifth: the thymus. I am increasingly convinced that from this chakra standpoint, the eucharist properly belongs not to the heart chakra but to what is traditionally known as "the third eye," or sixth chakra. Hence, part of the difficulty here was indeed a mismatch of ritual to chakra. Anointing precisely matches the high heart passage.

CHAPTER 16:
WHY FRANCE?

1. The grail legends themselves vary in their explanation of what this sacred object might have been. According to some traditions, it was the cup from which Jesus and his disciples drank at the Last Supper. According to others, it was the chalice in which Joseph of Arimathea caught Jesus's blood as he hung on the cross.

2. In some of the more recent feminist scholarship, particularly that of Margaret Starbird, this young girl is now suggested to be her

daughter (her skin is dark because of their ten-year exile in Egypt between the crucifixion and the time of the their arrival in France). See Starbird, *The Woman with the Alabaster Jar* (Santa Fe, N.Mex.: Bear and Company, 1993), pp. 60–61. Sarah Kali has long been revered as the patron saint of the gypsies and is often claimed to as the true subject of numerous black Madonna statues that dot the churches of France.

3. The most famous version of the legend is preserved in the thirteenth-century *Legenda Aurea* (*The Golden Legend*) of Jacob de Voraigne, the sourcebook for the vast majority of popular medieval iconography.

4. Lynn Bauman, Ward Bauman, and Cynthia Bourgeault, *The Luminous Gospels* (Telephone, Tex.: Praxis Institute Publishing, 2008), p. 104.

5. *Luminous Gospels*, p. 109.

6. *Luminous Gospels*, logion 57, p. 104.

7. Rainer Maria Rilke, *Letters to a Young Poet*, trans. Stephen Mitchell (Boston: Shambhala Publications, 1993), p. 54.

8. Rilke, p. 53.

9. Manuscripts circulated remarkably widely among the liturgical centers of the Continent and England in an era still five centuries before the invention of the printing press, so it is often difficult to pinpoint where a text originated. The most likely French candidates are Limoges and St. Benoit-sur-Loire, but the great Benedictine Abbey of St. Gall in Switzerland is also a strong contender. For a good general introduction, see W. L. Smoldon, "Liturgical Drama," in *The New Oxford History of Music*, vol. 2 (London: Oxford University Press, 1967), pp. 175–90.

10. The allusion to treasure here refers to another staple of *The Da Vinci Code* mythology: the conviction that the Cathars somehow came into possession of the legendary coffers of the temple of King Solomon in the Holy Land, which still lies buried somewhere in the rugged wilderness around Montségur in the south of France. The closest parallel I have yet discovered to the concept of parallel orders of celibates and householders living together in one community of love is in the remarkable Ephrata Cloisters, founded in eastern Pennsylvania during the eighteenth century by Conrad Beissel, a spiritual descendent of Jacob Boehme. For more on this fascinating connection, see Arthur Versluis, *Wisdom's Children* (Albany, N.Y.: State University of New York Press, 1999), pp. 100–11. The Essenes also practiced a form of parallel orders of celibates and householders, but the tone of these experiments is much more

ascetical than alchemical—that is, it is grounded in the classic distrust of the body and an equation of sexuality with impurity, rather than on a true Fifth Way paradigm of the transfiguration of sexual energy through the practice of kenotic love. For more on Essene sexual practices, see Barbara Thiering, *Jesus the Man* (New York: Atria Books, 1992), particularly pp. 87–89.

11. Apparently he did so unwillingly, under direct orders from the pope.

12. Quoted from Roland Murphy, *The Song of Songs: A Commentary on the Book of Canticles or the Song of Songs* (Minneapolis, Minn.: Augsburg Fortress, 1990), title page.

13. As we shall see shortly, both the "set" and "props" for John's staging of the resurrection drama derive directly from the Song: the specific fragrances and perfumes with which Mary Magdalene comes to anoint the body, and the garden itself (the other three gospels merely place the scene graveside). In addition, the dialogue between Jesus and Mary Magdalene deliberately alludes to and in fact paraphrases the lover's lament in song 3:1–4, where Jesus's comment "Do not cling to me" (John 20:17) seems to be a response to the lover's proclamation in song 3:4: "I found the one whom my soul loves, I held on to him and would not let him go" (Murphy, p. 144).

14. This theory has been set forth, almost as a fait accompli, by the brilliant and idiosyncratic British genealogist Sir Laurence Gardner, in his *The Magdalenic Legacy* (New York: Barnes and Noble, 2005), p. 26. It has yet to win recognition among Old Testament scholars, but that may be attributable in part to the fact that the academic community is traditionally slow to recognize insights arising from outside its ranks.

15. I am struck by the coincidence that the Persian poet Rumi was two years old in 1209 when the Albigensian campaigns began in Languedoc. In March 1244, when they finally came to an end with the fall of Montségur, he was a rising young scholar in Konya, Turkey. In December of that same year Rumi met his beloved teacher Shams y Tabriz, who initiated him into the pathway of spiritual love and changed his life forever. It is as if the Fifth Way baton had changed hands, as Rumi's profound mystical poetry carried the theme of transformation through kenotic love to newfound depths of spiritual rapture.

16. This celebrated proclamation, immortalized in any number of contemporary posters and greeting cards, is taken from Pierre

Teilhard de Chardin's "The Evolution of Chastity" in *Toward the Future* (1973) English trans. Rene Hague (London: William Collins Sons and New York: Harcourt Brace & Company, 1975), p. 87.

17. I discuss both of these remarkable communities at greater length in my book *Chanting the Psalms* (Boston: Shambhala Publications, 2006), chapters 14 and 16.

CHAPTER 17:
THE WISDOM MARY MAGDALENE

1. Song of Songs, 3:1–4 and 8:6–7. I am quoting here from the New Revised Standard Version, the version I used in my libretto.
2. This liturgy is available online as a downloadable text from Episcopal Church Publishing Company. Titled *A Solemn Liturgy of the Passion for Good Friday with a Biblical Passion Libretto,* it is available at www.churchpublishing.org (ISBN 978-0-89869-561-8).
3. Bruce Chilton, *Mary Magdalene: A Biography* (New York: Doubleday/Image, 2005), pp. 93–101.
4. T. S. Eliot, "East Coker," from *The Four Quartets,* collected in *The Complete Poems and Plays* (New York: Harcourt, Brace, and World, 1952), p. 129.

APPENDIX I:
MARY MAGDALENE AND THE SONG OF SONGS

1. Quoted from Roland E. Murphy, *A Commentary on the Book of Canticles or The Song of Songs* (Minneapolis, Minn.: Augsbur Fortress, 1990), p. 6. Murphy's original source is in *The Mishnah* (London: Oxford university Press, 1933), p. 782.
2. On both of these points, see André Lacocque, *Romance, She Wrote: A Hermeneutical Essay on the Song of Songs* (Harrisburg, Pa.: Trinity Press, 1998).
3. Lacocque, p. 11.
4. Lacocque, p. 209.
5. Speaking of brides, incidentally, there is no conclusive evidence anywhere in the poem that this pair is actually married—or for that matter, that their relationship is actually consummated. For many centuries scholars attempted to shoehorn the Song into an epithalamium format (a set of songs for a marriage celebration), but it has consistently refused to be so constrained, and the consensus among modern commentators is that it is supremely and

insouciantly a celebration of "free love." Again, this is a telltale Fifth Way trait, and an observation worth filing away for when we enter more deeply into the conversation between this text and Mary Magdalene's own Fifth Way path.

6. This chiastic pattern maintains itself throughout the entire Song: not rigidly, but with sufficient visibility to dispel any suggestion that the Song is simply a random collection of separate love songs. Around its thematic epicenter (4:12–5:1) are those two symmetrical passages of absence in 3:1–5 and 5:2–6:3. In the next concentric "ring," canticle 2 is counterbalanced by canticles 6 and 7. In each of these symmetrical units the male lover comes bounding onto center stage ("like a gazelle, like a young stag," in the words of 2:8)—full of amorous passion and praise. In the outermost ring, canticles 1 and 8 similarly parallel each other with their reference to the woman's personal situation (a vineyard keeper, mistreated by her brothers) and in their identical echoing of the poem's core theme, the freedom of love.

7. Murphy, p. 101.

8. Murphy, p. 190. From this point forward in the text, unless otherwise noted, quotations from the Song will be from this Roland Murphy translation.

9. At stake here, of course, is the notorious issue of "supersessionist" interpretation, the longstanding Christian proclivity to read Old Testament texts as foreshadowing New Testament events. This kind of religious imperialism implicitly devalues the intrinsic meaning of the texts themselves within their authentically Jewish frame of reference. It has only been within the past half century— and by no means universally—that Christian scholars have begun to repent of this arrogance, and I have no wish here to again raise the specter of an earlier and now thoroughly discredited school of interpretation. In its place, however, I would like to propose a potential new resolution to this centuries-old tension in what I call "imaginal prefiguring."

In imaginal time, remember, causality is no longer linear but holographic—or to use the literary term we've been exploring in this text, chiastic. The image of a pebble thrown into a pond comes to mind here; from the initial point of impact the influence fans out in concentric rings, traveling "forward" and "backward" at the same time. In the metaphysical language we have been exploring (particularly in the Gospel of Thomas) that causal epicenter, or "origin," occurs in the imaginal world, beyond space-time. From there, events fall into time in a chiastic pattern, with symmetry (synchronicity from the point of view of this world) as the key indicator of their intrinsic relatedness.

I sometimes illustrate this principle of imaginal causality to my students by reference to the story of Zaccheus, the "short man" in Luke 19 who climbs a tree to get a better look as the Teacher passes by. Jesus spots him up in the tree and calls, "Zaccheus, come down! I will dine with you tonight." Did Zaccheus's climbing the tree *cause* Jesus to notice him and issue the dinner invitation? Or conversely, did Jesus's prior intention to dine with Zaccheus that night magically *cause* him to climb the tree? In linear time these two possibilities look like alternatives, but in imaginal time they are joined at the hip. The pebble thrown into the pond is the two men's simultaneous heart-intention to meet. From that epicenter, the process falls into time as two "progressive" actions. But the fundamental causality is not progressive but purposive.

With regard to our question at hand, Mary Magdalene and the Song of Songs are joined at the hip by the reality of the Song's triumphant final proclamation, "Love is as strong as death." That is the imaginal epicenter. From there they fall into history as two halves of a single concentric ring: an Old Testament love song and a New Testament love story, both sharing the identical Fifth Way earmarks of hiddenness, mystery, messiness, and irrepressible freedom.

In this way, it becomes possible, I believe, to talk of an "imaginal causality" or intentional resonant field around these texts without needing to establish within this field a direction of linear flow. It is to link the texts by the same hermeneutic that Wisdom herself seems to favor. Like fragrance itself, "the transparent nothing that pervades all things," she simply makes her presence known.

10. There are many feminist scholars, of course, preeminent among them Margaret Starbird, who consider the black Madonnas to be cryptic references to Mary Magdalene. Having sat before several of these statues, however, particularly the powerful Madonna of Chartres Cathedral, I can only report that I do not personally believe this is so. The energy emanating from them seems clearly to belong to the Blessed Virgin, albeit in a much more earthy and procreative form than is typically allowed in the classic theological formulations. I believe that the blackness, in this case, does indeed stand as a cryptic reference to a fecundity that is more "mother" than "virgin."

11. Bruno Barnhart, *The Good Wine* (Mahwah, N.J.: Paulist Press, 1999), p. 224.

12. Barnhart, p. 216. Curiously, however, Barnhart resists the obvious conclusion that Mary Magdalene is Jesus's literal bride, and he insists that the nuptial union is to the divine Sophia, or wisdom. I have discussed this point in chapter 14.

APPENDIX 2:
THE ANOINTING ACCORDING TO JOHN

1. While scholars have traditionally assumed that Luke's account is the source for John's, more recent Johannine scholarship reflects a shift toward the view that John mirrors sources at least as early as Mark, particularly in his account of the Passion. According to Harry Maier, a professor of New Testament studies and my colleague at Vancouver School of Theology, the story of Mary and Martha most likely circulated in a number of independent traditions, and there is no reason to assume that Luke and John are in conversation here.

2. "Sitting shivah" for her deceased brother in accordance with Jewish funeral customs, she would not be permitted to leave the house until specifically summoned by her husband. See Michael Baigent, Richard Leigh, and Henry Lincoln, *Holy Blood, Holy Grail* (New York: Delacorte, 1982), p. 308.

3. Peter Ellis, *The Genius of John: A Composition-Critical Commentary on the Fourth Gospel* (Collegeville, Minn.: Liturgical Press, 1984). Ellis's work builds in turn upon an earlier study by J. Gerhard, "The Literary Unity and the Compositional Methods of the Gospel of John" (PhD diss., Catholic University of America, 1975).

4. Barnhart's justification for this "seven days of creation" schematic is that John's chiastic core is the brief episode in 6:16–21 where Jesus is seen walking on the Sea of Galilee. This suggests in his mind a link to Genesis 1:2 ("The earth had no form and was void; darkness was over the deep and the Spirit of God hovered over the waters") and allows him to trace an unfolding theme throughout John's gospel that Jesus is indeed the new creation. See Barnhart, *The Good Wine* (Mahwah, N.J.: Paulist Press, 1999), pp. 34, 37–38.

INDEX